FROM HASHTAG UNITED
to
WEMBLEY

PHIL HEARN

Acknowledgements

I am very grateful to all those who have supported me in writing this book.

Firstly, my wife, Sonja, who has supported me from start to finish and has had to listen to me rambling on about Hashtag United, Chipstead, Cheshunt and many more clubs.

Special thanks to Veronika Korchemna (veronikakorch98@gmail.com) for creating such a marvellous cover, to Charlotte Delmonte (www.charlottedelmonte.co.uk) for your impeccable graphic design skills and to my lifelong friends, Chris and Jon, for their open enthusiasm which included match visits.

Lastly, and most importantly, I dedicate this book to my special friend, Max Maxwell. Thanks, Max, for your unending humour, critical honesty, and enduring editing skills! Looking forward to seeing you when I next get to Thailand!

Disclaimer

While all the events in this book took place, they are inevitably a reflection of my personal recall. Most names and some characteristics have been changed. Some events have been compressed or embellished, and some dialogue has been recreated.

Contents

About the Author

I was conceived, born and raised in Charlton, South East London. It has meant that I am a lifelong suffering supporter of Charlton Athletic. Enough said. In the 1980s, I lived in Bromley and started supporting Bromley FC in the Isthmian League for a few years. From that moment, my love of non-League football grew and grew.

Once I had semi-retired, I could achieve my ambition of writing a book about non-League football. A 1970s book by Brian James inspired me in which he followed the winners of each round of the FA Cup from Tividale to Wembley. I copied the idea for the 2021-22 FA Trophy, starting at Hashtag United.

The book has allowed me to visit various towns in England, travel on many trains, observe and meet people, and try to find the funny things in life. And, of course, most importantly, watch some non-League football and enjoy the camaraderie of non-League football fans.

My website, www.fatrophy.co.uk, continues to follow the highs, lows and funnier moments of non-League football.

CHAPTER -1

GOAL

Sunday 22nd May 2022 – FA Trophy Final

*T*hen comes the game-changing minute. A strong attack ends with the striker shooting into the side-netting; some of the crowd think it's a goal...but no. Moments later, a long ball finds the opposition number 18 bursting from midfield. The exposed defence allows him to square the ball across the penalty area for his fellow striker to plant home confidently in the top corner from close to the penalty spot. He wheels away to celebrate in front of his rapturous fans.

Wembley erupts!!!

CHAPTER 0
WARM-UP

Saturday 21ˢᵗ August 2021 - FA Cup Preliminary Round - Chipstead v Faversham Town

*P*layers warm up before they play. So, I decided I needed a warm-up as well before starting my FA Trophy trail. I am following the FA Trophy from the very first qualifying round, hitching onto the winners of each tie all the way to the final at Wembley. Where I will be travelling is in the lap of the gods. I will be travelling to all the games by train, which, you may argue, puts my journey as well as my destination in the lap of the gods. I will watch Chipstead play Faversham Town in the FA Cup

Preliminary Round for my practice run.

As a supporter or competitor, I have never found practice matches particularly enjoyable. However, this is different. I've chosen Chipstead's FA Cup game, as I will start my FA Trophy trail to Wembley watching Chipstead at Hashtag United. Chipstead is not too far from where I live, but I am pretty sure I have never been to Chipstead nor Hashtag United for that matter in my entire life. I'm awake and ready to go at 6am. To ensure I was ready, I had reduced my usual Friday intake of Rioja to one glass, albeit settling for a largeish one. I am clear that today is just a practice run for the 1st Qualifying Round of the FA Trophy, which is still a lifetime away in five weeks. It isn't even the first round of the FA Cup for the 2021-22 season; 348 teams have already competed in the FA Cup in what the Football Association names the Extra Preliminary Round. That round has already ended the Wembley dreams of clubs such as Leicester Nirvana, Romulus (but not Remus), Odd Down, Tadley Calleva, not to mention Horsham YMCA, who went all the way to Jersey to lose to the Bulls by 10-1. I kid you not. 10-1, no Jersey bullshit.

Thanks to the Football Association's grading system, Chipstead and Faversham Town averted the need to play in the Extra Preliminary Round. Tie 114 out of the proverbial hat for this Preliminary Round game paired the Chips with the Lilywhites. First of all, let's clarify one thing; this is Chipstead in Surrey, not the Kent League team with the same name. The two Chipstead clubs suffer from the same problem as Ashford Town (Kent) and Ashford Town (Middlesex) and, to a lesser extent, Newport County and Newport (IOW). Both of the combatants in my chosen game are in the Isthmian League. Chipstead compete in the South Central Division while Faversham Town compete in the South East Division, but both divisions are at the same level, known as Step 4. The most famous son of Chipstead is Steve Sidwell. He went on to play Premier League football with Reading, Aston Villa, Chelsea, Fulham and Stoke City. The club, to its credit, runs teams for all age groups, down to under-sevens.

As with all the FA Trophy games ahead, my trip to Chipstead will include a tour of the home club's neighbourhood. This will be my standard modus operandi on my trail from *Hashtag United to Wembley*. With Google Maps, I decided to start my trail in Woodmansterne. Woodmansterne is not Chipstead, I concede. However, Chipstead Valley Road runs through the centre of Woodmansterne, so I plump for beginning my adventures there.

As my train pulls into East Croydon, it is bustling. I can't help wondering what these people are doing on a Saturday. Further, I can't help noticing the smattering of Crystal Palace shirts on Platform 3. As a lifelong Charlton supporter, I have never liked Crystal Palace. I know it's irrational, and I should know better at my age, but anything red and blue seems distasteful. Actually, I go further. It *is* distasteful. I don't consider myself a fashionista, but I would never wear a red and blue t-shirt. I know the expression "blue and green should never be seen", but "blue and red, I'd rather be dead" is more apposite as far as I'm concerned.

I change trains, catching another to Purley. By contrast, Purley Station is quiet and quite dull. There are no queues at the coffee stand, but I don't feel any need for refreshments. I have over twenty minutes to wait for the final leg to Woodmansterne and decide to use the men's toilet, which means returning to the platform I was on a few moments beforehand. I use the lift to save my worn-out knees. As the door closes, a man in a hat appears from nowhere and presses the button to re-open the door. I'm not in a hurry, but it briefly annoys me. I am sure there have been occasions when I have pressed the 'door close' button if I have seen someone coming. Am I the only person that pushes the 'door close' button in a lift when you hear someone approaching?

The experience in the gents' toilet exceeds expectations, as marketing gurus say. It is clean and as comfortable as public toilets ever get. The man at the next urinal departs, applying the tiniest splash of water to his hands at the sink, and deciding that the hand dryer is unnecessary. I take a more leisurely approach and make use of the soap and water. My eye catches what looks like a repurposed Durex machine. It appears to have had several options reflecting the selection of condoms that the public demands. Now, it ostensibly offers a choice of nappies, except that all the options are the same. Modern man has clearly come to Purley. Well, almost. Modern man cannot cope with nappy variants in the same way he can choose from a selection of condoms. I return to the platform where my train to Woodmansterne departs without any need for aggression at the lifts. The train arrives on time and pulls away from its platform adjacent to a plant preparing aggregates. My knowledge of aggregates stops at two-legged football games, but it looks like a messy, dusty business.

The train stops at Reedham on the way, a place I have never heard of. The most remarkable thing at Reedham is a small block of apartments, spitting distance from the platform. If the football results were on the television in one of the overlooking rooms, you would be able to see the scores, even with my eyesight. Perhaps the apartments are full of retired trainspotters who no longer want to stand out in the cold on the end of platforms. Unlikely, I suppose.

I am soon at Woodmansterne Station. I am the only passenger to leave the train. I make my way to Chipstead Valley Road shortly afterwards, mentally ascribing the acronym CVR to the road. It is appropriately named; the land rises steeply on one side and steadily on the other. Rather than setting off towards Chipstead, I am drawn towards a row of shops and other outlets. The parade of shops is unremarkable and like any other small town. The first outlet is the local fish and chip shop. It is appropriate that it calls itself Mr Chips, but I am not sure if this is a reference to the town of Chipstead itself, the nickname of Chipstead FC, or just a shrewd marketing ploy to tell you that the owner sells chips. Its website address is rather lengthy, too - *www.mrchipsfishandchips.com*. It's possible, of course, that the owner's name is Mr Chips. I secretly hope it is and that Mr Chips wants the world to know through his website that he doesn't just sell chips but also fish with chips. Maybe, Mr Chips felt it was a kind of calling in his life. I keep walking aimlessly for a minute or so; it is time to say, "Goodbye, Mr Chips".

I notice the Smugglers Inn, which someone describes online as "a friendly little pub with a great atmosphere, reasonable prices". As I pass, it is closed. To be fair, it is only 11.30am, so there's plenty of time to get that great atmosphere going. Across the road, I notice Raise The Bar, which is most definitely open. It has a dark exterior and has the air of a trendy bar selling craft ales at inflated prices. I like the bar's name, and when I am close enough, I can read that they offer a personal trainer. Who needs a personal trainer to drink beer? On closer inspection, it is a place to get fitter, not fatter. Nearby, outside Londis, two men are firing up what I assume to be a barbecue. I can't imagine why they are doing this, particularly as rain is in the air. In fact, it is unlikely that even the least conscientious fitness geek will come out of Raise The Bar and fancy a burger off the barbecue. Curious.

As the fine rain becomes a little more persistent, I come to a point on CVR where I seem to be moving from Woodmansterne into Chipstead. Woodmansterne, while being decent enough, clearly is a step down the ladder from its neighbouring Chipstead. I wonder whether I should have bothered wandering around Woodmansterne; it has a different feel.

I reach a pub called the Midday Sun. It's 50% correct. It is midday, but there is no trace of sun. Outside the pub is a single boot on the pavement. How can someone lose a boot? It presumably means that someone is or has been walking around with one boot unless, perhaps as a prank, someone has hidden the boots in two different places. It's a substantial boot; the owner would be walking around with a wobbly gait, wearing one boot. I will never know the reason for the abandoned boot. And then, I wonder if the owner only has one leg. Or, perhaps, he or she just got semi-legless in the Midday Sun last night.

It's strange when you go somewhere you don't know. I am surprised when I see a signpost indicating that Sutton is four miles away and Reigate five miles away. It has been years since I have been to Sutton. The last occasion was possibly when I missed an open goal in the dying minutes of a 3-2 defeat. For clarity, I was not playing at the ground of new Football League members, Sutton United. I believe I was playing against Old Suttonians 4th XI in a Cup game. I wonder if anyone else on the planet remembers that long ball into the Suttonians' penalty area that I brought down smartly only to scuff the shot wide of the post. I even had time to see the keeper give up hope, looking forlorn at the thought of extra time in the bitterly cold December weather.

As the rain worsens, I reach a small road that leads to Chipstead Station. I am starting to feel damp and cold, although I am mindful that this is a practice run, and I may have to watch Bishop Auckland play in a blizzard later in the season. I need to toughen up. I am grateful to find a coffee shop that doubles as a bakery. It offers a different sort of warm-up. It is empty, but I get a friendly welcome as I purchase a cup of Earl Grey and a piece of Bakewell tart. It is truly delicious. The silence breaks when a young woman comes in with her young son. His mother suggests he has a doughnut while she has a cup of coffee. The son has an enquiring mind and cannot choose from the overwhelming choice of goodies; I can see his point. He gestures at various items, showing a degree of uncertainty. The helpful assistant identifies Portuguese custard tarts, cream horns and more as he points at the items on offer. Finally, the boy hesitates for a noticeable time and chooses a jam doughnut. The mother is kind and gentle enough not to remind him of her earlier recommendation.

I finish my delicious Bakewell tart, consider buying a Portuguese custard tart to take away, and prepare to leave. You can tell you are in Chipstead proper now. The rose and geranium soap is the minimum the locals expect in the toilets I visit before departing. Thankfully, it has stopped raining, so I am ready for the final push to Chipstead FC's ground. And, by golly, a push is what it needs. If you make a 90-degree turn from a road through a valley, there is only one way to go. Upwards. The road from the valley to Chipstead's ground will ultimately take me to High Road, Chipstead's ground location. It's not called High Road because there is a McDonald's and WH Smith on one corner with Next and Fat Face side by side. It's simply a road that is high. The road ascends steeply and winds from side to side. Ronald McDonald would not make it up this hill. And, as for Mr Smith or the man with a fat face, it's doubtful. It gradually becomes scarier as the pavement disappears and cars the size of tanks come clattering down the hill, a surprisingly high percentage with personalised number plates.

As I climb the steep ascent, fearing for my life, I pass houses with names that probably add ten percent to their sale price – The Rookery, Greensleeves, Rosthwaite and the more logical High View. There's no doubt that the residents of this road could have clubbed together and diverted Messi from the clutches of Paris St Germain to Chipstead FC if they had wanted. I finally reach the top of the hill where High Road awaits, together with a welcoming sign for the White Hart. It's a more than decent pub, serving good food and a choice of decent ales. If gin is your tipple there is a sign to help you, kindly informing the world that Emmie recommends Bathtub Gin with Mediterranean Tonic. The heading on the board reads 'Gin of the Moment', although I misread it at first as 'Gin of the Month'. I deduce that Emmie may change her mind at any moment. Although I am curious about Emmie's recommendation, my slightly damp clothes do not conjure up images of having a bath in Italy with a gin in my hand. I opt for the more basic well-kept Brunnings & Price bitter.

I decide to sit at the bar and realise it's the first time I have propped up one since pre-Covid days. The staff behind the bar and those managing the restaurant are sharing jokes. I ask a customer if he is going to the Chipstead v. Faversham game as he looks ready to watch sport in drizzle, but he is a rugby chap heading across the road to the local rugby club.

"I didn't know they played football round here", he informs me. I am tempted to reply that I didn't know they played rugby round here, but it might sound wrong. "Enjoy your soccer", he says in what now seems a falsely jolly voice. "It's football, not soccer", I reply. Well, I don't, actually, but I can't stop myself saying, "Enjoy your rugger". Unnecessary, I know. The rugby man laughs over his shoulder, departing with a false "Ha, Ha". It's one better than "Ha bloody ha", as I note how annoying I find people who say abso-bloody-lutely or use an alternative swear word in the middle. I ponder whether I did my bit to stand up for non-League football.

Behind me, a group is debating welding and smoothing. I learn that you can save two thousand pounds if you do something connected to welding and smoothing yourself – some chance of me doing that. I assume smoothing is a technique rather than something you do to yourself. As I disconnect from the welding discussion, what appears to be a group of Japanese tourists appears at the door, looking hesitant and nervous. They are unsure whether to come in, use the antibacterial liquid near the door, or wait outside. Rescue comes in the form of a helpful staff member, who negotiates the spelling of a proffered name and matches it to the table reservations coolly. Soon after being ushered in, more Japanese tourists arrive. I can only say that they are far more polite than us Brits. Perhaps, they have come to see Chipstead play Faversham Town.

The lady behind the bar asks if I would like another one, but it's time to leave. I am on business. I walk down High Road towards Chipstead's home patch. The views are breathtaking. After all, I am in an AONB. At one time, I worried that AONB stood for an Area Of No Beer, but this area deserves its tag as it is genuinely an Area Of Natural Beauty. It's a short walk to the ground. The cricket club is at one side of the entrance with the football ground on the other side. The bar, called the Muddy Boot, is just outside the turnstile area. I enter to join nine others in the bar, sit down with my second pint of the day and watch the end of the Liverpool game on the television. I can see the turnstile area through the window and spot a sign reminding me that this is a family club and that I need to moderate my language. Abso-bloody-lutely, I will moderate my language.

Another sign spells out five things to remember:

1. There are kids
2. This is a game
3. The coaches are volunteers
4. The referees are human
5. This is not the World Cup

Frankly, it's hard not to be disappointed. I was hoping for a child-free afternoon, watching Brazil play Argentina, managed by pressganged coaches with a robot referee officiating. Now, that would be a game, as point 2 correctly states.

As 3pm approaches, I finish my pint and walk no more than twenty yards to the turnstile. Before the game commences, there is a minute's applause for a much-loved Chipstead fan. I must admit I prefer a minute's applause to a minute's silence. However, I am sure the referee did not blow his whistle to end the applause for nearly a minute and a half. Let's hope his timekeeping during the match is better.

There is no need for the five ground rules; everyone is very well behaved, and it's immediately apparent that it isn't a World Cup game. Someone pierces the silence with "Want it, Chipstead", but with no venom, as the sound floats away. Faversham Town start well, earning two dangerous free-kicks. It's not long before Faversham skipper

Harry Harding puts the ball in the back of the home side's net, but the referee spots an infringement that surprises the home faithful as much as the celebrating Faversham players. The visitors find the Chipstead net again before the quarter-hour mark; everyone knows that the referee and linesman have got their objection right this time. Faversham continue to press with their number 9, Roman Campbell, easily misheard as Roman Candle, giving the Chips' defence a difficult time. It's not long before Campbell scores a third disallowed goal after a neat flick-on by Manny Osuwasemo. I'm not sure I've ever seen three disallowed goals in the first 23 minutes. The Chips are enjoying a charmed life as a deflected shot narrowly clears the bar with the keeper stranded. There is a gloomy air among the home supporters, an expectation that it is only a matter of time before the visitors go ahead.

The siege on Chipstead's goal starts to abate for the last fifteen minutes of the first half. In fact, very little is going on. Looking around the ground at the hoardings, I can't help noticing that most signs use a font far too small to read what is on offer. Diamond Electrics and NR Electrical Contractors don't make the same mistake. Appropriately, a power surge from the Chipstead defence by Simeon Dennis puts Karn Miller-Neave in a good position. The move ends in a tidy save from the Faversham keeper, Luke Watkins. It gives the home fans something to cheer them as they seek their half-time cuppa.

I join a queue where everyone except me asks for chips, only to be told that chips are not ready. "I'll have burger and chips without chips", quips one fellow. Returning with my tea (no Earl Grey this time), I overhear the home supporters discussing the prospect of a replay. They don't know where Faversham is and consider alternatives such as Essex and Kent as possible locations. For some reason, I keep quiet even though I know where Faversham is. There's no need to pinpoint Faversham with 45 minutes still to play.

Faversham start the second half well. Their tricky number 11, Steve Okoh, weaves in and out of the home defence and looks likely to get in a good scoring position. He weaves once too often, leaving the ball behind. On the hour, another chance goes begging – one of those situations where the ball flashes across the goal and the incoming forward slides in, failing to connect by a whisker. It looks impossible to miss. It's still 0-0.

Things slowly change. Chipstead's experienced captain, Chris Boulter, takes steps to tighten the defence. The odd half-chance starts to come Chipstead's way. With ten minutes left, a low cross is deflected, and Watkins makes an excellent save to keep the door shut. It's now Chipstead winning the corners and Faversham making the desperate blocks. The home side breaks the deadlock when a cross after a short corner is deftly headed into the net by captain Boulter with six minutes remaining. Two minutes later, the home supporters' concerns about navigating to Essex or

Kent are forgotten when a pass is pulled back from the byline for Miller-Neave to slot home. Before anyone can catch their breath, it is 3-0 as Kieran Lavery dribbles into the box and fires home. It's breathtaking stuff and wholly unexpected. The game ends with some pushing and shoving by the corner flag, but it has not been a niggly game. I imagine they call such altercations an argy-bargy in Chipstead. The whistle goes, and the home fans look as pleased as punch. Given that the attendance was 76, no one leaves early to beat the crowds.

The 3-0 scoreline astounds everyone. Like the players, I need to warm down after the game. The only difference is that my stretching is no more than reaching to pick up a pint in the Chipstead bar. I check my phone to see which train to catch at Chipstead station and discover that all trains are cancelled. The laps of the gods will, I am sure, play out in many mysterious ways on my trail to Wembley.

CHAPTER 1

QUEEN

Sunday 26th September 2021 – First Round Qualifying – Hashtag United v Chipstead

I am excited. The news is full of the fuel crisis and queues at garages, but I am on my way to Sevenoaks Station as I make my way to Pitsea. My wife is dropping me at the station. She tells me about work-related matters; little of the information she is offering lodges in my brain. I may not be the best listener in the world, but my head is full of the day ahead. Did I say? I am excited.

As a nine-year-old, I remember the day the mighty Chelsea came to Charlton Athletic in the 4th Round of the FA Cup. It was a hard winter, and postponements meant the 4th Round tie was on a Wednesday night. I recall spending the whole afternoon at school watching the clock. The evening was memorable, not for the result, but because I saw Bobby Tambling, Eddie McCreadie, Peter Bonetti and others playing at The Valley.

Today was different. I would not be seeing the superstars I usually see on television. This adventure starts a trail, following the winners of each successive round in the 2021-22 FA Trophy. My itinerary is utterly unpredictable. I was excited about the unknown route to Wembley I would take but, more importantly, I have always loved Cup ties. I like the draw itself, the finality of winners carrying on and the losers having to wait another year.

The first FA Trophy was won in 1970 by Macclesfield Town when they defeated Telford United. As in 1970, this year's final, fifty-two years later, will be taking place at Wembley. 1970 was a long while ago. While I remember it clearly as a young man in my late teens, it was the year of many significant events. The first Jumbo landed at Heathrow that year, and Prince Charles joined the Royal Navy. Martin Peters became the first £200,000 footballer when he joined Spurs from West Ham, while his former teammate and England captain, Bobby Moore, was arrested at Bogota prior to the 1970 World Cup finals. Eighteen-year-olds got to vote for the first time, Ted Heath became Prime Minister, and Tony Jacklin won the British Open. Jimmy Hendrix, The Who, The Doors and many more appeared at the Isle of Wight Pop Festival. *I hear you knocking* by Dave Edmunds was the Christmas Number One in the charts, although things went downhill after that, with Benny Hill and Little Jimmy Osmond claiming the top spot in the subsequent two years. 1970 was indeed a long while ago!

My journey starts at Hashtag United. It was an easy choice. There were nineteen 1st Round Qualifying ties (they are not 1st Qualifying Round ties, by the way). When I saw the draw, my eyes immediately landed on Hashtag United vs Chipstead. It fitted perfectly. I am following the brainchild of Brian James, who in 1977 wrote the book *From Tividale to Wembley*, following the FA Cup. He chose Tividale as he had no idea where Tividale was. Although I cannot for one moment claim to be ahead of Brian in journalistic skills, I am one step ahead since I have heard of Hashtag United. I was sure that they played in Essex, but that was the extent of my knowledge. Also, the name Hashtag United is somewhat different from the norm. The Football Association was unwilling to allow a team with such a name into the Football Pyramid at first. However, the owner somehow persuaded the FA powers by citing other clubs not associated with cities, towns or villages.

The hashtag was a term adopted by Twitter as recently as 2007. Previously, a hashtag symbol was simply known as a hash, mainly to denote a number or a 'sharp'. C# will be familiar to those with elementary music training as well as software programmers. Americans have long referred to the hash as pound or pound sign; presumably, they find a pound sign too challenging to write. However, there have been other uses around the world – for example, it is known as hex in Singapore. It's also been known as an octothorpe, but if you believe Wikipedia, there are many other names - crosshatch, crunch, fence, flash, garden fence, garden gate, gate, grid, hak, mesh, oof, pig-pen, punch mark, rake, scratch, scratch mark, tic-tac-toe, and unequal. I think we'll leave it there, even though hak and oof deserve more research. If you were to say "oof" after scratching yourself on a sharp fence in a pig-pen, you could use five hashes.

The game takes place on a Sunday as Hashtag United are tenants of Bowers & Pitsea, who had a home game on Saturday. The landlords quite reasonably take priority. My journey to Pitsea is not easy; there are rail engineering works at my end of the trip and around Pitsea. Whereas this might make the journey more daunting or a miserable affair, I am not in the least perturbed by it. It's part of my adventure, I assure myself. As the Japanese say, *senri mo michi mo ippo kara*, which roughly translates as a journey of a thousand miles begins with a single step. I wonder if I will cover a thousand miles on my route to Wembley. I somehow fancy that I will.

My visit to Hashtag United is a mouthwatering opener for my FA Trophy trail. The word 'unique' is often overused and misused, but I think it's fair to say that Hashtag United is a unique club. They were founded in 2016 by Spencer Owen, a YouTube star. The club started playing friendlies for charity. Unsurprisingly, Spencer was, and is, highly active on YouTube, publicising his club with match commentaries, interviews and news. Tags' players are in the limelight more than some Football League players. The club boasts a women's team, teams for various age groups and an eSports team. Indeed, one of their former eSports players, Tom Leese, a top FIFA player, was recently transferred from Hashtag United's eSports team for a reported fee in the region of £50,000. On YouTube, Hashtag United have over 500,000 followers. To put this in context, this represents more followers than Leicester City, who won the Premier League in 2015-16. And, if you are wondering what eSports is, it's playing the FIFA football game on a computer competitively.

The morning is bleak as the 8.47 to London Cannon Street leaves Sevenoaks. It is an uneventful journey. A middle-aged couple wearing almost identical colours struggles with a crossword puzzle. In my commuting days to London, I enjoyed taking a peek at a fellow traveller's crossword, using telepathy to help them with any answers. It is a nice feeling when they get one that you have delivered to them by thought transference. At least, you can imagine that. The couple's modus operandi seems to be that he whispers possible answers, and she accepts or rejects his offerings. For one clue, he whispers a solution, but she corrects him, whispering, "no, no, no, it's...", but I can't make out her alternative. It sounds like "red horse", a dangerously strong Filipino beer. I suspect she said "race horse" or "racecourse". I'll never know unless I buy the same paper.

The Sunday service means I need to transfer from London Cannon Street to London Fenchurch for my train towards Pitsea. An app tells me I can do this in 50 minutes by Tube. I decide to walk; it is only about fifteen minutes on foot. The City of London looks strangely deserted on a Sunday. Whereas the West End of London keeps buzzing all weekend, the City has its shutters down with few signs of life. My walk down Fenchurch Street itself is probably my first for 40 years. On that occasion, with two colleagues, I met a NatWest Bank Manager who recklessly loaned us enough money to start a business. The meeting at the office lasted no more than ten minutes and ended with much shaking of hands. "A quick beer?" suggested Mr Bank Manager. No one could fault Mr Bank Manager for his honesty and directness. Beer soon arrived, and it was quick. In fact, it was lightning quick. I believe five pints in one hour at lunchtime stretches the most seasoned drinker. I could only assume that NatWest's way of screening out creditworthiness at that time was by setting small endurance tests; in our case, five pints in one hour. They were clearly loaning money to bright young things with stamina. Algorithms and credit ratings came later. I struggled to keep up with the pace, but I can remember relief at the end of the fifth pint when Mr Bank Manager clapped his hands and said, "Right, I must get back to work. Nice to meet you". I still remember thinking that if this pace kept going much longer, I would soon be a crumpled heap on the floor.

As I pass the East India Dock Arms in Fenchurch Street, it looks just how I remember it. I wanted to know if there was a plaque on the wall in the pub recognising the epic drinking event, although I fancy Mr Bank Manager performed this ritual every day. Fenchurch Street looks more cheerful than I remember it. Next to the bank, there is now a pleasant courtyard with coffee shops. Across the road from the bank there is, unsurprisingly, a Pret with a Veg Pret a couple of doors away. I didn't know Pret had branched out to a specialist veggie outlet. Their management obviously thinks they need to keep these two types of customers apart. Nothing is open, though; this is the City of London on a Sunday.

No sooner has the train pulled away than I need to use the train's toilet facilities. They are spotlessly clean. I am impressed. I use the sink with three sections labelled 'soap', 'water', and 'dryer'. A generous glob of soap falls into my palms, but disappointment follows. There is no water, and the dryer does nothing. Not that I want dried soap on my hands. I slump from being impressed to unimpressed. I cannot decide what to do until the toilet paper comes to hand. My hands still feel slimy as I rejoin the carriage. In these Covid-ridden times, it's a bit like the Russian roulette of the hand gels at the entrance to every shop; some are OK, some are like water, and others are slime you cannot remove. The fourth and, arguably, more annoying outcome is a squirt of liquid that somehow fires in several directions, including over your clothes. My mind returns to the game later in the day.

A man out of my sight is making arrangements to meet a workmate tomorrow at nine o'clock, but the conversation is uninspiring and barely worthy of eavesdropping. After stopping at West Ham, the lifelessness breaks when a young lad joins the train and is quickly on the phone. He looks about twenty. He joins the train while talking on the phone but quickly ends the call. Immediately, he calls someone else and starts to arrange a meeting time for the pub to watch the Liverpool game later in the day. He tells his friend that he had broken up with his girlfriend the previous night. He does this matter-of-factly, without drama and without providing any detail. He describes it as 'no big', which I take to be short for no big deal rather than any reference to the size of his ex-girlfriend.

We pass the back streets of West Ham and Barking. The houses look the same as the ones I remember around West Ham's old ground when I used to see Trevor Brooking ply his trade occasionally. The friend returns the conversation to the meeting time; there's nothing more to be said about the breakup with my fellow passenger's girlfriend. The conversation ends without me noticing. Now it is time to tell his mother that he has split up with his girlfriend. He adopts the same matter-of-fact approach, but Mum has none of it. She is questioning why he has split up with such a nice girl. He tries to end the conversation by repeating, "Yer, right, Mum", but she persists and asks him to reconsider his decision – if, indeed, it was his decision.

We reach the next station, Barking. It's a weird sight, seeing a carriage full of people impersonating dogs. I drift out of the conversation with Mum; when I return, the dialogue is a rerun of what I heard previously. I glean that the ex-girlfriend's name is Amy and that it was his decision. Mum is asking an extraordinary number of questions about Amy - the time she goes to work, whether she still goes to the gym and whether her brother still goes fishing. He opts for minimal responses to the torrent of questions; Mum is not dropping the matter. The conversation moves on to when Amy got her hair cut shorter and whether he liked her short hair. It feels as though we are seconds away from the poor lad telling her to shut up. I quietly congratulate myself on keeping any information about girlfriends in my youth well away from my mother. "Look, Mum, I've got to go", brings the conversation to a juddering halt. It's time to end the call and talk to someone else. I don't like to speculate about who receives his next call, but it crosses my mind that it may be Amy's replacement. I wonder if she is ready for his Mum.

.

We are soon at Dagenham, which many people associate with Ford motor cars. For me, it is the memory of the Dagenham Roundhouse. In its day, around the early to mid-1970s, it was a major music venue. I can recall seeing an unknown Cockney Rebel playing there; the band had so little material that all they could do was play some songs twice. Singer Steve Harley, who still tours, finished with a solo version of Marlene Dietrich's *Falling in Love Again*. How can I remember details like that when I can't recall what I ate for dinner last night? Nektar, Stray, Mott the Hoople, Man and Greenslade were other bands I remember seeing there.

The train leaves London suburbs behind and passes through Upminster. The land is flat here. There are wheat fields on either side. It's a pleasant view; West Ham feels a long way off. I feel like I am travelling on a Thalys train through the Netherlands. The sight of a windmill reinforces the notion as we pull into Upminster station; there is not much 'up' in Upminster. We stop at West Horndon, a place I have never heard of. West Horndon appears not to have any cousins, such as East Horndon, North Horndon, or, simply, Horndon. The train crawls into Laindon Station, which is not the end of the line, but as far as the train goes today. Some workers in high-viz jackets peer at railway tracks. I am left to face the dreaded Sunday bus replacement service.

Without anyone to guide us, the passengers cross a

bridge like sheep and exit the station to the car park, where two buses await. Would sheep really have the nous to cross a railway line by a bridge? Most people choose one of two identical-looking buses. Without any clues as to which bus I need to get to Pitsea, I go with the crowd – the book, *The Wisdom of Crowds* by James Surowiecki, taught me something – I hope! The queue to join the bus moves slowly as a woman checks tickets more thoroughly than you might expect. A nearby café called Wakey Wakey looks tempting. It offers tea and breakfasts until I realise the owners presumably couldn't wakey wakey this morning as it is not open. Eventually, I progress to second place in the queue for the bus. The tough-looking woman checking the tickets looks suspiciously at the dodgy-looking youth in front and questions him about his ticket. It transpires that he is just dodgy-looking and has paid the required fare. When it comes to my turn, she realises that I am the epitome of trustworthiness and gives my ticket no more than a cursory glance. Maybe, the grey hair convinces her I am not a fare dodger. "Ooh, from Tunbridge Wells", she coos, revealing that she did look at my ticket more carefully than I thought. "That's a long way", she adds. I smile. I can't think of anything to say other than thanking her. At least I have chosen the right bus.

The bus stops at Basildon Station before heading to Pitsea. I have never been to Basildon before, but it looks exactly as you would expect Basildon to look. I suppose I should provide you with a fuller description of what Basildon is like; you will have to live with it being Basildon-like – sort of all right and not all right all in one, if that helps. Three of us get off the bus at Pitsea. The two other elderly passengers who disembark appear to be solo travellers until the man shouts to the woman, "Wait for me. I am sorting out the papers". I can't imagine what papers he needs upon arrival in Pitsea. He puts different documents into what look like colour-coded plastic folders, seemingly doing his office filing while on the move. She looks impatient at this bureaucracy and keeps walking ahead, occasionally pausing to let him get nearer before steaming ahead again. It's a sort of game of cat and mouse. It's rather like the *Tom and Jerry* cartoon, in which Tom the cat almost catches Jerry the mouse, but never quite succeeds.

I encounter an overwhelming array of road signs upon turning a corner, pointing to London, Southend, Tesco Superstore, and more. There is little to help this pedestrian as upward-sloping walkways and subways offer no clues about the way to my immediate goal, Pitsea town centre. I plump for the wrong one and have to backtrack and walk along a path with loose gravel which leads upwards but under the main A13 dual carriageway. I feel as though I am tackling Spaghetti Junction on foot. The route takes me halfway to where I want to be but then abandons me, so I have to cross some waste ground under the flyover. I am sure this is not the recommended way to get across to the throbbing heart of Pitsea, which I can see a couple of hundred yards away. Finally, one busy road separates me from Pitsea's main shopping area. It's not pedestrian-friendly. The drive-in McDonald's on my side of the road is indicative of the best way to get what you want around here. There also seems to be a drive-through Poundland. Surely not.

I briefly sit down on a wall to make notes about things you are reading about right now. Seeing me sitting on a wall, a kindly young lady, no older than twenty, asks me if I am OK. I feel absolutely fine. She re-checks that I am OK. Do I look ill? Is it the way I am sitting on the wall? It's a kind thought, and I thank the young lady. I finally cross the road and have a chance to look at the Dil Tandoori, even though I do not want a curry. A big sign in the doorway has a heading of 'Food allergies and intolerances' with small text below. Right now, I have quite a few intolerances that I could tell them. Firstly, getting across a series of junctions which are not pedestrian friendly. Secondly, the Sunday bus replacement service. Thirdly, the drive-through Poundland. I need to stop. I sound like a right Moaning Minnie.

An assortment of outlets sells everything you might want, covering food, haircutting services, flowers, betting facilities, pharmaceutical supplies, and tyres. My eye catches the sign of the famous Pitsea Market. I enter, thinking that a cup of tea would be welcome after my travels on trains and buses. There are adverts for designer clothing at bargain prices. However, the first stall I see mainly sells sweatshirts with slogans. They are the sort of slogans that might be funny for two minutes, or even ten minutes, but feel tiresome after hours, days or months. On one rack, there is a choice of three sweatshirts. Customers have the option of two sweatshirts with the single word 'King' or 'Queen' on the front or a wordier option, 'The Bitch is Back'. The regal options come with a gold crown above the single word, whereas the 'Bitch' one rightfully has no crown. My imagination struggles to imagine anyone buying a 'King' or 'Queen' sweatshirt and gives up at the thought of buying the 'Bitch' one. Did the young lad on the train buy Amy that sweatshirt as a joke that backfired? I search the market to buy myself a sweatshirt with the word 'God' on it, but I can't find one. Of course, I don't want such a sweatshirt because I think I am God. God forbid. I want to walk around the market wearing the God sweatshirt taking a zigzag or random route so that someone might observe God moves in mysterious ways.

It's time for a sausage sandwich or a sausage roll. I pass several cafes, some of which have seats, where I can get a cuppa, but I feel dubious about the quality. I spot a Costa Coffee at the back of the market and play safe, even if I am acting a little snobbishly. While the quality may be more assured in Costa Coffee, I suspect the service is much snappier at the cafes in the market. The queue is not particularly long, but I become aware of three or four customers immediately in front of me making complaints. One person complains about the type of milk used, while another has a missing flavouring. Another customer has the wrong items on the bill and is querying the price. A couple is ranting at the beleaguered Costa team; I'm not sure why. Things are not going well, and the Costa team show signs of duress. When the transaction for my tea and sausage sandwich goes through with only the mildest hitch – I did say I didn't want milk three times – I am quietly relieved as I find a spare table. The bill complainers are still pointing out errors. I get as far as I can away from the dispute, which is still raging.

After taking a bite from my sausage sandwich, I study Google Maps to plot my route to the Premier Inn, my resting place for the night. I find a route that avoids walking along a busy dual carriageway. I choose a road parallel to the dual carriageway leading to a park and onto my hotel. Suddenly, the peace breaks as a shout of "Fuck this" comes from the till area. The man disputing his bill has had enough. The outburst is loud enough for the café to go quiet instantaneously as everyone stops their conversation and looks over to the till area. The angry customer has lost temporary control of his arms as they come into play to clarify his feelings to the under-fire Costa team. I don't know if the staff resolve the matter, but he marches to a nearby table with steam coming out of his ears. Maybe, I should buy him a King sweatshirt to cheer him up.

The walk towards my hotel is uneventful as I pass much modern housing. I spot a West Ham flag in the garden of one house. Its background resembles Gay Pride colours rather than the famous claret and light blue. Coincidentally, a local bus passes simultaneously with a similarly coloured flag supporting Basildon Pride 2021. Basildon is the big brother of Pitsea who lives next door. Flags are clearly a big thing in Pitsea. One resident wants their England flag in pristine condition as it flutters away on a washing line, presumably awaiting ironing. Two houses beyond, someone has carefully placed two England flags as markers for their garden's northwest and southwest corners. I wonder how many flags come out in this area during the World Cup. Or are they just leftovers from the delayed 2020 Euros? Have they cleaned the flag hanging on the washing line so they can fold it neatly and put it away for next year's World Cup in Qatar? Do they iron the flags? So many unanswered questions.

I come to Northlands Park, a pleasant enough place to walk through. It has one of those gates that narrow at the top, preventing motorcyclists or cavalry from entering. I have to turn sideways to get through; perhaps the Council are trying to exclude overweight people as well. I arrive at the Premier Inn, where a cheerful young woman greets me. With minimum fuss, she takes my bag and shares a joke with me. I retire to the adjoining pub, the Watermill, for a much-deserved pre-match pint. I steal some electricity to recharge my phone before setting off to the ground for the big game between Hashtag United and Chipstead. As I stand up to leave, I realise that one of my feet has pins and needles, causing me to hop and stumble for the first ten yards, ricocheting off a wall. No one seems to notice. On my one-mile walk to the ground, I can feel the excitement kicking in again. This walk really feels like the start of my journey to Wembley.

I decide to shoot a short video before the game and enter the ground, paying the £5 entrance fee. The lady on the turnstile is remarkably amiable, and the air of friendliness continues as I enter the ground. There is a family atmosphere inside with parents and children enjoying themselves; this is different from the business-like atmosphere of Premier League football. I've seen it at other non-League grounds, and it is always heartening to observe. I immediately recognise the Hashtag United owner, Spencer Owen, kicking around with young boys and girls on the pitch. How refreshing. I suddenly stop in my tracks as I realise a mistake. In the adrenalin rush of shooting my short video, I left my rucksack in the car park on the other side of the turnstile. Fortunately (yet again), I am not at a Football League ground. The retrieval is as simple as someone opening a door in the bar and letting me back in. I am thankful for the reunion with my rucksack, which contains....well, nothing much.

As the teams come out for the game, I notice that the

sum of the numbers on Chipstead's shirts is 66. This fact is an unnecessarily complicated way to tell you that their shirts are numbered 1 through 11. The numbers of Hashtag United's shirts are from 2 to 19; I can't be bothered to add the numbers on their shirts; I estimate around one hundred. Chipstead start well. A lunging tackle in the early stages prevents Chipstead's talented centre forward, Tom Collins, from giving the visitors an early lead. Just after, a blindside pass by Kofi Anokye-Boadi nearly puts Collins through for the opener, but the assistant referee promptly raises his flag just when a goal looks on the cards. You feel that Anokye-Boadi is the puppet master in this game, as everything revolves around his adroit passing and positional play. His shot from the edge of the penalty area is well-saved at the quarter of an hour mark; it only seems a matter of time before the visitors take the lead. However, Hashtag United briefly rally. A long ball to Kiernan Hughes-Mason just needs a toe on it to give the home side an undeserved lead. Hashtag stretch Chipstead again shortly afterwards, but the attack is thwarted by a foul by Chipstead's big centre-back, Michael Olarewasu.

I overhear someone in the crowd pass comment to their neighbour that Chipstead will score soon. It isn't the most fantastic prediction I ever heard as it had looked likely since the start, but, sure enough, Jensen Grant slips a pass through to Tom Collins, who scores with ease to give Chipstead a 1-0 lead after 25 minutes. A second goal doesn't look far away.

Collins almost sets up a teammate for a tap-in, but the chance passes. It's not long before Hashtag concede a free kick on the edge of their penalty area. Tom Collins does enough to put the ball around the wall to give the Chips a 2-0 lead; the home bench looks disgruntled at how easily their opponents scored. If there's a pivotal moment in the match, it is in the 40th minute when Chipstead deftly clear a good chance for Hashtag United off the line. It's their first excellent chance. A free-kick follows for the Tags, taken by number 14, Kris Newby; it just clears the bar.

At halftime, I get the chance to talk to a visiting Chipstead supporter. He is confident that it will be 5-0 by the end. I venture a 4-0 prediction. I suspect both of us will be wrong. When I saw Chipstead recently in their FA Cup game against Faversham Town, they looked sure to be on course for a 0-0 draw and then scored three goals in the last eight minutes to turn the result upside down. I seek out the loo and soon discover that my flies are undone. I have sat through the first 45 minutes of my FA Trophy trail with my flies undone. I suppose it is marginally better than the time I ran a training course with my flies undone for the whole morning session. As Basil Fawlty would say, "It's OK; I think I got away with it", albeit in a somewhat different context.

If there are any doubts about the outcome of this game, they disappear when Tom Annetts strikes a volley beautifully to make it 3-0 after 47 minutes. It is hard not to feel that you have seen the goal of the season. A clumsy tackle injures the impressive Anokye-Boadi, who has had a good game; the transgressor is substituted after receiving a caution to avert the risk of a red one. With over twenty minutes left, Chipstead's substitute, George Craig, neatly slots home a fourth as he jinks into the penalty area. As Kenneth Wolstenholme would have said, "They think it's all over…It is now!". However, the crowd isn't on the pitch.

As the game winds down, another rash tackle by Olarewasu results in a blatant penalty for the home side. The referee, Peter Wilson, must have thought about producing a red card but opts to wag a finger; to be fair, it has been a free-flowing game. Craig takes the penalty and sends Kerbey in the Chipstead goal the wrong way. A group of children behind the goal chant "Hashtag United" in the hope, perhaps, of inspiring a late three-goal comeback. As the game draws to a close, there is still one more moment of excitement. The Hashtag United keeper, Jamie Jackson, comes out of his box, dribbles past two Chipstead forwards and then squares the ball across his own penalty area. It's almost a gift of a goal, but the chance slips away. The whistle goes for full-time soon afterwards. 4-1 feels about right to me.

After the game, I meet Hashtag United's Commercial Director, Neil Smythe. Having arranged to meet Neil, I am surprised when asking someone if they know Neil Smythe. "That's me", he responds. We talk about the game and the disappointment with the result. Although Hashtag United have made two steps up the League Pyramid in the last three years, Neil is confident their form will pick up. Everything you see and hear points to the Club being well run. I hope he is right. The Chipstead players look quietly happy after the game. Young Tom Annetts, the scorer of the world-class goal, is pleased to be named Man of the Match. Deservedly, in my opinion.

Chips' manager, Rob Kember, hears the story of my adventure and observes that I will be following Chipstead until they lose. "If you lose", I correct him. I bid farewell to several Chipstead players and supporters and look forward to meeting them again at Aylesbury in thirteen days. I return to the Premier Inn.

The Watermill Inn next to the Premier Inn serves me well in the evening. I am tempted to absorb a glass or two of Rioja to accompany my wholesome pub food. However, I am ready for an early night as I plan to walk to Bowers Marsh in the morning, which will take me over an hour and a half. I will be heading to see the Bowers Marsh RSPB bird sanctuary after my breakfast of sausages, bacon, hashtag browns and chips.

I wake to pouring rain; my enthusiasm for a long walk is low. Thankfully, it suddenly stops, and I decide to take a route that revisits the Bowers and Pitsea ground where Hashtag United play. There is a typical small row of shops near the ground – a convenience store, a bookie, an off-licence and the grandly named Golden City Chinese restaurant. Maybe, more. I enter the seemingly unnamed convenience store to buy a bottle of water. The Asian lady serving in the shop is most friendly and speaks with a pleasant sing-song voice. She seems grateful for the 45p I spend. I continue my walk towards Bowers Marsh, passing the Co-op Funeral Services building. They display a sign offering a 24-hour service. I wonder if this means they take 24 hours to pick up the body or whether they are open 24 hours per day. If it's the latter, I wonder if the slogan 'We are dead helpful' would be worth sending to their Marketing Director in exchange for a small fee. Pitsea and Vange Royal British Legion are immediately next to the Co-op Funeral Services. I can't stop myself from wondering if there is a discount for British Legion members. Further, I can't help thinking that Vange sounds like a dull place to live. When I google Vange, I learn that Vange is a 'Human settlement in the United Kingdom'. Strange. Well, not strange, but why describe it as that?

The route means I have to walk parallel to the A13 dual carriageway for over half a mile. It's not too noisy as I am a hundred yards or so from the traffic. There is little to see; the highlight is a big outlet selling wood. If you find wood fascinating, it may raise your excitement levels. For me, it raises my ignorance levels. The yard offers 'Waneylap Panels for £15 inc.' I have no idea what a Waneylap Panel is or whether it is good value at £15. I make a mental note to check on Google later. Close to the Waneylap vendor, a small hut sells' beigels' according to a sign. It is shut. I assume they sell beige bagels, utilising a pun to lure customers in. I am not a great lover of bagels, though, beige or not. I notice an abandoned red bike on the pavement. I realise this is the third or fourth abandoned red bike I have seen during my visit to Pitsea. When I saw the second one, I assumed they were poorly made bikes that break down easily, but I now understand that they are part of a Boris Bike-type scheme, which means you can hire a bike and dump it wherever you like.

I cross over the A13 and see the Queen Elizabeth Bridge spanning the Thames at the Dartford Crossing in the distance. The walk to Bowers Marsh is longer than I imagined, but you soon escape from the dullness of the A13. I reach the bird sanctuary, expecting to find a café, pictures of birds, guides and more. There is nothing more than a sign with a few arrows pointing in various directions. A man walks past me and points out a sparrowhawk looking for brunch. He asks what birds interest me. I have no idea why I reply, "sparrowhawks". I admit I was expecting more razzmatazz than Bowers Marsh Bird Sanctuary offers. Although there is some nice open marshland, the sort of thing I like, I only walk around for three-quarters of an hour or so. I call a taxi driver, who is keen to tell me that he has never picked up anyone from this location.

George, a fine East End gentleman, speaks in short,

sharp sentences, clipping many words. He takes some time to come to terms with the fact that I have walked to Bowers Marsh, but nods approvingly when I mention that I had come to see the football the previous day. I explain that I had seen Hashtag play Chipstead. "Oh, at BNP" was the reply I heard. I immediately think he is questioning my political allegiances or that one of the clubs has a link to the BNP. Is he one of the people with England flags in the front garden? "Bowers and Pitsea's ground", he offers when he realises that I am struggling. The conversation gets closer to flowing, and George clearly loves his football.

"I'm West Ham, I am", he offers. "I remember Bobby Moore, Geoff Hurst and Peters", he continues. I couldn't help wondering if he knew Bobby Moore and Geoff Hurst well but wasn't on first-name terms with Martin Peters. He tells me a series of things that I already know in a way that sounds like he is giving away secret information.

"Of course, West Ham play at the National Stadium nowadays", he wrongly informs me. He tells me there's a lot of money in football these days, and Man City are megarich. "So, who won?" he asks, after telling me that Man City are megarich. "At the Hashtag game", he adds. I tell him the result, but he isn't overly bothered by my reply. The taxi pulls up at my hotel. As I was about to leave the cab, he asks which team I support. I can't resist saying, "I'm Charlton, I am". He laughs. "Like Bobby and Jack Charlton". He is pleased with his joke as we part company or, maybe, he was laughing at Charlton. George constitutes a nice way to round off my trip. Even if he has been a bit predictable, he was very likeable.

George won't make it as my favourite taxi driver of all time. That honour will forever remain with a driver in Kota Kinabalu, Malaysia. As I got into the taxi, an elderly gentleman wearing the traditional long loose tunic, Baju Melayu, greeted me. He asked me if it was OK to put on some music. I agreed, expecting to have to tolerate some traditional Malay music. Instead, Iron Maiden's loudest crashing music came out of the speakers. "OK, if louder?", he asked. I agreed. His head soon nodded up and down in time to the music. George could have made the spot of my number one taxi driver if he had put on music. I would have been ready for Chas & Dave's greatest hits, and George could have surprised me by playing Swan Lake. It would have been a winner.

I take the train back to Fenchurch Street. It's Monday; the bank is open. Calling and seeing if the bank manager wants a quick pint is tempting, but I expect he has to fill in time sheets, meet sales targets and has a no alcohol policy during office hours. Funnily enough, I do not want five pints in one hour. Not today. Not any day.

CHAPTER 2

HATS

Saturday 9th October 2021 – Second Round Qualifying
– Aylesbury United v Chipstead

*I*t's the second round of the FA Trophy or, to be more precise, the Second Round Qualifying. The tie between Aylesbury United and Chipstead takes me to Buckinghamshire. In the last round, Chipstead's 4-1 victory away to Hashtag United was played at a ground the home team shared with their landlords, Bowers & Pitsea. And Chipstead's next tie is against Aylesbury United, another team that groundshares. Aylesbury United play at Chesham

United's ground, approximately thirteen miles away from their old home in Buckingham Road, Aylesbury.

I decided that my explorations need to take in both Aylesbury and Chesham. Departing on Friday before the game, I first seek to learn more about Aylesbury. My journey across London means that I start with a train to Charing Cross; it's a journey I have made a thousand times before. I'm seated opposite a young woman reading Pandora's Jar, a book focusing on women in Greek mythology. A man on the other side of the aisle has commandeered all four seats, seemingly treating the luggage racks and seats as a kind of walk-in wardrobe. He has various items of clothing hanging from different places and a bag, half-open with hairbrushes, toiletries and wires waiting to burst out. But, really, there's not much happening, and the view out of the window is so familiar to me that I notice little.

A lady joins the train at London Bridge with a speaking carrier bag. "I'm strong and sturdy", proclaims the bag with a picture of an elephant on it. She forces the man with the travelling wardrobe to reorganise his possessions, causing a small black bag, possibly containing a shaver, to fall to the floor with a clunk. One stop later, the wardrobe man gets off the train. I missed him gathering up his dispersed items, but I did catch him looking through the window from outside to make sure that, in his haste, he hadn't left his nail clippers behind, a tie on the seat, or a spare pair of underpants in the luggage rack.

The Tube journey across central London to Marylebone is uneventful. Wearing masks is compulsory on Tube trains, but two men decide to break the rules. One looks around and notices that everyone he can see is wearing a mask. Looking slightly ashamed, he reaches inside his jacket and tries to put on a mask without being noticed. The other man stares blankly into space; he has no intention of being shamed into abiding by the laws, by-laws, rules, or whatever they are.

Upon arrival at Marylebone, I have enough time to grab something to eat. I choose Pret a Manger from the various outlets available, as I am, as their name says, ready to eat. It's only a small kiosk with two lines forming an orderly queue. A man pushes from the back, jostling some people in my row, to ask the Pret staff if they sell smoothies. "Not sold", replies the East European-sounding lady tersely, which produces a loud "Hrumph" and a swear word from the jostler. He causes several in the queue to show irritation at his pushiness, but no one says what they think. Or, at least, I don't say what I think. I sit down to eat my lunch on a bench opposite Bagel Factory, an outlet I have always thought of as being named ill-advisedly. Who wants to be reminded that they are buying a factory-made bagel even if it is factory-made? To my left, the man on the bench stares at a crossword with a pen poised in his hand. He looks stumped; he is just staring at the puzzle. Without warning, he suddenly writes in seven or eight answers. Maybe more.

I recall that, many years ago, I also waited to write in answers to a crossword until I had a few in case I looked stupid. The stranger's answers start to come with ease. Perhaps, he had a mental block, or are my telepathy skills at work even without seeing the clues?

Five minutes before its scheduled departure time, an announcement tells me that a three-carriage train to Aylesbury is ready to board. When I get to the platform, I see more than three carriages. Belatedly, I realise there are two three-carriage trains there, meaning I have to accelerate to get to the far end. Just as the train is about to depart, two men join it and sit opposite each other alongside me. The taller man has one of those exaggerated smiles. After speaking, his face changes to a big false smile. It's a bit creepy; he would scare people if this were a horror film. The shorter man has a gruff voice that is hard to hear. It's a growly voice that reminds me of those American gangster films where you turn up the volume on your television but still can't understand a word of the dialogue. Mr Smiley has been back in the UK for two months after living abroad for seventeen years. Perhaps, false smiles were prevalent seventeen years ago, or he has been living in a land of false smiles for seventeen years. Their sentences are short and sharp, moving quickly from one topic to another, mostly about sports. Intermittently, one or both use their phones to make a call. Mr Smiley has brief discussions about financial matters; the false smile disappears during these calls. It's hard to tell why Mr Growly is growling. The conversation switches from Miami Dolphins to Anthony Joshua before lurching to an international golf tournament. It then moves to actually playing golf, and Mr Growly mentions his golf club. He talks about the slacks you need to wear to play golf at his club. I've not heard the word 'slacks' for some time and certainly not in such abundance.

I feel as though I am witnessing the filming of a crime novel. Mr Smiley says "ten, just ten" as he organises another financial transaction on his phone. I wonder if he is talking about ten thousand or ten million pounds. Ten thousand must be too low-key for Mr Smiley. The crime idea takes hold in my head. I catch myself looking at Mr Smiley's pockets to see if there is a concealed weapon; it would appear not. I notice that Mr Smiley is smartly dressed in an expensive suit, or, at the very least, an expensive-looking suit. In contrast, Mr Growly is wearing jeans and a plain navy blue sweatshirt.

The train travels alongside the Metropolitan Line on its route towards Aylesbury. If you have ever wondered where they keep underground trains at night, there are oodles of tracks with out-of-use carriages in this area. We stop at Harrow-on-the-Hill, one of four stations in the UK with three hyphens in their names. Two hyphens are two a penny, but the other three triple-hyphenated stations are Chapel-en-le-Frith, St Annes-on-the-Sea and Walton-on-the-Naze. Harrow-on-the-Hill sounds nice, but from the train, it disappoints. It does not have much of a hill to shout about.

Mr Smiley ends yet another quick phone call and points two fingers towards his eyes, saying to Mr Growly, "I've got 20-20 vision, you see". I have no idea why. We speed past Northwood and Northwood Hills Tube stations, but I can see Mr Smiley and Mr Growly starting to fidget. Mr Smiley makes his umpteenth phone call and comes off the phone, bearing an even bigger false grin. "Asked me for a job. Bloody laugh that. No chance", says Mr Smiley. "Is the Pope a Catholic?" replies Mr Growly. I want to ask him how the Pope being a Catholic relates to a job request, but it would seem a bit forward.

They continue fidgeting in preparation to disembark at Rickmansworth. I fancy the rest of the journey will not have so much to intrigue me. "He's 63, for Christ's sake", adds Mr Smiley. "Far too old". I pass no comment on whether 63 is old. Sure enough, as the train pulls into Rickmansworth, they leave their seats. As I look up, there is a sign with the words "Quiet Carriage" and the need to avoid phone calls. As if that applied to my two 'friends'.

As we leave Rickmansworth, I consider what a rickman used to do for a living and what a rickman might be worth, so to speak. I discover that it's merely a corruption of a landowner called Ryckmer from Saxon times, and worth means farm. Disappointing. The train passes through a series of towns en route to Aylesbury, all of which I have heard of, but I would have no chance of putting them in the correct order without the aid of Google Maps. As you progress through Chorleywood, Chalfont & Latimer, Great Missenden and Wendover, you are treated to magnificent views. Sheep and cows loll around in fields as we pass rolling hills on either side. The Chilterns are, indeed, an area of natural beauty. After leaving Wendover, there are sheep, more sheep, horses and then some more sheep - in that order.

I arrive safely in Aylesbury and make my way to my hotel, The Travelodge. Google Maps takes me to Market Square, and I realise that I am close to some of the places I intend to visit. According to Google, the Bucks Museum is a place not to miss, so I head there, just off the square. A friendly young man leaps up to greet me as though I am the first person he has seen all day. He is attentive, smiley (in a more normal way than Mr Smiley) and desperate to please. He follows me like a puppy dog as I wander around the reception area. He apologises that a major refurbishment is taking place. He suggests it would be better to come back in November but cannot guarantee the refurbishment will be finished by then. A down-to-earth woman butts in and, with an air of sarcasm, says, "that's what we are hoping anyway", referring to the grand opening in November.

I explain my reason for visiting Aylesbury and that I am writing about the town. I can tell my interest in Aylesbury fascinates him until I slip my particular interest in the FA

Trophy and football into the conversation. If he is plugged into the mains, I must have kicked the plug out as he wilts at the mention of football. He perks up suddenly, but it's not on my account. Obscured from my view, a woman in a wheelchair arrives with another woman. He powers back up, generously offering to help them to the upper floor via the lift. I fancy there is no history of Aylesbury United FC in this museum. The fussing of the two women ends abruptly when the wheelchair controller brusquely says that she will let him know when they need help to get upstairs. I am back in the middle of things. Mr Friendly-But-Not-Footbally feels he needs to engage in more amicable dialogue with me after being rocked by the FA Trophy topic. "You'll find the Reincarnated Rubbish display very interesting". Having teased me with the offer of reincarnated rubbish, he leaves me to myself. I fancy he is pretending he has urgent business to attend to just to get away from me.

Some 18th-century paintings of the Octagon Pond near Aylesbury and Long Canal catch my eye, but they do not keep me for long. I climb the stairs to the first floor to see the Reincarnated Rubbish Exhibition – and, to be fair, it is pretty good. There is a fish made of plastic bottles, an African wild dog made of metal drink cans and butterflies, a chameleon and a quagga. Quaggas (or is it quaggae?) were zebras that appeared to be half zebra and half horse, which the crossword-solver at Marylebone could not fathom for nine down. Some crafts are displayed at the other end of the upper floor, created by people far more talented than I am, but are mainly uninteresting. The woman in the wheelchair arrives at the upper floor but dismisses the Reincarnated Rubbish Exhibition as unworthy of her time.

"Isn't it just?" says Mr Friendly-But-Not-Footbally in reply to my gushing "absolutely fascinating". If he could show some enthusiasm for FA Trophy football – falsely or not – it would balance my exaggerated zeal. Did I really say "absolutely fascinating"? I leave and feel an obligation to make a donation. I had already received a gentle nudge. "It's absolutely free", I was told on arrival, but "you can make a donation if you wish". I press some pound coins into a large plastic cube. The two members of the welcoming committee smile benignly as I exit. I fancy they are judging me somehow, but I will not lose sleep over it.

I decide it is time to check on the Kings Head pub in Market Square. It oozes history and has an impressive courtyard. Several people are sitting at tables enjoying an afternoon drink, simultaneously imagining, I presume, they are basking in a pleasant Mediterranean climate. I go inside. I order a pint of Beechwood, an ale brewed in Terrick, just outside Wendover. It's a tasty pint, I decide, as I take the first sip before sitting down in a corner. A group of six people is sitting at a nearby table, laughing and enjoying typical pub banter. Judgementally, I suspect they have been drinking all afternoon. Their conversation flits from topic to topic. The dialogue moves on to comics of yesteryear, by which I mean Beano and Dandy as opposed to Arthur Askey and Sid James.

Someone poses two questions: "What comic did Roy of the Rovers appear in, and what colours did his club, Melchester Rovers, wear?" This is right up my street; they can see my ears prick up. I know the colours, but I am uncertain about the comic. Red and green, and Dandy, is the best guess from the gang of six. Someone looks to me for help. Like an old friend, I am welcomed to their table. Introductions become prolonged as jokes flow, and Dave takes time to explain why he is Dave when his real name is Donald. Or, maybe, it was vice versa. My answer of Melchester Rovers wearing red and yellow stripes is met with mutterings of "of course" and a claim by a woman of being "almost right" with "red and green". As for the comic that Roy appeared in, I am 80% certain it was Tiger. Google confirms that my knowledge of comic footballers was correct.

Of course, Google comes into greater play to ratify everything as I learn more about Roy of the Rovers. Although Melchester Rovers played most frequently in red and yellow striped shirts, red shorts and red socks with two yellow hoops around the top of the socks, it was not unknown for Melchester to wear kits with subtle differences. You can find red shirts with one vertical yellow stripe down the left-hand side, red shirts with two yellow hoops, red shirts with a yellow shoulder flash and red shirts with yellow short sleeves. But, there are some even bigger surprises; Roy occasionally wore blue shorts when wearing the red shirt with yellow sleeves. I was beginning to wonder why Melchester Rovers never needed to change colours due to a colour clash, but deep research reveals otherwise. Even when Melchester Rovers played a team in red, the referee usually adjudged that they did not need to change colours, but on a rare occasion, you could see Roy in an all-white kit with a couple of red and yellow hoops around the middle of the shirt. If this detail gives you the impression that Roy was a boyhood hero, I will have to disappoint you. I frankly found him a bit tiresome.

I limit myself strictly to one pint at this stage of the day as there is much important business ahead for the afternoon. Donald (or David) offers to buy me another pint and is, I think, hoping I might stay as the others had had enough drink and laughter for one Friday afternoon. I decline, but I am amazed at how much fun I have had in such a short time. As I depart, a chorus of cheerios and waves fill the bar as we part like long-lost friends.

My next destination is back around Market Square. Market Square has shops and two malls around its perimeter with various street vendors in the middle, selling samosas, kebabs, fish, flowers and more. I don't visit the malls, but the food outlets look tempting even though I am not hungry. On the eastern side of Market Square is a statue of Benjamin Disraeli. Disraeli was Prime Minister of Britain for two stints and is acknowledged as the founder of the Conservative Party. Some will be thankful for that; others will not. He was an MP for Buckinghamshire from 1847 to 1876. Just off the square, more surprisingly, is a statue of David Bowie – or, more accurately, David Bowies. The bronze sculpture shows different alter egos of Bowie. The reason for its presence is a bit tenuous. It transpires that Bowie first performed his Ziggy Stardust act at Friars, Aylesbury, in 1972.

Disraeli is making a point of facing away from Bowie. Then again, Bowie has tucked himself around a corner just off the square, so Disraeli would have had to crane his neck to see him. Still, as Bowie and the great Freddie told us, I am *Under Pressure* and need to move on. There are yet more statues to see as I cross the main A41 road that runs through the centre of Aylesbury, in order to get to my hotel, the Travelodge. The hotel sits alongside the canal next to Aylesbury's main theatre, the Waterside. I meet Ronnie Barker, seated on a wall, looking upwards to his left. He doesn't look particularly relaxed in his Norman Stanley Fletcher garb as he looks up at the theatre. Ronnie started his career at Aylesbury Repertory Theatre, which means he can greet patrons of the Waterside Theatre and those staying at the Travelodge, although he appears to be staring over my shoulder as I approach him.

I check in to the Travelodge, receiving a warm greeting. After dropping my bag in my room, I am ready to start a sad journey to the former home of Aylesbury United Football Club. My walk takes me back through Market Square and out of the town up Buckingham Road. Buckingham Road does not have much to offer except a steady stream of traffic. I pass what appears to be a deserted car showroom or furniture outlet; the area to its front is abandoned and overgrown. It looks like a symbol of what is to come. There is a sign pointing towards the abandoned outlets for TP Smart Repairs. It's unclear what they repair smartly or whether the proprietor is (or was) TP Smart.

After walking for over twenty minutes up a straight road, I reach a busy roundabout. There's a Nisa store here and an off-licence called Mak Wines, possibly owned by a dyslexic Scot. There's also a fast-food outlet called Favorite Chicken, which claims to offer Britain's tastiest chicken. I inwardly groan at the American spelling of 'favorite', just as my spellchecker groans as I type this. It is doubtful that it is Britain's tastiest chicken even if it is jolly good. I recall stopping at a shop near Melbourne in Australia with a sign telling the world theirs had been voted eighth best sausage in the State of Victoria. More honest, I would agree, although directions to the purveyors of the seven superior sausage-makers would have been helpful.

After the roundabout, you come to the Horse & Jockey pub, which has a Premier Inn alongside it. This hotel would have been ideal if Aylesbury United still played at the Buckingham Road ground. A road off to the right leads to the former stadium. There are houses opposite the ground's locked gate. The stands and floodlights are still in place, though nature has taken over the pitch and, indeed, the terraces, entrance and former walkways. There have been several applications for building houses on the site, but the Council is sticking to its diktat that the land usage is for leisure purposes only. The landowners have offered Aylesbury United the chance to buy the ground for £800,000, but that's a bridge too far for a small club. There is, therefore, an impasse. It's an unhappy situation that still upsets many supporters, even though the eviction was fifteen years ago. There's a fantastic video on YouTube about Aylesbury United's old ground organised by a group of people who visit derelict sites - *https://www.youtube.com/watch?v=170238SHw4c*. In it, the police eventually ask the 'derelictioners' to leave as they are trespassing, but it couldn't have been more amicable. I find a path by the river that allows me to gain some access. Getting closer, it seems so sad. The playing area is overgrown with bracken and other plant life that has gained a stranglehold. The stands and terraces are similarly dense as a jungle. I don't try to get from one side of the pitch to the other, but it would be a difficult, if not impossible, task. I sincerely hope Aylesbury United can play here again sometime soon.

My next destination is the Aylesbury Duck pub. In my opinion, you can't go to Aylesbury and not find out more about Aylesbury Ducks. Disappointingly, you can't buy a real Aylesbury Duck in Aylesbury; you have to go to Wendover. The easiest route to the Aylesbury Duck pub is through a park alongside the River Thame. Be careful not to confuse it with the River Thames. It's a pleasant enough walk with dog walkers and parents pushing children in pushchairs. I pass a dog-walking gentleman, who could easily be mistaken for Colonel Sanders – you know, the Kentucky Fried Chicken chap. He walks with a bit of a limp, but I have no idea if the real Colonel Sanders walks with a limp as you only ever see his head. A hundred yards ahead of me, I notice a woman changing her footwear, which appears a strange thing to do in a park. As I get closer, I realise she is changing from her trainers to her Wellington Boots as the path is flooded. With only one pair of footwear to last me until after the Aylesbury – Chipstead game, I have to turn round after briefly considering paddling to the other side of the flooded area.

The re-routing means I have to walk through a housing estate, which offers little to distract me. I pass a parked truck with the words 'Salt Kitchen' on the side with the strapline 'Sinful but salty'. The proprietor has been on Masterchef no less. I'm impressed. A young woman in front of me is waving a stick around; I'm not sure if she is water divining or searching for metal objects. I think she is the youngest person I have ever seen performing either of these activities. Good for her. I cross over to ask her what she is doing, but as I cross, she crosses too as if to avoid me. I decide it's rather threatening to turn and confront her.

My Google Map app takes me down Brunswick Close. I anticipate reaching a dead end ahead. However, Brunswick Close is not a close and leads to Jackson Road, the location of the Aylesbury Duck. A sign on Jackson Road unnecessarily tells me I am in a 'designated public place'. The Aylesbury Duck pub is at the end of Jackson Road, although I discover it has been renamed the Cotton Wheel. Outside, the pub looks fine, but as I venture inside for a pint, I can tell that it is not the place for me. It's only 5.30pm, but the pub looks more like a pub does at closing time, and several customers look like they have been there for some time. Two Aylesbury United programmes in glass cases on the wall catch my attention briefly. One is from a 1983 friendly against Oxford United, the programme costing 20p. The other programme costs 6d (2.5p in today's money); it comes from 1973, but there is nothing on the programme to indicate the opposition. I am slightly curious why these two artefacts appear on the wall. Undoubtedly, the day Aylesbury United played Bobby Robson's England side is far more worthy of note. England won 7-0 at the Buckingham Road ground in front of 6031 paying customers in that game. Peter Beardsley scored four while Gary Lineker, Trevor Steven and Dave Watson each scored once. The game did not boost Robson's charges before the Euro 88 tournament as England recorded three defeats to the Republic of Ireland, Netherlands, and USSR. Still, it was a memorable game for the Aylesbury United supporters, even if Gary Lineker allegedly has no recall of the game. I down my pint at the Cotton Wheel and look for a taxi back to the Travelodge. As a bus appears almost instantly, I take the cheaper option.

My evening entertainment takes me back to Market Square, where there is a good choice of bars and restaurants. The first pub I pass looks too busy, the next too quiet, and the third appears to have an age cap of about twenty. My eyes lock onto a pub that looks potentially too trendy for me. It turns out to be quite the opposite. It's the Rockwood, which has a mixed clientele and the most helpful lady running the bar. There are four local ales to choose from, none of which I recognise. I describe my taste in beer, and she makes an excellent recommendation, which I take back to a quiet corner.

Soon after taking my place, a group of four people in their forties or fifties approach the next table. I don't know why one of them asks me whether anyone is sitting there. Quite clearly, no one is sitting there, but I provide the affirmation the gentleman needs, and they sit down. They are a group of two men and two women, whom I presumptuously take to be two couples out for the evening. One of the men is leading the dialogue, and his voice is familiar, but I can't fathom why. Suddenly it comes to me; it's Louis Theroux. Does the other guy supply firearms or peddle Class A drugs? Or, is one of the women a sex worker?

Louis wouldn't come here for nothing. From the corner of my eye, I take a sly look at Louis. He has those thick-rimmed glasses, but he has jerkier movements than Louis. It's not him.

I can't resist a second pint; I need to double-check that I am not in the company of Mr Theroux. However, it's not long before a curry to satisfy my hunger takes priority. I lose interest in my neighbours as Google provides me with the details of an Indian restaurant called Desire. I throw back my pint somewhat too quickly and set off, checking directions to Desire. I discover that it is 50 yards away! The food is good enough but unspectacular. As I leave Desire, I make an unplanned return to the Rockwood, perhaps to reward them for two fine pints earlier. I find that Louis and the reprobates he is interviewing have left. It's getting near bedtime, or, more accurately, my bedtime; I prefer a glass of wine now that I am full of curry. The same lady assures me that their Rioja is a good one and, more to the point, she is right. It's a good nightcap, but time for bed. Many others in Market Square have plans for much later revelry than me, but it's not unruly or overly loud as I say goodnight to David Bowie and Ronnie Barker. I feel as though I should have porridge for breakfast tomorrow.

The next morning, I am awake at 6.30 as I want to get to Chesham, where Aylesbury United now play, early enough to explore the town before the game. I check my phone to see how far I walked the previous day as I have a mild obsession with knowing. 9.4 miles is displayed, further than I thought. It's a mild and harmless obsession. I met someone once who would get annoyed if they forgot to take their phone with them when they went upstairs without it, meaning that one flight of stairs would be unrecorded. I kind of get their logic of having to go back downstairs to get the phone and return upstairs so the missing flight is recorded, but there is a flaw in their thinking somewhere.

Although a bus connects Aylesbury and Chesham on weekdays, there is no such option on a Saturday. You need to take a train to Chalfont & Latimer and then an overground Underground for one stop to reach Chesham. It's a misty morning, and in places, my view of the rolling hills outside is limited. Watery sunshine seeps through trees before another bout of mist swirls through gaps in the trees. At Chalfont & Latimer, I change trains and await the Tube to Chesham. The Chalfont & Latimer to Chesham track is the longest stretch between stations on the entire Tube network. Furthermore, it's a single track all the way. The Tube journey to Chesham passes between rolling hills and some near perpendicular hills. It seems strange to look out of a Tube window and see a man walking a dog and a group with backpacks scaling steep hills.

We pass through a dense wood known as Chesham Bois. As a French scholar, although many years ago, I know that 'bois' is French for woods. I'm never sure whether Chesham Bois is pronounced in the French manner or like 'boys'. I remember meeting a posh chap years ago, pronouncing Theydon Bois as 'Theydon Boys'. Maybe, I should not rely on how posh people pronounce foreign words. I can probably avoid saying the word, so it's a non-issue, but mispronunciation bothers me more than most people. It seems like yesterday that, as a naïve eleven-year-old, I had to read aloud the word 'bosom' in class. I was good at spelling but had always assumed that it was spelt 'buzzom' or something similar. When I pronounced the word to rhyme with blossom, it caused hilarity in the class, followed by the English teacher mocking me. I will definitely avoid saying Chesham Bois today.

Coming out of Chesham Station, it is strange to disembark from an underground train into a country town, having passed open fields, hills, and dog-walkers. It's hard to imagine that the train was at Aldgate and taking weekenders around Central London to Madame Tussauds and the like only an hour ago. I wander towards the town centre, taking in a poster for T-Rextasy playing at Chesham's Elgiva Theatre. It doesn't tempt me, but I notice I'm too late anyway as the show was on the previous night. I decide to walk to the town centre rather than riding a white swan. As I enter the main pedestrianised area of Chesham, the first shop I see is displaying information about a Council development grandly called 'The Chesham Masterplan'. The Masterplan is apparently about expanding the housing stock and commercial premises shoe-horned between the steep hills that surround Chesham. As I read some of the Council's outpourings of benefits to the local community, someone comes up behind me and says, "you wonder who writes this absolute twaddle". The voice comes from a young man in his early thirties, who turns to walk away but snaps, "In a word, completely corrupt". It isn't the right time to explain that 'completely corrupt' are two words as they are spat out with some venom.

There is a market in full swing with a vast array of goods on sale. People are strolling around wearing their best Saturday morning smiles, carrying raffia baskets and canvas bags. The canvas bags are more interesting as they often have words on them. One looks like it has the word 'Laundryman' on it; another has the words 'Some people need a high five'. I wonder how she would react if I gave her a high five, not that a high five is easy when both her hands are full. To be fair, her bag just says that some people need a high five. It would be presumptuous of me to assume she needs a high five. Maybe, they are just trying to avoid the ten pence charge for a plastic bag. However, I fancy they have walked around with fancy bags for years here.

The Giggly Pig market stall sells more types of sausages than I have ever seen before. It's hard to imagine what the pigs get giggly about unless they find the randomness of whether they end up with honey and mustard, ginger and onion or whatever is hilariously funny. The next stall sells dog treats with offerings of goose feet, deer antlers, goat's ears and rabbit ears. There is something rather macabre about this stallholder's wares. I picture him lying in wait in secret hides as badgers, hedgehogs, and bunnies pass by. I really would not want to see the garage of this stallholder.

To some extent, you are trapped in the centre of Chesham. The roads out of Chesham appear to require climbing monster hills. White Hill looks as though you might need crampons and jumars to scale it. I move towards the busier end of the pedestrianised area and pass a shop called Mini Amsterdam. Unsurprisingly, it sells goods connected with CBD, vaping and the production of goods found in Amsterdam's coffee shops. More surprising are their other merchandise areas, which cover phone and computer repair services, home décor and toys. Perhaps some of these terms have alternative meanings outside my vocabulary. Before taking on the busy end of the town, I drop into Nero; I haven't had my mid-morning cuppa. As it is busy downstairs, I make my way upstairs to a lifeless room.

After Nero, I move into the busy part of the town. There has previously been an air of festivity, but now there is a full-on carnival atmosphere. People wear colourful and unusual hats while a Mexican band walks through the crowd, playing cheerful music and displaying excessive Saturday morning frivolity. Amid the carnival atmosphere, more serious-looking people manage stalls raising money for Disappearing Palestine and Saving Chesham. I find an alley where a string quartet plays *You're My Best Friend* before launching into Mozart's *Eine Kleine Nachtmusik*. The quartet is performing outside a jewellery shop. You can get a free beer or a glass of bubbles if you watch the four young musicians for a while. It's a tempting offer until I realise you are quickly guided inside the shop once you have accepted a free drink. I decide to pass.

I pass the Mexicans, who still look cheerful, playing up-tempo rhythms. I get a real sense of community; it's as though everyone knows everyone – except me, that is. A man patiently teaches children how to spin plates as more behatted people pass me. Then, I see the sign. It's Chesham Hats Off Day or, more accurately, *Hats Off! Chesham*. Everyone seems to be breaking the rules, though, as hats are more on than off. It doesn't seem to matter. A sign informs me that Chesham was Chiltern Region's Britain in Bloom town every year between 2010 and 2017. There's no room left on the sign to add any more years, so I am left to wonder if Chesham's form dipped after 2017, if they won but didn't bother to make a new sign, or, possibly, because the sign was full, they just gave up.

As kick-off approaches, I stop off at the George & Dragon for a pint. I opt for a pint of the curiously named Side Pocket For A Toad. The pump features a toad with a pipe in his mouth and an overflowing frothy pint in his hand. I sit in a quiet corner, enjoying what turns out to be a well-kept beer. I see a poster for Mouth on a Stick, but the event was some weeks previously. I wonder what happens at

Mouth on a Stick night, eventually discovering that it is the name of a band. Two men enter the pub. One wears a tall, red hat with yellow stars and a body resembling an alien life-form. The other man is wearing a t-shirt that says, "I'm not fat. I've invested in this". The second part of the claim may be true; the first is stretching it a bit far, rather like the t-shirt's material. An older man and woman enter the pub and take a spare table near me. They don't appear to know each other well and act nervously in each other's company. I give them the names of Janice and Roger; I have no idea why. Janice is clear that she only wants a light lunch but cannot decide what to eat.

"You choose first", she says to Roger. "Fish and chips for me", retorts Roger, giving her no extra time to consider. The indecision goes on for some time. Perhaps, they should try Mouth on a Stick, deer antlers or goose feet. Roger is standing, poised to go to the bar to order. She suddenly opts for the curry.

"Hardly a light lunch, Janice", I think to myself. Their conversation is stilted, and they change topics frequently. I learn that Janice makes her own spelt bread and eats healthily. "Not today, Janice", I think. Roger prattles on (there's no other word for it) about where he has been, and Janice seems to be taking a false yet fading interest. Their food arrives as the waiter asks who wants fish and chips and who wants the curry.

"Fish and chips is mine", bellows Roger. "Oh, did I

order curry?" asks Janice.

"Of course, you did", I say. Actually, I didn't, but I realise I've been eavesdropping too much. I decide to leave. I pass another couple who haven't spoken to each other since I arrived. I walk through the bar to the gents and pass Red Hat, who is guffawing as he invests further in his belly. I catch the punchline of his anecdote or joke, "Yes, all of them had it", causing four or five men to laugh aloud, one or two holding their stomachs. Perhaps, he could start the joke again for my benefit as I try to work out what joke would have such a punchline.

I return to the fresh air. Once again, the non-Mexican Mexicans are there, causing me to divert round another stall as they approach me, looking as cheerful as ever. I escape the merriment of *Hats Off! Chesham* and make the short walk to Chesham United's ground. As I pass through the turnstile, two gentlemen greet me, selling green and white scarves, hats, badges and other Aylesbury goodies. "Who do you support?" they ask. "Well, neither team", I start to explain.

Before I can explain my Wembley trail, one of them jumps in and says, "you must be FATrophyHound. I'm following you on Twitter". I have never received such a welcome upon entering a football ground anywhere. We discuss Aylesbury United's predicament of being unable to play at Buckingham Road before I take up my chosen place on the terraces, leaving the Ducks' vendors to sell more green and white merchandise.

Chesham United's ground is in a pleasant location with hills and fields behind the goal to my right. I take a seat in the stand and await the arrival of the two teams and the officials. At 2.55pm, everyone except a missing linesman is ready to parade onto the pitch. He eventually squeezes through the players to lead them onto the field as a burst of Come of You Ducks comes from the speakers. Ducks' captain Jack Wood receives a pre-match award for making 500 appearances for the club. He has the second-highest number of appearances for the club. Cliff Hercules, a name I recall, holds the record of 669 appearances, during which he scored 301 goals. He scored his 300th goal after he had officially retired from the game. Cliff is an Aylesbury United legend, having filled the roles of caretaker manager and Football in the Community Officer. Cliff's son, Max, is in the line-up for today's game.

Straight from the kick-off, Aylesbury United look the sharper team. An early free-kick for the Ducks, taken by Jensen Grant, rattles around the penalty area. Shortly afterwards, their no.9, Ty Deacon, turns well but shoots inches wide. Max Hercules and Ty Deacon are troubling the visitors' defence in these early stages, and a goal looks imminent. Matt Kerbey in the Chipstead goal fails to hold another free-kick, but again the visitors escape. Just as Chipstead appear to be getting more possession, Hercules gets inside his full-back and is brought down; the referee, without hesitation, awards a penalty. The Chipstead bench and players feel the decision is harsh; I would agree, but I think it was a penalty without the benefit of VAR. Hercules gets up to take the penalty, but Kerbey makes a Herculean effort, diving low to his right to keep the score at 0-0.

A long-range shot from Hercules after 22 minutes looks to be goalbound until it just goes over the bar. I was starting to imagine a 1-0 or 2-0 halftime lead for Aylesbury when Andy Kabuikusomo makes a solo run at the Ducks' defence, dribbling with his right foot. The ball runs away from him briefly, but as he regains control, he is able to swing around and score from the edge of the penalty area with a left-foot shot. Chipstead have gained an undeserved 1-0 lead.

Deacon continues to cause the Chipstead defence problems. On one occasion, he is fouled when in a good position, resulting in a yellow card. Then, he takes advantage of a defensive slip, which Kerbey in the visitors' goal rescues by narrowing the angle. In the last ten minutes of the half, Chipstead become more menacing. Kabuikusomo looks strong as he runs at the home defence powerfully; Davis in the Aylesbury goal blocks one effort well. Michael Olerewaju fires just over for Chipstead before the interval. Moments later, an injury causes Olerewaju to leave the arena. The half ends with action at both ends, but Chipstead have the one-goal advantage. One wonders what would have happened if Aylesbury United had converted the penalty when they were in the ascendancy.

The second half starts quietly, but, out of nowhere, Aylesbury's Deacon slips through an accurate pass to Sonny French, who makes no mistake, putting it past Kerbey. One-all. Chipstead respond quickly as Kabuikusomo has a shot charged down by Jordan Jenkins. A neat move follows with a cross by Jake Bewley, which flies unimpeded across the Aylesbury goalmouth. Kofi Anokye-Boadi, Chipstead's no.10, starts to influence the game more. His interchange with Lee Stubbs produces a sharp save from Davis. A break from Aylesbury results in French being pulled down on the edge of Chipstead's area. Someone in the crowd near me growls at the referee, while his friend, in a familiar voice, more reasonably points out that "we would do the same." Are Messrs Growly and Theroux in attendance today? Kerbey pushes the resultant free-kick over the bar to keep the score level.

One of the best moves of the game almost puts Chipstead back ahead as Kabuikusomo, Anokye-Boadi and Chips' full-back, Simeon Dennis, combine well. As the 90-minute mark approaches, there are fewer chances. Free-kicks break up the play, and penalties look inevitable. The referee blows for full-time; it is down to penalties.

Both teams score with their first two penalties, but then Jeremy Boakye misses for Chipstead as Davis guesses right and is right. It is Aylesbury United's second chance to get ahead in the game with a penalty. Alas, Deacon, who looked so dangerous, particularly first half, is the one to miss to keep the scores at 2-2 in the penalty shootout. It's an impressive save from Kerbey. Bewley slots Chipstead's fourth penalty to the keeper's left, but Aylesbury miss yet again, which leaves Chipstead's leading scoring, Tom Collins, the task of completing a victory. He looks confident and not without reason as he scores comfortably.

Overall, it has been an even game. Chipstead looked more solid in the second half and rode their luck in the first period. It was an opinion echoed by the victorious manager, Rob Kember, after the game.

After the game, I spoke with some Aylesbury United fans about their Buckingham Road ground. While some, not unreasonably after fifteen years, are resigned to never returning to their old home, others still campaign under the #BringTheDucksHome hashtag for a return. They are a warm and friendly bunch of supporters at Aylesbury United; I promise to come back if Aylesbury United ever play in Aylesbury again. Although *Hats Off! Chesham* made for a fun morning, Aylesbury United's fans would like to be back home with or without their green and white hats. My day with Aylesbury United is over, and United's hopes of FA Trophy glory are also over.

So, it's hats off to Chipstead for winning their second FA Trophy tie. As David Bowie might say, they have been *Heroes,* and it is time to walk back to Chesham Station and travel *Station to Station*. I'm in a good enough mood to be happy carrying a bag with the message 'Some people need a high five'. My last thought is about Aylesbury United. I'm all for #BringTheDucksHome; I fancy the England cricket team will have to use that hashtag in Australia this winter.

CHAPTER 3

PONCHO

Saturday 30th October 2021 – Third Round Qualifying –
Chipstead v Whitehawk

It's Saturday morning before the Chipstead-Whitehawk tie; it's raining cats and dogs. In fact, it's raining so hard, it's more like cows and sheep. It's the sort of day when a poncho might come in useful. The 'cats and dogs' idiom seems to have as uncertain a source as my enthusiasm for walking several miles to Chipstead's High Road ground. You can take your choice as to the etymology of the saying. Some believe the Norse God of wind, Odin, often pictured with dogs and wolves, somehow got coupled with the Greek expression *cata doxa*. *Cata doxa* means 'contrary to experience or belief' according to Mr Wiki, which seems like a long-winded and tenuous connection to me, especially as there is no letter 'c' in Greek, only 'k' (kappa). Alternatively, you might believe that people kept household pets in the rafters in days of yore, although I have no idea why anyone would keep a pet in the rafters - cats and dogs would surely flee the roof space if it rained heavily. Don't believe that? How about cats and dogs floating down the street in bygone days when it rained heavily? Again, this appears unlikely. Nevertheless, these explanations are more coherent than the Welsh equivalent, which roughly translates as 'raining old ladies and sticks'. Anyhow, suffice it to say, it's pissing down this morning.

My wife drops me at the station, but I get soaked in the 50 yards I have to run to the platform. To be fair, it's scarcely a run, more of a fastish waddle. As I board the train, I consult my BBC Weather app to see whether this rain is likely to persist. Ahead of me, I have a planned six-mile walk from Kingswood Station to Chipstead's ground. Another aspect of walking in the rain scratches at the back of my mind. To keep dry for walks before each game, I have bought some waterproof trousers (sensible) and a waterproof poncho, a source of much hilarity amongst my family. When the whole family finds whatever I am doing funny, there is only one thing to do – laugh along. It was one of those jokes that, I fear, has longevity. Each time the poncho is mentioned, it brings identical smirks and sniggering. The poncho, maroon in colour, is in a small plastic case in my bag, ready for use. I have refused to take it out until I need it. "Can you take a selfie when you use it?" various family members say through muffled giggles. I don't care much if the picture of an old man in a maroon poncho goes viral as long as it keeps everyone happy.

As I sit on the train, it is desperately gloomy outside. The BBC Weather app offers no cheer. It tells me there is a 98% chance of rain when I arrive at my destination in Kingswood. The poncho looks sure to come into play today. Even the golfers we pass at a local course are wearing so much clothing it's hard to imagine they can swing a club. As I become more alert to my surroundings, I realise that the only passenger near me is a man, half sleeping and half stirring. He looks terrible; I'm no doctor, but my expert diagnosis says it's a whopper of a hangover. I can only imagine that he fell asleep on the last train the previous evening and stirred in time to catch an early train home. His phone rings, which wakens him enough as he clumsily puts the phone to his ear. He mumbles into the phone at the caller, who questions his whereabouts. The only word I could catch was "train". On his arm, he has a tattoo, which appears to be his name. I wonder whether he would have been better served by putting his home address on his arm as well.

It continues to rain old ladies and sticks everywhere. I check my bag to ensure that the maroon poncho is safely in the bottom of it. There is a sense of relief when I find it there. Today, my route requires me to disembark the train one station after Chipstead at Kingswood. I plan to walk to Tadworth and then towards Chipstead across Banstead Heath. I intend to avoid the boring A217 dual carriageway, crossing it in order to go straight up Chipstead Lane and White Hill to Chipstead FC's High Road ground. Knowing that Chipstead's ground is at the top of a hill, I take Google Map's caption of 'mainly flat' with a pinch of salt to go with the cats and dogs. I know only too well that a steep hill will be part of the walk at some point. En route to avoid dehydration, I have located the Well House Inn in Chipstead Lane. I have budgeted enough time to get a pint to help me up the hill to Chipstead's home.

At another station on the train's journey to East Croydon, two elderly walkers join. They look better prepared than me. Their rucksacks appear to have various useful objects hanging off them, with four thermos flasks between them. Their waterproof kit looks substantial with less potential for amusement than mine. Their rainwear looks classier than my £7 poncho as they rustle and clatter towards two spare seats. They look totally unbothered by the incessant rain; I'm starting to get ever so slightly miserable about it. A ticket inspector suddenly appears in our carriage. I place a mental bet with myself that Mr Hangover has no ticket. The inspector gently stirs the now sleeping Mr Hangover, who wakes with a bit of start before closing his eyes again. The ticket inspector, an expert in deciphering mumbling, establishes that my mental bet of no ticket is right. Mr Hangover also appears to have no money. However, more mumbling satisfies the ticket inspector as he passes a cursory glance at the QR code on my phone. Can this man read QR codes with his eyes as well as translate mumbles with his ears? A true genius. Or, more likely, he just wants a quiet life.

As we approach East Croydon, where I will change trains, I spot an outlet of Buildbase, the sponsors of the FA Trophy, through the window. In my ignorance, I had assumed that they provide sheds and that their products do what they say on the tin. In fact, they seem to sell everything related to DIY, which probably explains why I know so little about them. I change trains at East Croydon station and grab an overpriced and tasteless cup of tea. One cheap tea bag and some hot water for £3 in a small plastic cup. I am beginning to sound like my mother. A man in a hurry bumps into me; he's wearing a Fulham tracksuit top and black shorts. If he didn't weigh so much, I might have mistaken him for a Fulham player late for the game. Although I leave my seat early to be ready to disembark at East Croydon, the Fulham player leaps out of his seat. He reminds me of airline passengers who click open their seatbelts and leap up the moment a plane stops at its bay after a long intercontinental flight. Do another ten seconds matter? Thinking about it, I am sure I have been guilty of this at times.

I have a 25-minute wait for my connecting train to Kingswood. I sit in a soulless waiting room with four others; the rain pouring down outside makes it worse. Repeated announcements tell the travelling public about the 'improvement works' which will cause a lot of disruption next week. The word 'improve' is repeated towards the end of each announcement. The sombre mood of the waiting room is broken by someone's phone playing an oompah band ringtone. It cheers me up briefly. I am not sure I've heard an oompah band ringtone before. I belatedly discover that my journey from East Croydon to Kingswood requires me to change trains at Purley, so I jump up and take the first train to Purley. I've had enough of the sombre mood, and the ringtone will not be as much fun the second time. Secretly, I'm hoping the same will be true about my poncho. Once I've given the family a selfie to snigger over, they may be sated; somehow, I doubt it.

I've still fifteen minutes to wait when I arrive at Purley. I decide to visit the toilets not only to pass the time but to pass…yes, you've got it. Confusingly, the sign on the door says 'Automatic door'. Beside it is another sign, which says 'press to open'. I press, and the non-automatic automatic door opens. By the taps, there is another sign which alerts me to the danger of 'very hot water', which is strange when there is only a cold water tap. I am bombarded with posters telling me it will be sorted if I see it and say it. To be frank, I am more suspicious of the claim than the likelihood of seeing something suspicious.

After availing myself of the facilities, I find a different waiting room where a couple whisper to each other. They must know that if they do anything funny or say anything unusual, it will appear in this book. They whisper in inaudible tones, using short sentences. I call them Peter and Sue; it suits them well, I feel. Peter and Sue look very respectable and refuse to do anything noteworthy beyond Peter scratching his nose with his middle finger. Isn't that a bit unusual? I try it myself; it feels OK, but I'm right; it also feels unusual.

With time to get across to my platform, I stroll to the lift, which tersely barks 'platform' at me. Then it says 'lift going down' more cheerily with an inflexion in the middle of 'going'. It continues in this cheery vein with 'doors closing' and 'subway'. I was half expecting 'subway' to be said in a monotone, but, no, there's an air of weekend heartiness about it. I walk under the railway line to another lift which will take me up to the platform. I am disappointed when I discover that the ascending lift is mute. How can I be sure where I am going?

Having fortunately arrived at the platform, despite the unhelpful lift, the train for Kingswood leaves seven seconds early - a small amount of time but enough for Neneh Cherry to sing about. Bad luck to those that cut it fine; the train will have departed. It stops at Chipstead Station, but as it edges out of the station, I suddenly notice something is different. Heck, the sky is blue. There is no rain. That two percent chance the BBC gave me has worked in my favour. The sun is shining. A 50-1 shot has come in (actually, it's 49-1). There is no sign of rain at all. Why did I waste £7 on a maroon poncho?

I alight at Kingswood; you can immediately tell this place is well-to-do. Upon leaving the station, there is a parade of shops. You cannot miss the Kingswood Arms just before the shops. It looks like a nice pub, offering a choice of three times cooked chips and sweet potato chips; it's a possible location for my dinner on the way home tonight. I am always put off by overly-descriptive food. Beds of rice, herbs from the meadow, curated selections, artisanal anything, flavours of autumn, pan juices and triple-cooked chips are not for me. You never see double-cooked chips or quadruple-cooked chips, do you? I check Tripadvisor, and nothing persuades me that it is the right place for me this evening, although it is handy for the train home.

Next to the pub is a restaurant called No.2 Restaurant, and pan juices are an unwelcome thought. My toilet humour finds this an inappropriate name for a restaurant, but just as my mind wanders off on this tangent, I realise it is called No. 12 Restaurant. I don't know where the other eleven restaurants are, but there's probably a good reason for calling it No. 12. It looks expensive and is expensive. White tablecloths never feel right to me if you are a solo diner. In fact, I don't like white tablecloths generally. I am sure they exist so that there is evidence of how much you spill. I move on to the adverts for activities in the Village Hall. I discover that a band called Atlantis is appearing on the 4th of December, playing their selection of golden oldies. I don't feel tempted even at the bargain price of ten pounds. My eye then notices an event this very evening. There is a farce called *Old Actors Never Die…They Simply Lose The Plot* taking place. Although the title is quite witty, and I do not doubt Lynn Brittney's ability to write a high-quality farce, I cringe at the memory of my parents finding Brian Rix's trousers falling down funny. This discovery writes off the Kingswood Arms as a possible eatery. I imagine the villagers of Kingswood flocking to the Kingswood Arms to satisfy their stomachs with triple-cooked chips before being enthralled by middle-aged men with trousers around the ankles. I continue to browse the parade of shops. I am not surprised by the number of beauty treatment suppliers and hairdressers in this parade of shops. Still, I am surprised that the largest shop is a pet store called Pets Corner, without an apostrophe. A sign makes it clear that dogs are as welcome as humans. I'm not sure how many dogs are trained to tap a card to pay for a shiny new lead or bone.

As I near the end of the shops, I cannot stop myself from looking through the estate agent's window. The houses in Kingswood seem to range from £1.5 million to £3.6

million; that price tag wipes out a significant proportion of the population as potential buyers. While looking at the £3.6 million mansions, I am startled by the sound of a car horn. It becomes apparent that someone has reversed into another parked car as they have attempted to manoeuvre out of their parking spot. There appears to be no damage whatsoever, but the owner of the tapped car has the look of someone who has had his car written off and acts in a surly manner. It is a bit of a farce in itself, wrapped up in a silent movie. The offending car's owner is remarkably affable, apologetic, and willing to pay for any damage. Mr Surly continues his silent role as Mr Affable repeats his lines. Mr Affable suggests that he can't see any damage. I think he's probably right. Mr Surly refuses to answer but then breaks his silence by asking if Mr Affable has a pen to write down his details. With no visible damage, the cost of any repair must, at most, be like loose change in the pocket to Mr Surly. No one has a pen, but I find myself standing there with pen in hand, having noted down the price of Kingswood properties in the estate agents. I feel as I though I have been caught red-handed with an illegal pen in my hand. I feel obligated to offer my pen, which Mr Surly takes with minimal recognition of my gesture. Mr Affable thanks me for loaning the pen to Mr Surly so that he can note down Mr Affable's details. Mr Surly demands proof of Mr Affable's identity, not of me, thankfully. Mr Affable cannot oblige, which turns Mr Surly into Mr Even-Surlier. Lynn Brittney ought to be here to get ideas for her next farce. I privately hope Mr Surly's trousers do now fall to the ground. I patiently wait for the return of my pen so that I can get a cup of tea at the nearby Watermill Café. Mr Surly speaks to Mr Affable again, claiming that you can often find damage later. Mr Affable goes along with this; he really is the most affable gentleman I have ever met. I eventually get my pen back. Mr Affable unnecessarily thanks me for allowing Mr Surly to use the pen. Mr Surly treats me as though he expects a pen supplier to be at his beck and call whenever he needs one. I want to say "tosser" aloud, but it remains in my head. Plus, it would have no effect on Lord Surly. Tosser. There you go.

The Watermill Café is pleasant and not overly ostentatious. It's busy, particularly as a group from the Tadworth Athletic Club occupies a large area with several tables joined together. It looks like an end-of-season booze-up, aside from the fact that they are eating healthily and drinking elderflower cordial. The friendly young lady checks for a spare table and tells me that I have to leave by 12.30, more than an hour and a half away. I tell her that I plan to be in a pub by 12.30 or just after; she gives me an "it's all right for some" look, revealing that her shift ends much later. I was only going to have a cup of tea, but the sausage sandwich served at the neighbouring table looks too good to miss, so I order one. I recall being in Beijing with my wife years ago in a restaurant where the menus were (understandably) in Chinese, and no one spoke any English.

After much deliberation, we ordered the same as the people at the next table using sign language. The people at the next table found it amusing, if nothing else.

The waitress told me there might be a delay due to the large number of athletes wanting their eggs benedict. There was no need to alert to a possible delay, as a sausage sandwich arrives in minutes. Looking around the café, I notice that the comfortably-off folk of Kingswood like to dress half-smart, half-scruffy. Expensive-looking polo shirts with overused jeans, t-shirts with the names of 1980s bands and casual jogging bottoms are the norm. I feel slightly overdressed yet wearing cheaper clothes - a strange paradox. I notice a Psychic Event will be taking place in the café on the 13th of November, the date of the next FA Trophy round, starting at 12 noon. If Chipstead win today's game and are drawn at home again, I could just about manage an hour or so of the Psychic Event. I thought about explaining this to the staff to see if I could get a ticket in the event of Chipstead winning and playing at home. Surely, the Psychic Event organisers should know whether Chipstead will win and gain a home tie. I finish my tea, pay and leave without indulging in any conversation about the Psychic Event.

As I open the door to go, a couple of grey-haired folk like me are leaving. "They do a good breakfast in here", the grey-haired lady tells me. I agree, although it is a funny time to reassure me about the quality of their breakfasts. "Oftentimes, we come in here…". She continues, but I stop listening. Of all the words Americans have invented, I find 'oftentimes' to be one of the most annoying; maybe, awesome beats it by a whisker. She rambles on about her 'oftentimes' breakfasts, but the words fall on deaf ears. I want to ask her why she has to use the 'O' word. We go our separate ways, and the next words I hear are the grey-haired man saying how nice it was to meet me. How polite they are in Kingswood, even if they lapse into unnecessary Americanisms. Apart from that tosser, Mr Surly, that is.

I walk back past the parade of shops, restaurants and other outlets and make my way out of Kingswood. As I leave the village and its big houses, I pass fields with horses. Every child in Kingswood probably has a horse – or, maybe, two or three. It is not long before I reach the A217 dual carriageway, which is dangerous to cross. Risking my life, I manage to take the road towards Tadworth. I pass streets of semi-detached houses, all with tidy front gardens. A sign prohibits reversing without a banksman. When I see a man with his young daughter reversing into a drive, I wonder if I should challenge the driver and check for his banksman certification. I wonder why people feel the need to put signs on their drive, such as 'no turning'. Is it to punish those who make a minor misjudgement in their directions or have over-relied on an errant satnav? The road is uninteresting. More worryingly, it is heading downhill, meaning I will have an even bigger climb to get up to Chipstead's ground on High Road.

I reach Tadworth and its station, where there are several shops. There's a butcher and baker, although no sign of a candlestick maker. I pass Castaway Travel, which occupies an overly large space. In a far corner, a woman sits, who, to be honest, looks like a bit of a castaway; perhaps, it adds to the authenticity. With the railway line in a deep cutting below, I see a sign pointing out, 'Thieves beware. Forensic Trap Device'. I am curious about a forensic trap device, even though I do not intend to carry out any theft on the railway, not least because it would require me to scale a very steep bank. I discover from Mr Google that it is a device used on railways to douse offenders with a chemically coded liquid, covering their skin, clothing and hair. It's a world I know nothing about, but there are some fascinating videos on the internet if you are curious.

Appropriately, as I leave Tadworth, I am a tad later than I planned. As I near Banstead Heath, I pass two pubs, the Dukes Head and the Blue Anchor. I cross the road to navigate the optimum route across Banstead Heath; without Google Maps, I would have taken the wrong path from the myriad of choices. Banstead Heath is beautiful. Dense woods surround the heath on sloping hills. Walkers, dog walkers and runners co-exist, but there is plenty of space for everyone. Someone calls for their dog - "Guinness!" - it looks up, but chooses to ignore the call. The owner calls Guinness three or four times with increasing volume. Guinness appears to be deaf. I suspect he is unhappy at being called Guinness when he has a mainly white body and a black head. The owner gives up on Guinness and walks on. Guinness decides of his own volition to follow. There's independence for you.

The sun makes it a pleasant experience as I walk across the heath. Thank goodness you can rely on the BBC's weather forecast. As I walk down another hill – this means even more hills to climb later – it starts to get muddier as I near the bottom. Google Maps keeps me on course, bringing me out at the roundabout on the A217 opposite Chipstead Lane. Getting across the A217 again proves difficult and once again life-threatening. I make it to the other side safely and without ending up on the alternative other side where the Psychic Event attendees might be contacting me.

Chipstead Lane is reasonably safe to walk down with a narrow pavement. I know the Well House Inn is not too far, and, sure enough, it appears just as the faintest doubts are creeping up on me. As I walk up to the bar, I am not ready to be served by a young lady in full Halloween regalia who appears unexpectedly on the other side. Recovering from the shock, I opt for a drop of the Shere Drop bitter. After a couple of sips, she kindly offers me a free bowl of soup; I show my gratitude. I am not clear whether this is to aid my recovery from the perceived shock or to test the chef's work as it is the first serving of soup of the day – or maybe, it is the chef's first day at work, and she wants to check that no one dies from the soup. Anyhow, the soup is delicious, even though I've never thought of beer and soup as good bedfellows. If the intention with the soup was to tempt me into something more filling, the plot fails, as I am soon on my way for the final push to Chipstead's ground. I could do with a push, too, as the hill gradually gets steeper. As hills go, it is just the right side of very steep. I pass the curiously-named Pigeonhouse Lane, and I'm soon leaping over puddles at Chipstead's High Road ground entrance. I see several Whitehawk supporters standing outside the bar in the October sun. They are laughing and are enjoying their day out. I enter the bar and buy myself a pint of local bitter, which is well-kept. I meet Trevor, Chipstead's social media man. I later discover that his duties extend to running the 100 Club, worrying about team sheets, and fetching ladders to retrieve a child's ball when it ends up on the roof.

Trevor invites me into a roped-off area for officials; it is probably the first time in my life that I have been in a roped-off area for officials. He tells me about the unexpected departure of Chipstead's star striker, Tom Collins, who has joined Hanwell Town. After presenting me with a Chipstead FC badge to add to my Wembley trail collection, Trevor has to rush off, wearing yet another hat, I shouldn't wonder. I leave the officials' area and join the Whitehawk fans, still laughing loudly. They seem to enjoy beer and plenty of laughter. I am introduced to a young lady, who will be wearing the shrimp outfit today; I am not clear why it is a shrimp outfit and whether it only comes out on Cup-tie days. I really must take my journalistic duties more seriously.

Whitehawk's fans call themselves the Whitehawk Ultras. They are anything but ultra-anything, pursuing an agenda of being anti-homophobic, anti-sexist, anti-racist and anti-fascist. Besides doing local charity work, they promote non-League football togetherness, relishing the chance to mix with opposing fans. It's a far cry from Premier League football, you might say. The Ultras have experienced ups and downs over the last ten years. Having risen from the Sussex County League, they were promoted to the National South in 2013. They were within a whisker of reaching the National League via the playoffs on two occasions. However, back-to-back relegations mean that Whitehawk currently play in the Isthmian South East Division.

Having seen Whitehawk seven or eight times at their home, I share tales about my visits. I recall the dramatic 5-3 win over Lincoln City in the FA Cup 1st Round when the mightyish Imps collectively lost their rags and got bundled out of the Cup. I also chatted about the funny and wholly clean songs Whitehawk supporters like to sing. I always liked the chant of 'the referee is a referee' whenever an official appears to make a mistake.

Kick-off comes quicker than expected; the chit-chat over a beer has made the time fly by. I take my seat five seconds after kick-off. In the opening exchanges, Stephen Okoh, Whitehawk's nippy winger, looks as though he may make it a tough afternoon for the home defence. The Chips create a good chance when full-back Marco Correia finds Collins' replacement, Kieran Lavery, who curls a shot just over the bar. Chipstead manager, Rob Kember, had shuffled his pack after a disappointing 5-0 defeat the previous week. Although Chipstead pass the ball around neatly at times, the visitors look sharper in the tackle and more incisive in attack. A Whitehawk header is blocked, allowing ex-Brighton and Egyptian international Adam Al Abd to curl a shot sweetly with his left foot into the top corner of the net. It is a well-taken goal in the 11th minute by a player who looks classy on the ball, even if he may have had far more pace in the past.

Chipstead look sharper in midfield as the half wears on, although they still look toothless in attack. Allen in Chipstead's midfield starts to inspire more movement from his team as Whitehawk sit back on their 1-0 lead. On the 25th minute, a quick break from a Chipstead corner has the Hawks in the position of five on three. As the ball breaks loose, a close-range shot hits the post, keeping the score at 1-0. A chant of 'We are Super Whitehawk from Whitehawk' resounds from the visitors' end. No.11, Lawson carves open the home defence yet again. Shortly afterwards, Lawson beats the offside trap as Kerbey in the Chipstead goal keeps the deficit to one goal. As the half draws to a close, Chipstead enjoy more possession, but when the whistle blows for half-time, the home fans cannot complain about the scoreline.

During the interval, the general consensus is that

Whitehawk are the better team. But, as the pundits say, it could be a game of two halves. It's a silly expression, in my view. Nearly all football games are games of two halves. Of course, there are exceptions; some games are abandoned after 40 minutes. Then, again, when I think about it, if you are a real pedant, it is unlikely that each 'half' is precisely the same length. From the kick-off, Chipstead look sharper, giving the visitors less time to settle. The danger from Whitehawk's two wide players fades and Chipstead start to threaten the Hawks' defence. Within five minutes of the restart, Chipstead have a flicked header diverted for a corner, and an effort from centre half, Olarewaju, cleared off the line and scrambled away. The game has a faster pace now; Andy Kabuikusomo works hard to get into the penalty area but has his shot charged down. Al Abd defends another dangerous situation after Chipstead's Kabuikusomo beats him for pace. Without wishing to sound like a know-it-all, I pass a comment to someone near me, promising an equaliser soon. As it turns out, I am a know-it-all. I receive a friendly pat on the back as Lavery fires home after Correia showed good pace down the right flank. Chipstead fully deserve to be level, compensating for their lacklustre first-half performance. With twenty minutes to play, the home side is in the ascendancy. As they confidently pass the ball, you can sense their newly found optimism, calling for return passes from teammates as Whitehawk defend deeper.

A late tackle by the goalscoring Lavery follows his

strike; there is a moment when you can sense that the referee is the most important person on the field. The Whitehawk players are thinking of a red card. In contrast, the Chipstead players try to coax the referee into seeing it as a mild offence. The Chipstead supporters wait nervously to see how it will pan out. The referee adds to the drama by leaving his hand poised over his pocket. Is it yellow or red? I reckon he is buying time to decide. If Mr Whay, the referee, firstly saw red, he mellows quickly as he pulls a yellow card from his pocket. The referee is a referee.

The game continues with Chipstead looking the more likely team to win. Kabuikusomo turns smartly with a quarter of an hour remaining, leaving himself in a good position. However, his shot takes an upward path. Moments later, Lavery controls the ball well on the wing and crosses for Kabuikusomo, who turns sharply again, only for a desperate block succeeding in keeping the scores level. I want to be a know-it-all again, but once a day is enough. The Hawks look like a side hoping to hang on, preferring the 50-50 risk of a penalty shoot-out. Their first-half midfield dominance is nowhere to be seen. Kabuikusomo is in the limelight again from a corner as, amid much jostling, he heads narrowly wide. Then, out of the blue, a back-header almost eludes keeper Kerbey as he scrabbles to his right to save a freak own goal.

The inevitable happens, though. A neat exchange of passes on the right of the pitch results in Miller-Neave finding space in the Hawks' penalty area. The attempt to halt Miller-Neave's progress was successful but unfair; hesitancy was not in Mr Wray's makeup this time as he points with authority at the penalty spot. After leading for much of the game, Whitehawk are experiencing a Halloween nightmare. Kieran Lavery takes the responsibility and gains the Freedom of Chipstead, so that he can walk his sheep through the town, as he puts the penalty past Stroomberg-Clarke in the Whitehawk goal. The keeper's effort to save the well-struck penalty is almost enough, but it just gets underneath his brave dive. I am slightly disgruntled that I didn't tell my neighbour that it would soon be 2-1, but I can feel smug inwardly. Inwardly, at least, I'm gruntled.

I reflect on my Wembley trail as the final minutes of the game pass. I have become attached to Chipstead. Before starting this journey, I hoped each winner from the previous round would lose their next game. I guess this was to maximise my exposure to different teams. I find myself gently supporting Chipstead, although I hope they get an away draw as I think about the next round. Much as I love Chipstead, I want to widen my horizons, as it were. In those final minutes, Chipstead continue to threaten, seemingly unaware that one mistake could lead to the lottery of penalties. Stroomberg-Clarke makes another good save, tipping a long shot over the bar, but his teammates cannot conjure up any chances at the other end of the pitch. Mr

Whay blows the whistle for full-time.

Trevor Stotten kindly offers to take me to East Croydon station at the final whistle. Firstly, though, he gets a break from his various duties of social media supremo, 100 Club organiser and worrying about team sheets. He sets off to get a ladder to retrieve a ball that one of the kids has kicked onto the roof. We clamber into Trevor's car and set off for East Croydon. I groan at Palace's win; Trevor celebrates. Both Trevor and I celebrate England's mauling of Australia in the T20 World Cup.

As I enter East Croydon, I notice there are people in Halloween gear around me. Halloween, or All Hallows' Evening, to be more precise, has had a strange history. The Irish and Scottish migrants took Halloween across the Atlantic to America. Then, America exported it back to the rest of the United Kingdom and many other parts of the world. All Hallows' Day on 1st November remembers the dead, including saints (or hallows) and martyrs. There is a drunken carnival atmosphere about the place; the revellers just see it as a chance to let their hair down, some with shocking hairdos. I feel a need to escape the exuberance of East Croydon, but as I check my phone, I note my hourly train home has been cancelled. It's all part of the adventure, I assure myself, googling frantically for pubs near stations on my route home.

Being skilled in finding pubs, I am not stranded or thirsty for long. As I sit sipping a pint of a local beer, it occurs to me that I haven't actually seen the centre of town on this visit. My mazy route means that I have missed the throbbing heart of downtown Chipstead, although I should stress the centre of Chipstead begins and ends quite quickly. It's a nice place to live; it even sounds like a nice place to live. If it was called Chipford or Chipton, I am sure house prices would be a couple of hundred thousand pounds cheaper. Even Chipborough, Chipington or Chipwell would reduce house values by one hundred thousand or more. It would take a name like Chipstead-cum-Sotwell to increase the cost of a home.

I find my mind wandering and wondering. It is a long while until Monday's draw when I will find out whether my adventure continues in Chipstead-cum-Sotwell, somewhere on the M25, or as far away as Truro City. Frankly, I don't care too much. I've already found the diversity of Pitsea, Aylesbury, Chesham and Chipstead to offer enough to bring plenty of fun. And, I have no control over how those balls will come out of the velvet bag if, indeed, they still use a velvet bag. My tangential thoughts mean that I have to rush to the platform to catch a train in the direction of my home. I hope no one sees me run or waddle to the station. But, if they do, so be it. No one has seen me in my maroon poncho. Not yet, anyway.

CHAPTER 4
APOSTROPHE

Saturday 13ᵗʰ November 2021 – First Round Proper –
Bishop's Stortford v Chipstead

The most memorable moment from the 1971 FA Cup Final for me was not a goal but a goal celebration. Anyone old enough and interested in football will remember Charlie George of Arsenal lying on the ground in the crucifix position after giving his side a 2-1 lead against Liverpool in extra time. Less memorable is the actual goal itself, a well-struck shot hit powerfully, dipping to the right of Ray Clemence in the Liverpool goal. Even less memorable is the nicely weighted pass to Charlie George by John Radford. For the benefit of those too young to know, Radford was an old-fashioned, 'Steady Eddie' striker from the days when journalists called goalscorers either centre forwards or number nines. So, why do I tell you this? Although John Radford is best known for his 379 Arsenal appearances, he also played in Bishop's Stortford's 1-0 win over Sutton United in the 1980 FA Trophy Final. Indeed, in 1987, Radford became Bishop's Stortford's manager in one of several stints at the club.

As I look at Bishop's Stortford's history, I get the feeling that Chipstead are stepping up a level for this game. But football games aren't decided on history; it's all about what happens on the day. The two clubs have only met once before. In the FA Cup in 2013, Bishop's Stortford came to Surrey and won 6-1 after going a goal down. We have all played in those games; I recall playing at Old Monovians with a weak team in my youth and losing 11-1 after scoring first. If memory serves me well (and I doubt it), I think we were only losing 2-1 at half-time. I can't quite remember my part in it. At different times in my uninspiring football career, I played as a relatively successful tap-in-from-one-yard striker, a dirty midfielder and a no-nonsense centre half. Bizarrely, the highest standard I played was in goal when I was called in as a last-minute replacement. Even more bizarrely, it was probably one of my better performances.

I'm looking forward to my trip to Bishop's Stortford, particularly as *The Sunday Times* recently voted the town as one of the best places to live. My journey to Bishop's Stortford means travelling to London and taking the train from Liverpool Street towards Stansted Airport. I did visit Bishop's Stortford around 1991 to see Bromley play at the home side's old ground in Rhodes Avenue. As far as I recall, the score was 3-2 to Bromley or maybe 4-2, although it could have been 2-2. I told you my memory was unreliable. Where have those 30 years gone since I used to follow Bromley in their Isthmian League days? I could run ten miles with ease in those days.

My journey to Central London passes uneventfully. I decide to walk from London Bridge to Liverpool Street. As I leave London Bridge, a tourist asks me the way to "Station London Bridge". I try to explain that she is already at London Bridge Station and point at the ground to reinforce the point. She looks at the ground in a confused way. Suddenly the Euro drops as she points at the sky, smiling. "Thank you, sir", she says politely. It is my turn to be confused. I can only assume that she realises London Bridge Station is between the ground and the sky. I set off across London Bridge.

Two men with posh accents arrive behind me as I walk past Bank Station. One of them sounds as though he was educated at Eton. He is describing his previous evening's liquid consumption to his fellow walker. He refers to an extra bottle of 'splendid' wine that he 'quaffed', which he admits sent him 'a bit whooshy'. I've not heard the word 'quaffed' for a while and never heard 'whooshy' before. I need to brush up on my posh-speak. Maybe, I should try the word 'whooshy' after a few beers in Bishop's Stortford this evening. The walk to Liverpool Street station looks as though it focuses on clientele who are coffeeholics rather than alcoholics. You could drink a half pint of beer in every pub between London Bridge and Liverpool Street and still be able to explain yourself upon arriving at your destination. I am no expert in the effects of coffee, but if you had a coffee at every coffee shop on the same route, I expect you would be highly charged with caffeine and highly charged in monetary terms.

I have plenty of time to spare when I reach Liverpool Street station and decide to take it over a cup of tea. I let my mind wander, but it is interrupted when I notice the distinctive and unmistakable looks of Ramesh Ranganathan, the comedian, at the next table. I do that thing where you want to double-check that it is Ramesh, but I try to avoid him seeing me. I take a few subtle glances, confirming that I am absolutely right. With some embarrassment, I find myself looking up Ramesh's Wikipedia page on my phone and immediately notice that his name is Romesh, not Ramesh. Sorry, mate. I have transgressed one of my own rules: never get someone's name wrong. However, I found it quite funny recently when a hotel chain sent me an email which began something like this:

Dear Title Surname
Forename, have you thought about taking the trip of a lifetime…

Romesh's webpage is not particularly informative; I already knew for some reason that he was a former maths teacher and lived in Crawley. This might give the impression that I have been stalking Romesh for years, but I also knew he trained under Jill Edwards as a comedian. And how do I know Jill Edwards? I enrolled for her stand-up comedy course, which was a victim of Covid. Small world, eh? Romesh and I could be on first-name terms. Perhaps, a double-act like Morecambe and Wise. Maybe, I should introduce myself now. Romesh sees me and makes eye contact. He wonders why I have taken four unsubtle glances at him. An urgent fifth glance at Romesh reveals that it may not be the unmistakable face of Romesh Ranganathan. The sixth glance, which is starting to unnerve the man who looks for all world like Romesh, confirms to me that it is not the comedian. Romesh is mistakable, or, rather, a bloke who looks a lot like him is mistakable. Suddenly the tables are turned. The lookalike is now glancing at me. I am wondering if he thinks I am someone famous. After all, it's an easy mistake to make. It has become a sort of dance as I try not to notice that he glances at me every twenty to thirty seconds. I have unnerved him. He looks as though he is trying to place where he has seen me and makes direct eye contact. He is trying to remember where it was. Was it the Brighton Dome? London Astoria? Scarborough? Blackpool? The shows must blur into each other. Except, of course, he is not Romesh Ranganathan and didn't appear at any shows.

My mind switches back to the two days ahead. I need to check the spelling of Bishop's Stortford properly. I have always assumed Bishop's Stortford was either Bishop Stortford or Bishops Stortford without an apostrophe. Indeed, Bishop Auckland has no apostrophe and no necessity for multiple bishops. Further, the good folk of St Neots have never felt the need to slip an apostrophe into their town's name. As I leave the café, I immediately see that the departure board shows Bishop's Stortford with an apostrophe. It's 1-0 to The Apostrophes. I wait for the departure board to display the platform from which I will be travelling and almost bump into the Romesh lookalike again. At least, I assume it is the same gentleman. I remember that Dolly Parton once failed to win a Dolly Parton lookalike contest. Is it something like that? If there is a Romesh lookalike contest, there are certainly some outstanding candidates. Thankfully, the platform number soon appears, and I can escape.

I board the train, noticing the itinerary in ticker-tape style on its side. Hmm, Bishop's Stortford is displayed as Bishops Stortford. That's 1-1 in The Apostrophes vs The

Not Apostrophe game. I realise that my train ticket will have the destination printed on it. To my surprise, there is no apostrophe on my ticket. It's 2-1 to The Nots. My overground train starts underground but soon emerges above the ground. The underground line running alongside the mainline tracks is now overground. I am sure I learned that more than 50% of the underground network is above the ground. In the daylight, we gather speed as we pass through Bethnal Green and Cambridge Heath. It's hard to see any green at Bethnal Green, let alone any heath at Cambridge Heath.

The first stop is at Tottenham Hale. It is unlikely that there are artisanal vendors at Tottenham, I reason. The word is far too close to Arsenal. Would a Tottenham supporter buy from an artisanal vendor? I doubt it. Two men in their late twenties join the train; they are deep in conversation about politics. One of them is keen to clarify where he stands politically. As his friend tries to pin him down on his political position, he attempts to explain by describing himself as slightly to the left of mid-right. I'm still none the wiser; it's a bit like those compass points west southwest and north northeast; it takes a moment for the brain to visualise the exact direction. His friend leans back as though satisfied with the explanation of 'to the left of mid-right' and doesn't pin him down. Maybe he would explain more clearly if he physically pinned him down. "I'm slightly more centrist", he confides, leaving my mental compass spinning. I wonder if he is left of the centre or just a shade nearer to the centre than his friend. Actually, I am not sure if he is a friend or not. I decide that it is all nonsense. Their conversation veers off into local council responsibilities and maintenance work of major roads. I lose interest.

My eavesdropping switches to a young woman who answers a phone call. She appears to have a Spanish accent, which becomes fascinating as she intersperses many English colloquialisms in her dialogue. She speaks beautifully, "I already have meats, cheese, crackers, olives der-der, der-der, der-der", using 'der-der' to explain she has plenty more. I like it, especially the way she says it. She threads 'much ado about nothing' into her discourse and 'biting the bullet'. I would love her to use the word 'palaver', but I suspect it's a step too far. She ends the call in a friendly but abrupt way, the way you can with a friend you know well. "Ciao. See you", she says, mixing languages with her pleasantries to conclude the call. OK, so she may not be Spanish after all. Her silence sends me back to the two politically-precise men who must be council workers as they debate subcontracted school maintenance. I've overheard some boring conversations, but this takes the biscuit. In fact, it would be more interesting if they discussed the biscuits they eat in the office.

The train hurtles through Cheshunt as the view turns to leafier suburbs. We pass the River Lea and several lakes on the right side. I make a mental note to sit on the left side of the train coming back to get a better view. It doesn't occur to me that it will be pitch dark when I return on Saturday evening. As we approach Broxbourne, I have good views of rivers and nature at its best. At Broxbourne Station, there is a local map with a big arrow showing that 'You are here'. I suppose it's more useful than a sign saying, 'You are not here'; that would be annoying.

As the train pulls into Harlow Station for its last stop before Bishop's Stortford, I find myself humming an old Genesis song, *Get 'Em Out by Friday*. I can recall Peter Gabriel singing:

I represent a firm of gentlemen who recently purchased this
House and all the others in the road
In the interest of humanity we've found a better place for you
To go, go-woh, go-woh

My mind flits back to Aylesbury United's fate at their old Buckingham Road ground and how they now play miles away in Chesham. Peter continued:

Here we are in Harlow New Town
Did you recognise your block across the square, over there
Sadly since last time we spoke
We've found we've had to raise the rent again
Just a bit

The sign on Harlow Town station clearly has an apostrophe in Bishop's Stortford, making it all square at 2-

2. We pass through Sawbridgeworth. I am aware of the town's existence, but, until today, I would not have known that Sawbridgeworth lies midway between Harlow Town and Bishop's Stortford. The train follows the course of the River Stort and, after passing meadows, woods, and open fields, soon arrives at Bishop's with an apostrophe Stortford – the sign at the station makes it 3-2.

Upon leaving the station, the first thing that you see is a big factory alongside the River Stort. I cross the river into the town centre with food outlets offering fish and chips and kebabs coming into view. The local kebab house has the name, Kebabery, which doesn't roll off the tongue as well as it might. There are two hairdressing salons, one named by the easily understandable pun, the Barber Chop, and the other more enigmatically called Ace of Fades. A beauty salon within yards of these outlets has a sign outside with the message 'Glow on, try us'. I am most definitely in the Land of Puns. The dentist lets me down, though. If the local hairdresser had qualified as a dentist, I am sure he would have called the establishment 'Mind The Gap'. The area over the bridge is full of small shops. Tat Lab, as you might guess, offers tattoos and piercings. The 'Lab' in the name makes me think that they are experimenting with tattoos rather than providing a reliable service. It reminds me of doctors practising; it never sounds right. Two vape shops within yards of each other indicate that the locals have replaced their cigarette smoking habit with vaping. As I continue along South Street, I spot the Crazy Razor, a Turkish barber who is presumably crazy or, at least, crazy with a razor in his hand. I am relieved that I don't need a Turkish barber today.

I head towards my hotel, but it is too early to check in. Exploration of North Street is the order of the day. North Street is a narrow street and as pleasant as any town centre. It is a narrow road in places, with traffic in single file queuing to escape to the outskirts of the town. I look for possible places to eat in the evening and notice Pizzaiolo, an Italian restaurant. Aside from being difficult to say, a pizzaiolo is a pizza maker. Try saying pizzaiolo ten times without hesitation; it's impossible. Perhaps, Pizzaiolo can sponsor the FA Trophy next year, particularly as Papa John's Pizza now sponsor the cup for League One and League Two sides. Papa John's, though, has missed a trick in my book. The cup should extend over four seasons.

Although North Street is a busy high street, the people do not seem overly hurried. There is a relaxed atmosphere as passers-by greet each other or stop to chat. I decide to explore North Street more fully on Saturday morning, although I've noted a place that looks ideal for a good breakfast. As I reach the end of the street, it starts to rain. I quickly buy a local paper and dive into the nearest pub. The Horn at the Half Moon sounds like two pubs rolled into one. From what I can gather, the Horn is where live music takes place, and the Half Moon is the pub. As it is mid-afternoon on a Friday, there is no live music, and a small clientele occupies three of the four tables in the front bar. I order a pint of Doom Bar and take a seat to look at the local paper.

The *Bishop's Stortford Independent* immediately strikes me as being a proper local paper. Although I appreciate that local papers are dying out, I dislike those that have merged, covering a wide area with news of towns and villages outside most readers' range of interest. This one is a proper one. I immediately discover how Bishop's Stortford conceded a late goal to Lewes Town the previous week to turn a potential win into a draw. There is a plea from the manager, Steve Smith, to 'Get behind the Blues in [the] Trophy tie' on the back page. As I thumb the pages of the *Independent*, I learn about a new development at Gilston to make a new town. I snigger to myself when I see a picture of an elderly person raising a glass after a virtual Orient Express trip. The virtual experience resulted from some care home workers using cardboard boxes, complete with fairy lights, to make it seem like a genuine day out. There was even a train driver to welcome passengers. I kid you not! God forbid I get old enough to be taken on a Virtual Singapore Grand Prix driving experience, using scatter cushions as the driver's seat and an umbrella handle as a steering wheel. And, of course, with fairy lights for the pits. If I do, I must tell my children not to allow my photograph to appear in a local paper. That would be the pits.

As I put the paper in my bag, I notice that *the Independent* has an apostrophe in Bishop's Stortford. Of course it would have one – it's 4-2. I finish my beer and leave the pub; the rain has passed. I take a walk around Market Square. I pass a large restaurant with an elaborate entrance called Piscio, although it is unclear what type of food it sells. Using my memories of Latin, I imagine it is an Italian fish restaurant. I use Google Translate to tell me what Piscio means, expecting an answer of 'I fish' or something similar. Google Translate is unequivocal in its reply. Piss, it replies. I decide not to put Piscio on my list of possible restaurants for Friday evening. I retrace my steps down North Street; this end has a different atmosphere from the high street area. It looks like it used to be the high street, but, at some point, Pizza Express, curiosity shops and other specialists moved in. Even the butcher's shop refers to itself as a 'butcher, grazier and farmer'. The Dog's Head is a big pub that looks suspiciously like a Wetherspoons. It advertises 'Wing Wednesdays', but not 'Thigh Thursdays'. Perhaps, this end of town is the Alliteration Quarter, which would be a fine thing to have in a town, given that the south end is arguably the 'Pun Quarter'. I've never really understood why areas in towns and cities are called quarters if there are not four of them, but who am I to challenge this?

Bishop's Stortford has a fascinating history. The Bishop's part of the town's name derives from the Bishop of London acquiring the place in 1060. During the mid-17th

century, at the time of the English Civil War, the Manor of Stortford was sequestered from the Bishop of London and sold for £2,845, a princely sum, indeed. At the time of the Restoration, it was returned to the Bishop of London. Bishop's Stortford became a major thoroughfare for road and water transport and was sufficiently convenient and close to London to become a trading post. In the second half of the 19th century, Bishop's Stortford's most famous son, Cecil Rhodes, set out to South Africa. He set up the British South Africa Company and, of course, the country Rhodesia. He has a lot to answer for.

I decide to cross the more northerly bridge in Bishop's Stortford. I want to check a pub and restaurant I earmarked earlier for my evening entertainment. As I approach the bridge, I see yet another vape shop – does every town have so many vape shops these days? I cross the bridge and walk up the slight upward incline of Hockerill Street. At the top of the hill at a crossroads, I can see the Cock Inn, a possible destination for this evening. Just across the road, I spot the Wiggly Willow café. I can't help thinking that the Cock Inn and the Wiggly Willow form part of Bishop's Stortford's Euphemism Quarter; maybe there really are four quarters here. I find the Zoo Hairdressers a surprising name for a coiffeur, but there is a picture of two camels humping in the front window to align with the quarter's theme. Actually, I'm making that up. There are no pictures of camels, but it would have embellished my tale. The Cock Inn proudly displays an old sign saying Circa 1547. Funnily enough, it is about ten to four.

I look through the window of the Cock Inn, and it looks as though it serves its purpose well. It has hand pumps for the beer and multiple TV screens to watch England play Albania in the World Cup Qualifier this evening. Across the road is the Ruby Indian restaurant, which looks ideal for some pre-match food. I feel prepared for my evening in Bishop's Stortford. I decide it is time to return to my hotel and head back down Hockerill Street. I pass the tanning shop, Sunbelievable, which ought to be in the Pun Quarter rather than the Euphemism Quarter. I walk closer to Wiggly Willow, which offers 'more than just a coffee shop'. Is this some sort of euphemism as well? Was it exiled from Alliteration Quarter?

After checking in at my hotel, I take a well-deserved rest before leaving for a Ruby Murray at the Ruby Indian Restaurant. I haven't booked a table, but when I arrive, three staff members fuss around me with assurances that they can squeeze me in. They pore over the table reservations as though they are planning a military operation. Meanwhile, a waiter reassures me they will find a table and asks me to be patient. "I was being bloody patient", I think unreasonably. When I explain that I will be quick as I will be crossing the road to the Cock Inn to watch the England game, everything is tickety-boo. It transpires that there is no squeezing required as I have plenty of room at my table. The curry is excellent, washed down by a pint of Kingfisher. The only blemish on my visit to the Ruby is a loud American. This man explains to his fellow diners that he always eats at the most expensive restaurants because those restaurants have the most to lose. It's a theory. Perhaps, I should tell the owner of Kebabery not to expect any American custom any time soon. Or, maybe the owner of Kebabery should charge £100 for a kebab.

A woman with long dark hair arrives at an adjacent table with her partner and two children. One of her children is a miniature clone of the woman. I am briefly fascinated by their similarity until the woman catches me looking across at her family. She smiles at me, leaving me to smile back, but I need to look away. I am still fascinated but keep my gaze on the American, who is stuffing half a naan bread into his mouth – at least, it looks that way. Halfway through eating the chunk of naan bread, which is hanging precariously from his mouth, he explains to a studious-looking woman that someone threw him a curveball. She looks befuddled by the term. I hope she bowls him a googly in return. Let's see what he makes of that. There's another exciting moment when an onion bhaji falls to the floor. The American and others scramble under the table, presumably to put that curved ball on the home plate while fortunately not crushing the ball. I pay, leave and cross the road to the Cock Inn to watch Gareth Southgate's army take on the Albanians.

As I enter the Cock Inn, I am briefly disappointed as, perhaps unsurprisingly, all the chairs and stools around the television screens are occupied. I look around slightly hopelessly until a friendly gentleman offers me a chair being used for coats and positions my chair in a plum spot. I am grateful for this gesture and go to the bar to get a pint. Before I've had time to have more than one sip of beer, Harry Maguire puts England ahead with a header that I fancy I might have scored in my day. The goal is greeted with muted cheers and a couple of shouts of 'get in there' and one man applauding a little longer than you would expect. Harry Kane makes it 2-0 less than ten minutes later, and an air of complacency spreads through the bar.

"These Bulgarians are not much good", says someone at the bar as I order a second beer.

"It's Albanian, you plonker", someone corrects him. Another pint and I might have cheekily pointed out that it's Albania, not Albanian. England are majestic and far too good for a somewhat disorganised Albania, whose poorly executed pressing game leaves gaps all over the pitch. England go in at half-time 5-0 up, and it could have been more; Harry Kane has chalked up a hattrick. The discussion at the half-time interval focuses on whether England can put away ten. It's hard to imagine England going hell for leather in the second half when they have another game a few days later, albeit against the even weaker opposition of San Marino.

The man who found me the seat believes England ought to score ten – or more. And, no excuses. Less than ten will be a failure, he tells me. Even though I think there is no pleasing some people, I indulge in chat about England, Tottenham, Charlton Athletic and Bishop's Stortford FC. He calls over Charlie, a regular Bishop's Stortford fan, to meet me when I tell him about my trail from Hashtag United to Wembley. As I sip my third pint of the evening, I am suddenly launched into the role of TV interviewer, seeking the opinions of Joe Public. I flounder. I ask Charlie what Bishop's Stortford are like in terms of ability. "They're shit", he replies, chuckling, but then, almost as an afterthought, qualifies it by adding, "in comparison to Spurs". "I suspect that Tottenham's player budget is slightly more than Bishop's Stortford's", I offer. "That's true", he chortles, "just a few quid".

He tells me that Bishop's Stortford have a couple of good-looking lads; I am not sure if he is talking about their football ability or physical appearance. Charlie's friend, Danny, joins the discussion. I drop into the conversation Bishop's Stortford's most memorable FA Cup performance, a 2-2 draw at Middlesbrough, followed by a 2-1 defeat in the home replay. It draws a blank look from Charlie and Danny, but then I realise they were probably toddlers in 1983. Without warning, we are talking about Charlton's ground, The Valley, and the fact that it is in a valley. Danny thinks it's a coincidence that The Valley is in a valley. I don't know how to explain that it is not a coincidence. I am unsure how the conversation switched to that topic.

The second half has my chair-finding friend switch from slightly negative to totally apoplectic as England fiddle-faddle around and play out the second half, adding no further goals to their commanding five-goal lead. "Pass the ball" is his main instruction, which ranges in tone from moany to shouting and, occasionally, shrieking and pointing at the TV. Southgate is lucky not to be sitting in the bar. England players pass the ball well, but they have that air of schoolchildren on the last day of term. The chairperson is orchestrating protests in the bar to little effect, claiming that England ought to be beating 'these amateurs' by ten or more. In a way, he is correct, but I'm feeling quite mellow and enjoying my beer too much to become over-excited. Football has become somewhat incidental to my enjoyment levels.

Just as I think he is beginning to mellow as well, he leaps out of his chair, shouting, "for Chrissake, shoot". The barman looks across, grateful, I suspect, that the game will be over in ten minutes. The chair-finder turns to me for support; I nod in agreement. The nod is not good enough; he demands ratification. "I am right, ain't I?" he says. I confirm that he is right. It's a somewhat unsatisfactory exchange of words. Suddenly, the chairperson becomes calm. With four or five minutes left to play, he shrugs his shoulders and settles back into his chair. As he does so, his blood pressure visibly falls, and he mutters resignedly, "it's going to be 5-0". I nod in agreement again, feigning a resigned look. He watches silently for the last few minutes. As soon as the referee blows the final whistle, he jumps up from his chair, smiling. "Ha, we won that easily, " he says, becoming light-hearted in his manner. As he makes a beeline to the bar for refreshment, I decide to leave. We awkwardly shake hands; I wasn't expecting him to offer his hand and I flap out my hand belatedly, more like a flipper. As I pass through several bodies between my chair and the door, someone shouts across the bar, "See you, mate". I look up and realise that it is Charlie. Or maybe, it was Danny. I am not sure.

The walk back to my hotel is about twenty minutes as I head back towards the town centre. I pass 'more than just a coffee', accountancy firms and shops, continuing over the River Stort bridge. As I reach the town centre, I see a queue of people waiting to enter what I assume to be a nightclub. I have never queued to get into a nightclub. Without warning, perhaps inspired by the waiting nightclubbers, I decide to grab a 'homebound' beer. A pub across the road from the nightclub appears to be a hospitable place to pass half an hour. I enter the Star, which, I soon find, serves a good quality pint of beer. It is busy, and I quickly see that I am not their Friday night target market. However, it has a friendly atmosphere and is spacious enough without being like a Wetherspoonian barn. As I purchase my beer, a young lady asks the barman if she can have four shots of some description. I cheekily tell her that she can't as she has had enough to drink and that I am a police officer. She laughs and says, "my dad is a policeman; he'd probably say I've had enough to drink too". I ask her not to report me to her dad for impersonating a police officer. She laughs. I find a quiet corner and ponder the offers shown in the bar. The Bottomless Brunch is intriguing (not to mention the Festive Bottomless Brunch). However, I am left to wonder what is crazy about their Crazy Sunday Topped Roasties. The beer slips down all too easily, but I am disciplined enough to know that, at my age, it is time to get back to my hotel room. At least, I think I am.

My hotel is more of a pub with some cabins in the car park. It is very comfortable and competitively priced even if the rooms are small. At the last moment, I decide to have a nightcap in the pub, even though I've had enough beers for the evening. As soon as I enter, I sense a convivial atmosphere with everyone sharing jokes. I find it easy to join in. I have had my fill of beer for the day, so I fall back on a nightcap of red wine. The Rioja on offer is a decent one. A group of four men joke about getting home. A young couple joins in the banter, celebrating that they are flying from nearby Stansted in the morning to Spain. It transpires that they are in the cabin next to me. Lisa, behind the bar, joins in the cheery atmosphere and asks me why I am staying in Bishop's Stortford. I explain my *From Hashtag to Wembley* adventure, which she describes as 'cool'. She not only appears keen to appear in this book but shows enthusiasm to offer another Rioja, which I don't need. I accept the offer. The camaraderie and humour continue, but things are thankfully coming to a close. The young couple decide it's time to leave – they've had enough booze for the evening and have an early flight. I say goodnight to Jack and Alice and wish them a good trip to Spain. "Oh yes," replies Alice with some gusto as they wave exaggeratedly by the door leading to the car park cabins. Five minutes later (or it seems like five minutes), I bid farewell to Lisa and several others. It is time for some rest; there's a big game ahead. I have to confess that I feel a bit whooshy or even somewhat whooshed. I enter my room, getting the combination lock on the cabin door right at the first attempt in the half-light. As I enter the room, I notice how thin the walls are. Jack and Alice are uttering the words "Oh yes" loudly yet again, but in, I suspect, a somewhat different context. I make tea, put on some headphones and crash out soon afterwards.

I am slow off the mark on Saturday morning but undamaged from the previous night's excesses. I plan to start the morning exploring the old Rhodes Avenue ground area and then seek a good fry-up in the town centre. Whether Cecil Rhodes liked to watch a game of football when he was in town is unknown. The old ground is not far from my hotel, so I walk southwards from Bishop's Stortford towards Rhodes Avenue. I pass the BS Escape Rooms; I assume BS stands for Bishop's Stortford, not the social media acronym.

As I look over to the Escape Rooms, it's hard to see an entrance, never mind an exit. Perhaps that's the escapology challenge. I reach Rhodes Avenue sooner than I expected. As has happened several times when I revisit places from years ago, I have no recall of the area whatsoever. The site of the old football ground has now been replaced by houses on roads probably named after town councillors. I can guess where the old ground was roughly by the newness of the houses, but there is not a lot to see. I wander back along Rhodes Avenue, noticing that the roads leading off on the older side of the road have more interesting names. Zambesi Road and Shangani Road are named after Zimbabwean rivers. Indeed, the Battle of Shangani was the first battle of the First Matabele War in 1893, with the 128th anniversary just a few days earlier than today. This battle was a particularly nasty affair where the British forces ruthlessly thwarted a surprise overnight attack by the Matabele. These road names are far more interesting than the town councillors whose names appear at the site of Bishop's Stortford FC's old ground. As I leave Rhodes Avenue to retrace my steps into town, I notice an establishment called Doody's. Doody's purports to offer archery, circus skills and maths days. If giving children skills with bows and arrows while dressed as a clown is a way to teach algebra, I'm all for it.

I return to modern times and pass Kwik Fit. Their sign lacks the expected punctuation mark, narrowing the gap to

4-3 to The Apostrophes. However, it soon becomes a rout as Bishop's Stortford Social Club knows about apostrophes, as do their next-door neighbours, to make it 6-3. I eventually arrive at South Street Pantry, which looks like an ideal place to consume much-needed sausages, bacon, eggs, baked beans and the like. Nearby, Kemsley Barbers warns the public that there are only 42 days left to Christmas, but it's not enough to make me panic about getting a haircut. For heaven's sake, I don't need one anyway. Breakfast is good. In fact, it is excellent and convinces my stomach that the Rioja last night was no more than a minor aberration. After breakfast, I potter around the Bishop's Stortford Saturday market. It has a mixture of mundane things and unexpected things. I'm attracted to a cake stall, which offers a sumptuous choice. I opt for the billionaire's cake with cookie dough. The vendor chit-chats idly with me and passes me my purchase; I can't believe how heavy it is to hold. My stomach wonders when it has to get to work on this highly calorific offering. "It's for later", I say to myself, as I hum to myself ", You can't get quicker than a Kwik Fit".

I wander around the town centre and the market before exploring, what I would call the back of the town near the station. This area is where you find the Allinson Bakery. Amusingly, they have a sign that offers jobs with the unintentional pun – various roles available at the factory. The factory owner is presumably well-bred and used his (or her) loaf to get to the top – probably, part of society's upper crust.

After a short break, I decide to set off for Bishop Stortford's ground; it's a walk of almost two miles from the town centre. Once again, the route takes me past 'more than just coffee', the Cock Inn and the Euphemism quarter. I notice a funeral directors next door to a hairdressing salon. The hairdressing salon offers extensions at competitive rates; sadly, the funeral directors next door can't offer extensions. The walk to the ground is probably the least exciting part of Bishop's Stortford. The road runs to the M11 and Stansted Airport with little to note unless you are interested in car dealerships and car washing services. I suddenly remember my billionaire's cake with cookie dough. I eat it as I walk along. It is delicious and as good as a meal. The walk continues unexcitingly.

Fortunately, the Nags Head is just over halfway along the route to break the monotony. The pub is on a bend in the main road, so I have to walk a few extra yards to use a crossing. I press the button and wait for a green man. A good two seconds after it has turned green, a car goes straight through the red light. I jump back even though I am at a safeish distance and involuntarily shout, using language I will leave you to imagine. It's the first real threat to publishing *From Hashtag United to Wembley*. The entrance to the Nags Head reminds me of the front of old-fashioned swimming baths. An array of signs offers everything you can imagine – perhaps, everything you can't imagine. I'm not sure I want a Fizz Friday or Burger Tuesday, but there are many alternatives. I liked the Fizz Friday alliteration – very much in line with expectations in the Alliteration Quarter of Bishop's Stortford. They could have developed the idea further with Taco Tuesday and Whopper Wednesday. There are plenty of drink offers, which might mean you need Sober Sunday if you are a regular customer. I enter the pub and mistakenly walk into the eating area. A young lady asks me if I want a table for two. I tell her I only want a beer; she smiles and points to the drinking area with both hands. Perhaps, she used to work at Stansted as a marshaller who guided the planes to their bays; it looks that way.

I buy my pint, sit down and recharge my phone. It's an OK pub, but I feel shoe-horned into a corner with little to amuse me. I am soon continuing my walk to Bishop's Stortford's Prokit UK Stadium. Just as I am about to give up hope of finding anything interesting on this road, I realise I am outside the Gü factory. I never realised Gü produces its splendid goods in Bishop's Stortford. I agree it's not particularly exciting, but it is something of a highlight after the tool hire and car wash outlets on my route. And, yes, I am rather partial to Gü's caramel cheesecake.

There is a signpost to the ground down a road to the left. It is more like an industrial estate with offices and factories for repairs and maintenance of planes. After a sharp ninety-degree bend to the right, I come face to face with a Bishop's Stortford FC car park attendant, who welcomes me to the ground. I suspect few fans arrive on foot. After a brief chat about the purpose of my visit, I approach the turnstile. The stadium has a stand on each side and plenty of space behind each goal.

I have a beer in a marquee, not realising I can get a beer in the main bar indoors. The lady serving the beer is busy on the phone talking to someone. While speaking, she uses her fingers to describe the shape of a card. I nod. She points a machine at me, tapping on the part where you place the card. The transaction goes through; she silently mouths "thank you". Just for fun, I silently mouth back, "thank you". It's a silent transaction.

It's not long before the teams are ready to come out onto the pitch. Two mascots and the players await the referee's instruction to march onto the pitch. It's unclear why there is a delay. As the referee makes his first stride, there is a passionate cry of "Come on, Blues" from the stand. And, then, another identical shout. I've not heard these gritty shouts at previous rounds. Bishop's Stortford fans expect more. As I look at the team sheet awaiting kick-off, my eyes are drawn to Jonny Giles playing in the number 7 shirt for Bishop's Stortford. The more famous Johnny Giles had an 'h' in his forename and wore the number 10 shirt at Leeds in Don Revie's days. Will similarities end there?

A good through-ball in the first minute stretches the Chipstead defence as they concede an early free-kick on the edge of their penalty area. The kick comes to nothing, but it's an early warning. Ryan Charles in the Bishop's Stortford attack looks dangerous in the early exchanges, but Chipstead look competitive all over the pitch. Breaking down the home side's left flank results in a devilish cross from Figuero-Correia; Bishop's Stortford are relieved to put away the cross safely for a corner. The short corner causes another scare as Chipstead look for an early goal.

After ten minutes, a move down the right results in the Blues' right back, Reiss Chandler, sending in a perfect cross for Jake Cass. His header is just saved by Kerbey in the Chipstead goal as Charles lurks around, looking for any scraps. A chant of 'Allez Les Bleus', which I misheard as 'Allez the Blues', goes up. I did wonder why there were mixed languages. Chipstead are beginning to get harried out of the game by a physically stronger team. A shot from Jonny Giles flashes across the Chips' goal. Shortly afterwards, Foxley receives a shrewd pass from Cass, but Kerbey manages to scramble the half-save away. I can't help noticing how Cass runs the channels well and pulls the visitor's defence around. Giles also shines as the pressure builds up on Chipstead; his neat turn and shot from the edge of the penalty area need Kerbey at his best to keep the score level. After 38 minutes, a tidy move brings the goal that has been on the cards. Yet another cross by Giles is headed down by Charles for Darren Foxley to tuck away, giving Kerbey no chance this time.

Chipstead need to keep Bishop's Stortford at bay until

half-time so they can re-group. However, the worst happens. Jeremy Boakye concedes a free-kick on the edge of Chipstead's penalty area. Jonny Giles takes a peach of a free-kick to give the home side a deserved 2-0 lead. Just before half-time, Chipstead get a rare half-chance. Andy Kabuikusomo intercepts a poor backpass, but the burly striker cannot capitalise. Chipstead desperately needed that chance to be converted.

After the re-start, Bishop's Stortford continue where they left off at half-time. Charles and Foxley combine well for Ben Marlow, whose header is blocked by Chipstead skipper, Chris Boulter, deflecting it for a corner. Moments later, Cass is denied another chance after a scramble in the Chipstead goalmouth. Although Chipstead struggle at times to cope with the home team's strength, it appears that the Blues are taking their foot off the gas midway through the half. Despite many Chipstead attacks petering out, a low cross by Kabuikusomo almost brings a goal. Shortly afterwards, a dogged run by Kieran Lavery produces a shot Blues' keeper, Jack Giddens, saves comfortably. It's now the turn of Bishop's Stortford to keep control of the game as Chipstead press forward. The home attacks are becoming less frequent, although their forwards still look dangerous when given a chance. Bishop's Stortford nearly sow the game up when Foxley's outstretched foot narrowly fails to convert an opportunity to make it 3-0. Immediately afterwards, Chipstead win a corner down the right-hand side. From the in-swinging corner, Kieran Lavery rises smartly to turn his header into the roof of the net with the clock on 90 minutes – it's 2-1. In a grand finale, Kabuikusomo puts through Joshua Berry, a substitute, but his long curling shot clears the bar. It is the first time that the home fans have looked nervous, but the final whistle quells the nervousness and Bishop's Stortford are through to the 2nd Round Proper.

The result feels about right. Bishop's Stortford looked a notch above their opponents from the Isthmian South Central Division for several periods of the game. Physically, the Blues looked stronger, making it hard for Chipstead to control the game. However, Chipstead's spirit shone through, and, as shown in previous games, they worked their socks off, running for each other. And, they almost sneaked a late equaliser to take it to penalties.

It's nowhere near the end of my journey to Wembley, but it's the end of my trail with Chipstead. In the bar afterwards, Rob Kember, the Chipstead manager, wishes me well and points out that the luck I have brought Chipstead has ended. "I knew we would score, but we needed to score earlier", he offers. It's been a pleasure to meet the Chipstead players, officials and supporters; I wish them well in the League and promise to see them again. I promised myself I wouldn't become attached to any team I encountered, but that was always unrealistic. The players, officials and management are a credit to the club and a jolly decent bunch.

I discuss everything from next round opponents to apostrophes in Bishop's Stortford's bar. The home fans favour a home tie against local rivals, Chelmsford City. Having counted the Apostrophes vs The Not Apostrophes and come up with a final score of 8-3, I learn no one in Bishop's Stortford cares. They refer to the town as simply 'Stortford'. Another wasted effort. I say my goodbyes and head to the bus stop to return to Bishop's Stortford station. Three bus routes serve the route to the station; none of them turns up. Mr Uber saves me and gets me back to the station in the nick of time.

CHAPTER 5
HAM

Saturday 27th November 2021 – Second Round Proper –
Bishop's Stortford v Leiston

*A*s I stand on Platform 2 of Rye Station, awaiting the 7.47am to Ashford, I wonder why the three other men, all travelling alone, find the need to catch this train early on a Saturday morning. The four of us are all shapes and sizes, probably from entirely different backgrounds, but we all appear to be focusing on our day ahead. The shortish, plumpish man, who some might describe as short and fat, looks at his watch edgily, even though the electronic board tells us that the train is running one minute late. The board increases the delay by 100% and indicates a two-minute delay, which causes the fat bloke to recheck his watch. The tall, wiry man in his thirties with wispy hair gazes into space, possibly considering how soon he can launch a rocket to the moon, while Mr Average-income-average-number-of-kids-average-weight-average-height-ordinary-looking-bloke paces around the platform. If he commits a murder now, I will be a terrible witness as everything about him is average. First, he is on my left, then my right, then back on my left. He suddenly stops and puts his carrier bag on the platform. The bag is open enough to see a toaster inside; at least, it looks like it. I wonder why. As the train crawls into the station, Mr Average-income-average-number-of-kids-average-weight-average-height-ordinary-looking-bloke strides up the platform, presumably preferring the front carriage. I board the train and make a bet with myself, at odds of 5000-1 on, that none of these fellow train-boarders will be seeing Bishop's Stortford play Leiston today.

I am travelling from Rye because this game is on a date when my wife and I are taking a ten-day break on the Sussex coast. There was a sense of relief when the draw took me back to Bishop's Stortford, as fate could have taken me as far afield as Truro City or Plymouth Parkway. I am looking forward to a second visit to Bishop's Stortford – or Stortford as I now call it. I have a busy morning planned, exploring different areas of the town. As I am on holiday, I am only making a day trip from the Sussex coast to Hertfordshire. My route to Bishop's Stortford looks tricky but, in practice, works well, as I plan to pick up the high-speed train from Ashford to London St Pancras before travelling north to my destination.

This first leg from Rye to Ashford crosses marshland, reclaimed from the sea in the 17th century. I imagine that it is a bleak place in winter. As the train passes open land on its way to its first stop at Appledore, I take pleasure from the fact that humans haven't invaded this corner of England, leaving its diverse wildlife intact. Amazingly, 600 plant types live in and around Dungeness, the seaboard town of this area, roughly a third of all plant species in Britain. Rare moths, bees and beetles are flying or crawling over the open land as the train chugs along, catching up on the two minutes it had lost en route to Rye. Streams, patches of water and rich vegetation compete for space as we continue to Ham Street, the second and only other stop before Ashford.

At Ham Street, two people board the train, both men on their own. Is there a gathering of single men in Ashford today? Having already considered whether anyone boarding the train at Rye is travelling to Bishop's Stortford, I can't help wondering if either of the two men boarding at Ham Street is heading to West Ham. Perhaps, both are. Realistically, it's doubtful either is going to West Ham, even though the high-speed train stops at Stratford, close to West

Ham's ground. The bookmaker in my head has come up with odds of 2000-1, which makes me consider gambling a virtual pound with my virtual bookmaker. The 'ham' theme sticks in my head, not because I want a ham sandwich or anything like that, but I find myself thinking of football teams with 'ham' in their name. After a moment's hesitation, I congratulate myself on thinking of Birmingham City, Gillingham and Nottingham Forest so quickly. I then realise there are loads of them – Rotherham United, Northampton Town, Southampton, Tottenham Hotspur, Wolverhampton Wanderers. Huh, it's easier than I thought and not much of a challenge. I feel a bit deflated. Now, I would like to stop this game, but the brain, which has given up as a bookmaker, can't stop as Fulham, Cheltenham Town and Oldham Athletic follow. Fortunately, the slightly distasteful thought of 'old ham' stops me in my tracks. As Dagenham & Redbridge lands in my thoughts from nowhere, marshland gives way to 'edge-of-town-ness' as we slow for Ashford International.

As I get off the train from Rye, I spot Mr Average-income-average-number-of-kids-average-weight-average-height-ordinary-looking-bloke walking ahead of me at a pace I can't match. He is either in a hurry or much fitter than me. Or both, of course. Although I was slightly worried about the seven-minute connection time at Ashford International, I needn't have been. The train to London is five minutes late, making it a chilly wait on the draughty platform. Unlike Rye and Ham Street, the passengers boarding at Ashford International are all types – couples, a group of young lads, families, a man with a dog and many more. As the modern-looking train with its slanty nose comes into the station, the experienced travellers score a slight advantage as they know where the doors will open. I'm just lucky as a door opens right in front of me. Before I have had time to settle down in an empty seat, and well before those with cases have sorted out suitable temporary storage, an invisible David, who describes himself as an On-Board Manager (probably an OBM amongst colleagues), welcomes us onto the high-speed train with the slanty nose. For clarity, the incorporeal David did not refer to the train as one with a slanty nose. He reassures us that CCTV is operating in the carriages for our security and safety. I neither feel more secure nor safer.

It's not long before David becomes more than a voice as he passes through the carriage checking tickets. He looks exactly as I imagined; I instantly feel I have met him before. He is above average height, has bushy greying hair, glasses and the manner of someone who always looks busy. I dangle my ticket in the air as David passes down the carriage. 'Perfect', he says as he high-speed-reads my ticket. My ticket is no better than anyone else's, though, as he says 'perfect' to everyone. That is until he comes to someone with an invalid ticket. David now looks sterner. David seems ready to be a tough, fine-imposing ticket inspector until the passenger's explanation satisfies him. Suddenly, it's all smiles with a friendly pat on the shoulder for the traveller. My 'perfect' ticket didn't qualify for a pat on the shoulder. David reverts to being a friendly OBM. As he disappears down the carriage, I can hear him churning out 'perfect' more times than I've had hot dinners.

About ten minutes later, the train is pulling into Ebbsfleet Station. A group of youngish lads join with beers in their hands. I offer to move my bag so one of them can sit down, but they prefer to stand and drink their beer because, as one of them explains, it's more like a pub atmosphere. It's far too early to consider a beer, as far as I am concerned. I deduce that they are en route to Arsenal for an early kick-off – so, obviously, you need an early beer. As the train slides under the River Thames and belts through suburbs, there is little to entertain me, to be frank. I find myself trying to think of other meats that appear in the names of football teams and struggle to think of any. At last, I think of Cowdenbeef. Sadly, Cowdenbeef (I will never think of them as Cowdenbeath again), are bottom of the Scottish League Two. I then come to pork, which conveniently rhymes with York. However, I am not particularly satisfied with this effort as Pork City sounds like an all-you-can-eat US-style restaurant for gluttons. We briefly stop at Stratford International, and before you can say Jack Robinson, we are at St Pancras International. Something about my journey from Ashford to London seems too quick. As I leave the train, Liverpool belatedly pops into my head as another meat-based team.

At St Pancras Station, I have what my father often used to refer to as a call of nature. I recall telling my teacher I had a call of nature at primary school. Miss Phillips was ready to react if a child wanted a wee, but a call of nature flummoxed her. Nowadays, kids use the same language, and everybody is on the same page. This call of nature meant I had to find the gents' toilets tucked away on the far side of the shops in the station. The fourth door is open, and I enter; it's all squeaky clean. In the nick of time, I notice no toilet paper. Seriously, there are not many things in life worse than being caught in a toilet with no toilet paper available – when you need it, that is. Maybe, the man with the toaster feels the same about not being able to make toast whenever he needs to. It reminds me of my experiences in Malaysia, where I have spent some of my life. In Malaysia, it is not uncommon for the toilet paper in public toilets to be in the main area, meaning that you have to grab enough sheets before entering your cubicle. No, I don't understand the thinking behind this, except that it might make maintaining supplies easier. It becomes a tricky problem if you forget. I can recall waiting for silence outside the cubicle so that I could make a break for the toilet roll dispenser in an undignified state. I managed to get back without being discovered with about two seconds to spare. Thankfully, everything at St Pancras goes to plan as I walk back through the station for the underground train.

The rest of the journey from St Pancras to Bishop's Stortford is much like my last journey to Bishop's Stortford. The only variation is that I am taking the Tube to Tottenham Hale to pick up the train to my destination this time. The change from underground to overground means you must briefly visit the outside world. Two things hit me; it's cold, and Tottenham Hale is more developed than I imagined. As I stand on the platform there, awaiting my train, a young couple near me are, what my father used to call, canoodling. He did use some expressions, my father. I'm not sure where canoodling starts or what follows when it finishes, but I make a mental note to find a different carriage as the heat is rising between these two young lovers.

After Harlow Town, the train stops at Harlow Mill. I don't think I stopped here on my last visit. It sounds nice, and my expectations rise, but there's nothing to see. As you pull into the station, there is a lot of graffiti. The word "Fatzo" appears in two places. Is this reference to Fat Rophy? Or, me?

As the train closes in on Bishop's Stortford, I reconsider my plans for my second visit to the town before today's game. I've explored the town centre, so I decide upon a quick breakfast at the highly commendable South Street Café before exploring the greener areas of Bishop's Stortford. On arrival, I head to the café, crossing the bridge to the town centre. I notice a takeaway called Chicken

Corner on the bridge, which, surprisingly, advertises pizzas in its window. It reminds me of a takeaway in Jomtien in Thailand that I used to run past called 'Just Burgers'. I always used to think that the owner regretted calling his establishment 'Just Burgers' after he decided to branch out into pizzas. Nearby is Dali's Fish & Chips. I wonder if the takeaway is inspired by Salvador Dali's *Mountain Lake* painting, which has a lake you can view as a fish. However, I don't think the surrounding hills appear as chips. Perhaps, Salvador wasn't the inspiration for this chippy.

I take longer over my breakfast than planned, but I have plenty of time to explore Bishop's Stortford. I walk up the High Street past Clinton's, which has a 'balloon in a box' offer. I can't understand the benefit of putting a balloon in a box, except, maybe, it transports more easily. I set off to the northwest of the town, heading up Windhill, which is appropriate on a cold, windy day. Bishop's Stortford is one of those towns that is not remarkably hilly, but some roads go up, down and up again like mini-versions of San Francisco, although that is stretching it a bit far. I pass the impressive St Michael's Church and The Old Monastery, where the Council debate things of importance. Opposite St Michaels is the Gourmeturk Restaurant. I don't think stringing together the words gourmet and Turk adds anything to its appeal. I assume that it claims to provide gourmet Turkish food, but I am not clear what makes a restaurant 'gourmet' or 'not gourmet'; presumably, that's for the diners to decide. I struggle to put the memory of *Fawlty Towers'* Gourmet Night out of my head. Indeed, the restaurant has either closed or is undergoing refurbishment. At the top of the hill, I cross the road and find a track that heads in the direction my head says I should follow. I can't explain why I take the track; it appears to offer nothing of interest in view. After around half a mile, I find a notice that tells me that I am entering the grounds of Bishop's Stortford College, a well-known public school. I read a warning that tells me I will be committing an offence under the 1996 Education Act unless I keep to the waymarked routes. It sounds like an idle threat, but the waymarked routes take me where I want to go and provide enough choice, so there's no need to challenge the claim.

As you walk through Bishop's Stortford College's grounds, it's impossible not to be impressed. The youths attending here are spoilt. Spoilt rotten, I would say. Besides pitches with floodlights, not just one, there are signs for the various astroturf pitches. It is a vast complex; I just hope the pupils don't grow up with an equally massive complex. I approach a woman doing some gentle runs and exercises. It looks like a mixture of Tai Chi and yoga, interspersed with slow-motion sprints. Can you have slow sprints? Whatever they are, they are not slow by my standards but snail's pace compared to Dina Asher-Smith. As I get closer to her, she stops. I am unsure whether this is through embarrassment or, more likely, to take a rest. I was planning to walk past, offering no more than a smile.

"Good morning", she says in a friendly way that slightly startles me. We get chatting, and I tell her about my FA Trophy mission. "Fascinating", she says in a way that is ambiguous in tone – she may or may not be fascinated. I can't judge. Without prompting, she tells me that she used to row and now plays a lot of badminton. We move on to the subject of the College's impressive grounds; she drops her voice to a whisper even though there is no one within 400 yards or more. "You don't have to walk where the signs indicate", she explains. I needlessly point out that I am about to leave the college grounds on the path we are standing on, so there is no reason for me to break any rules. "The Council and the College are like that", she says, overlapping her middle finger over and her forefinger. In a conspiratorial way, she adds, "I could tell you a lot more", but I get the feeling she doesn't want to, and she hasn't told me much. Although I am here to gather knowledge about Bishop's Stortford, I don't wish to play the role of an investigative journalist. She wishes me a good day and more convincingly adds, "enjoy your football". "I will", I reply in a cheery tone, starting to regret that I didn't ask more about the Council and College shenanigans if that's what they are.

I emerge from the grounds into a cul-de-sac, which offers nothing of interest. As I walk back towards the town, I come to the main and goods entrances for Bishop's Stortford College. A sign invites people to the open day, which is currently in progress. I consider taking a nose around, but you have to make an appointment – and have, I suspect, a bank balance ending with several zeros. Buses with waiting drivers are ready to transport the elite youth of Hertfordshire and beyond to a sporting event or another activity. The drivers wait outside the main entrance for their cargo. It suddenly seems colder as I think more about my afternoon on the terraces at Bishop's Stortford's ground. The college's motto is *verbum dei*, the word of God. I smile as *deus, frigus est* (God, it's cold) goes through my head. I unexpectedly arrive at the original track that led me to the college grounds, my mental compass fooling me briefly. I pass a young Bishop's Stortford student in uniform, canoodling with a young lady. I suspect canoodling in school uniform breaks several arcane rules, leading to horse-whipping in public if reported. He clearly thinks it is worth the risk. I decide to try to stop the word 'canoodling' coming into my head again for another ten years; I have no idea why it has surfaced today.

I'm heading to the north of the town to stroll through the parks and castle area of Bishop's Stortford. The Sworder's Field runs into the Castle Gardens. It continues into the Grange Paddocks, where there is a modern leisure centre. I start in Sworder's Field, using a track that leaves the northernmost of Bishop's Stortford's two main bridges. I follow the River Stort, which the men in suits at the Town Hall diverted away from the town centre when the Jackson

Square Shopping Mall was built in 1969. I walked in this corner of Sworder's Field on my last visit to Bishop's Stortford two weeks ago. It was warm enough that day for people to sit by the river drinking tea and coffee bought from a pop-up café in the park. No one is in sight today, and there is no popping up.

An information guide tells me that I can see bats and mayflies, but I can't imagine they will come out in this weather. I see a sign for the Markwell Pavilion and the Elsie Barrett Clubroom. The Elsie Barrett Clubroom was initially built for the benefit of blind people. Nowadays, you can rent it separately or as two rooms, together with the Markwell Pavilion. However, there are some restrictions. You cannot hold dog training sessions, although I find it more extraordinary that 'Only Guide Dogs are permitted at this venue'. I've never heard of a hall only for guide dogs; maybe, I am misreading the sign. You can also hold birthday parties there, but not if the birthday person is aged 16 to 21. Presumably, the logic is that parties for those under 16 would not involve alcohol and parties for those over 21 would have learned how to manage their alcohol intake. Rash assumptions, I would suggest. Parties for those aged 12+ need a £300 deposit, but under 12s are exempt from this. The signs indicate that committees have thought long and hard about the goings-on here. Finally, there is a touch of the killjoy as helium balloons are not permitted. Is this why there is a market locally for balloons in a box? I get a mental picture of a dissenter on the committee, shouting in a squeaky voice, "we should allow helium balloons".

I follow the signs to the castle, expecting to see moats, turrets, a portcullis and donjons. Waytemore Castle will disappoint you if you have the same expectations. All that remains of the castle is a grass bank and some remaining fragments at its top that you can barely see. There's some doubt about the castle's history. Some believe the Normans built it, others the Saxons. The most accepted view is that it dates from the time of William the Conqueror. There were further developments in the 12th and 13th centuries before being used as a prison in the 17th century. It may have acted as a dividing line between the House of Wessex and the Viking Danelaw to the north. In the 16th century, it fell into disrepair and, arguably, only remains at all due to its Grade I listed status. Suffice to say, you would need to be seriously into castles to enjoy this one.

I continue north from the castle; it is bitterly cold now with drizzle in the air. Much of the land has been turned over to nature, and there is a wilderness on one side that must be home to an array of different creatures. It reminds me of the rewilding experiment in Sussex, which the wonderfully-named author Isabella Tree explains in her book, *Wilding*. In the distance, I can see the Grange Paddocks Leisure Centre and some football pitches. There is a game taking place. I briefly shelter in the Leisure Centre to make some notes, partly because of the drizzle gaining momentum. The rain stops within minutes, so I leave the Leisure Centre entrance; a sign at the exit thanks me for being active. I start to cross a field in the direction of the football match. The referee puts the whistle to his mouth as I get within twenty yards of the pitch. He makes one of those blasts that go up, down, then up again with a long final flourish. There is no question that it is full-time. I don't know which team won, but the team in green and black are slouching less than their opponents, who don't have the thrill of victory to keep them warm.

A lad in green and black comes away from the pitch, moaning at his father, "it was really cold out there". The sympathetic mother wraps duvets around her son and makes soothing noises, saying, "you'll soon warm up", as she provides a hot water bottle for her little cherub. The father replies, "it was cold watching", and marches towards the car park.

I return to the leisure centre through the car park and onto the main road, which I note, is called Rye Street. Coincidence or what? I continue north from the town centre, but there is little to see. When I reach a roundabout, my morale rises as I see a pub, a place to warm up a bit. As I get nearer, disappointment sets in as it looks closed. It appears to be one of those pubs that have morphed into an Indian restaurant. Usually, they don't look right to me. I have trouble reading the name in big letters on the side of the building. I realise that UNTBATTE is the middle part of Mountbatten. It's time to turn around and plot a route to the ground.

Google Maps is a fine invention as I can see the different routes to the Bishop's Stortford ground. The shortest route looks devoid of any interest. My main criterion for this judgement is that no pubs or shops are on the way. I take a more exciting course, bringing me out near the Nags Head, the pub I visited briefly before the Chipstead game. Google Maps soon has me traipsing down a slightly muddy track. Ahead, I see trains flashing across the path but no sign of a bridge. Just as I think that Google Maps has led me astray, I realise that this is a foot crossing with a mini traffic light system to tell you whether it is safe to cross the train line. I don't like it much; this is a busy line to Cambridge and Stansted Airport with trains hurtling past at high speed. I cross safely and immediately meet a friendly black labrador. Or, rather, I meet a friendly man with a friendly labrador. It's hard to judge whether the man or the dog is friendlier. As an owner of three labradors, I find it hard to pass one without showing some interest. I emerge from the track onto a road with smart houses next to the river. I am not allowed to fish here under any circumstances. I misread the map and have to turn round, meaning I meet the friendly man with the friendly labrador a second time. The friendly labrador remembers me, and it's a happy reunion. I also pass a DPD van for the second time, almost stepping out in front of it in a careless moment. Maybe, crossing the track is safer than a road. I find my way to a busy main road, which Google tells me to follow until there is an alley on the other side of the road.

I miss the alley and end up on a private road with small cul-de-sacs shooting off in every direction. I retrace my steps and find the passage. How could I have missed it? The route to the Nags Head is through a housing estate. I see the DPD driver making his 99th delivery of the day; I think he recognises me. He appears to be driving cautiously. Even though it's starting to drizzle more, I am relieved that the road brings me closer to the Nags Head than I expected. I need to warm up. Illogically, perhaps, a cool pint of beer will help. Upon arriving at the Nags Head, I suddenly realise that the rain has been invading my back. The back of my coat is soaking, and my jeans are damper than I thought. There's a slight squelch as I sit down. I get talking to a couple and exchange moans about the cold weather. We chat and become good friends. Our friendship is sealed when I ask them to keep an eye on my belongings while I use the toilet. Upon returning, we talk some more; nothing profound or consequential, but plain old friendly pub talk. Without warning, they leave without saying goodbye while I'm looking at my phone. I'm a bit annoyed for some reason.

Within minutes of their departure, a man with thinning hair in his fifties, I would guess, wanders towards the vacated seats, looking dazed. He has a dreamy air about him. He gives the appearance of someone transported from another planet, or perhaps having taken part in some time travel, and looks puzzled at being in the Nags Head. I have never met anyone who has come from another world or travelled through time to the best of my knowledge. He asks me if the seats are free. I could confirm that there is neither a fee for sitting there nor anyone sitting there. Perhaps, he is dazed and confused. I make a hand gesture to indicate he is welcome to sit at the next table, even though I have no jurisdiction over his decision. It turns out he is from the planet Earth and that he is going to see the Bishop's Stortford v. Leiston game. We get chatting, and I explain that I am on my Wembley trail. He is more direct than I expected at first and asks why.

"I've always wanted to write a book, and I love non-League football", I reply to answer his question. I continue, "I also liked the idea of not knowing what is in store for me". "It wouldn't be on my bucket list when I retire", he replies, as though he has carefully thought about his bucket list already. He clearly has thought about it. He lists jumping out of a plane, flying in a helicopter and walking from Land's End to John O'Groats without hesitation. "Oh, and I'd like to go to the Antarctic. You can fly there, you know". He is on a roll now and looks animated, a different person from the dazed time traveller of a few minutes ago. "And, see polar bears in the wild. And, the Galapagos Islands. I'd like to do that". I feel that it is churlish to explain that if he wants to see a polar bear in the Antarctic, he will need experts to capture one and fly it from one pole to the other. It's unclear whether the Antarctic, Arctic and the Galapagos Islands are separate trips.

Perhaps, a boring business meeting on Monday morning has just entered his head, but he snaps out of his dreams of retiring and working through his bucket list. "I reckon they'll win today", he says, assuming I realise he is a Bishop's Stortford supporter. "What do you think?" I blurt out a scoreline without much thought; my head is still thinking about polar bears in the Antarctic – or, even the Galapagos Islands. "2-0", I offer without much thought. Maybe, it's a business opportunity - a sort of polar bear on tour experience where the animal travels with you to exotic parts of the world. I put it aside, though, as it doesn't seem fair on the polar bear. My friend from another planet suddenly disappears into yet another different world as he consults his phone at length. I disappear into my own world as we fall silent. Maybe, there's not much more to discuss, or he finds me too dull. I find myself boring sometimes, so it's not unwholly reasonable.

As I get up to leave, the alien reconnects with me. "Live like it's the last day of your life", he says in a jokey way. "Indeed", I reply cheerfully. I utter an unsatisfactory false chuckle and wish him well.

As I leave the pub, I think more about living like it's the last day of your life. What a depressing day that would be. I am unsure what I would do if I knew today was the last day of my life, but I wouldn't be jumping out of a plane.

I arrive at Bishop's Stortford's ground and head for the bar; it's far warmer in the bar. Have I told you about the cold weather yet? The bar is full of supporters from both teams. The Leiston supporters are a friendly lot, and I talk to two or three of them. A man with thinning hair interrupts politely to tell me that Leiston is pronounced *Layston*, not *Leeston*. I calculate about ten mispronunciations on my part since my arrival in Stortford. We discuss their league status and the fact that they play in the Southern League Premier Division, meaning they must travel from the Suffolk coast to places like Banbury, Bromsgrove, Tamworth and Hednesford. If you don't think that is burdensome, take a look at a map and the roads connecting Suffolk to these places. They would rather be in the Isthmian League, but their appeal was turned down. They do not seem overly confident about the prospects in today's game, even though they have a mid-table league position. The Leiston supporters I am talking to cite 4-1 defeats away to Hitchin Town and Coalville Town in recent weeks as reasons to be pessimistic against in-form Bishop's Stortford. As soon as I mention that they looked dangerous up front against Chipstead in the last round, I feel a sense of guilt for increasing their pessimism. These Leiston supporters are thinking in terms of 4-1 yet again.

Conversely, a Bishop's Stortford fan is full of positivity and equally full of cliches. He tells me about someone playing in the hole, how a previous game was a game of two halves and that there are no easy games at this level. He wonders if Leiston will park the bus (I think they came by car), but Stortford's forwards should have enough in their lockers. Stortford, he tells me, always give 110%. I feel that it is churlish to say that you can't give 110% and explain he has made a schoolboy error. I decide to show him a clean pair of heels and move across the bar into acres of space.

As the teams come out, shouts of 'Come on Blues' are ambiguous as both clubs are known as the Blues, although I remember from my last visit that supporters usually refer to Bishop's Stortford as Les Bleus. Two spectators discuss Football Focus during the warm-up; one is aghast that two women presented today's programme and turned off in protest. Whatever next? Women playing football?

The Blues playing in blue, Bishop's Stortford, start strongly. The home side have a viciously cold, strong wind blowing in their favour, while the visitors' defenders have heavy drizzle in their faces. It's not ideal weather for good football, but it doesn't bother Bishop's Stortford. In the first two minutes, Leiston's defence struggles with a looping cross that bounces menacingly around their penalty area. Leiston's defence clears another attack immediately afterwards, but they more closely resemble a team desperately hanging on to a lead with a minute to play. Sure enough, after five minutes, home favourite Frankie Merrifield pops up unmarked to head a goal at the near post from Jonny Giles' pinpoint cross.

It's not long before a free-kick from the right catches the wind and almost makes it 2-0 as Leiston keeper Sam Donkin desperately saves the goalbound effort. However, the wait for a second goal is brief. After nine minutes, Frankie Merrifield escapes his marker again and heads home a corner at the near post. It's already becoming a tall order for Leiston to recover this game, particularly with their leading goalscorer out of the team from a training injury. Another cross from Giles fails to find Merrifield or anyone else this time; the score remains at 2-0. At this stage, only the optimistic Leiston supporters are dreaming of a 4-1 defeat. At the quarter-hour mark, another dangerous cutback by Giles causes panic and draws a clear-cut penalty. Donkin denies Merrifield a rapid hattrick with a smart dive low to his left.

Out of the blue, Leiston supporters suddenly find they have something to cheer. A good break from midfield finds Adam Mills, who picks up the ball just outside the home team's penalty area after a well-timed run. His curling shot plants itself neatly in the corner of the net, giving Jack Giddens little chance. Maybe, it's a lifeline that never looked likely in those first fifteen minutes. It occurs to me that, to date, both teams have scored in each of the five ties in my FA Trophy trail.

After this goal, the game becomes more even, which is more than can be said of the wings of planes coming into land at Stansted Airport. The high winds cause two pilots to opt for another attempt at landing. I recall coming into Gatwick many years ago on a flight from Newcastle when it was blowing a hurricane. On the first attempt to land, the wings wobbled scarily, causing off-duty airline staff to scream. Our BA pilot was a cool cat. He became the last to land that evening, albeit after three attempts, taking great delight in telling us that the Air France pilot had turned back to Paris. England 1 France 0 was the subtext.

The rest of the half is more even. Adam Mills, shining in the Leiston midfield, picks out Brendan Ocran, but the assistant referee flags offside just as Ocran gets into a good goal-scoring position. Not to be confused with Mills and Boon, Mills and Barnes combine well to generate panic in the home defence. This dispels any romantic notions of an easy passage to the next round for the Bishop's Stortford team. Leiston get themselves in a defensive tangle just before half-time, but the chance goes begging. As the half draws to a close, the rain becomes heavy. Another Giles cross almost produces Stortford's third goal, and a corner is headed over by defender Ryan Henshaw. A chant of "Allez Les Bleus" hopes to stir their heroes to greater things. "Allez Les Bleus?" queries a visiting supporter. "Fucking pretentious twats".

A third pilot decides this is not the right time to land his tin can of passengers on this approach and circles back over the Hertfordshire countryside. You wonder whether

Bishop's Stortford have wasted an opportunity to kill off this tie after such a strong opening period. The half-time whistle is a relief as I hurry into a warmer area. On my way indoors, I meet the Leiston fans. "It's your game, here, with that wind second half", I suggest to one I met earlier. "3-2?", I proffer. With the look of someone who has seen too much disappointment over the years, the Leiston supporter turns his mouth down like the grumpy emoticon. "Maybe", he says unconvincingly, as we go our separate ways. I suspect he is still thinking of 4-1 in the other direction.

After half-time, I return to my seat, drying it with the sleeve of my jacket. I expect Leiston to surge forward with the wind at their backs, but the game is bogged down in midfield as a series of fouls breaks up the play. Behind me, I notice that there is a new supporter. He appears to be the club moaner. "Pass it to the left", "play the easy ball", "don't mess about there", "for Chrissake", and "wide, wide, WIDE … too late" are a selection of his early second-half moans. Every club has a few moaners, although you shouldn't confuse them with the excitable fans, who can moan and be enthusiastic in equal measure. The other two categories, of course, are the enthusiasts and the passives. The passives are a bit of a mixed bag, I find. Some scarcely react when their team scores; others may be silent moaners. The moaner gets up, either making his way to the gents or unable to take any more. He doesn't reappear. I don't notice his absence for a while, and I feel a little disappointed. And, perhaps, just a little worried about his wellbeing.

A goalbound shot by Giles is blocked, but it is not long before Darren Foxley scrambles the all-important third for Bishop's Stortford. The game continues, but it is scrappy and, perhaps, more like what you might expect on such a stormy day. 4-1 looks to be on the cards, though. A long ball finds Bishop's Stortford substitute Christopher Harris one-on-one against the Leiston keeper, but his shot hits a post. As the ball comes out, Ben Marlow places a shot precisely as though he is trying to strike the other post. If that's his intention, he is successful. A scramble ensues as Ryan Charles has his goalbound effort saved well by Donkin. It's a let-off, or three let-offs, for the visitors.

For those more interested in meteorological matters, there is a weird weather phenomenon after 75 minutes. A high clearance by Bishop's Stortford's defence suddenly gets held up in the high winds and looks about to return the ball from where it came. After hovering briefly, the ball is caught in a vortex and then carries on its path towards the Leiston goal. There is a brief moment when half the players scattered around the pitch start to prepare for a header in case the ball comes their way. The Leiston central defenders look more surprised than most as the ball gathers speed towards them.

After 80 minutes, that 4-1 scoreline becomes a reality. The Leiston defence looks heavy-legged as two defenders fail to clear an easily defendable situation. Foxley threads a pass through to Harris, who fires into the far corner of the goal. Two minutes later, it is 5-1. With the proverbial acres of space, Ryan Charles shoots from long range. The shot looks stoppable, but you get the feeling Donkin thinks it is one of those days. Bishop's Stortford have a couple more half-chances, but the game seems more like a friendly now. The whistle goes for full-time. The crowd disperses home or to the bar; the players are ready for a bath and you can't blame them. There is no doubt that overall, Bishop's Stortford deserve to win, although I felt that Leiston had a brief period when they looked to be in the game.

I grab a pint at the ground afterwards, but my cliché-ridden friend does not return to the bar. Let's hope he didn't fall into the hole. Another Blues fan talks to me about the game and tells me Stortford deserved a fourth in the first half. When I say that the score was only 2-1 at half-time, he points out that it was 3-1. I tell him he is wrong, but he has that look of someone who knows they are right. I know I am right, but I decide not to press the point. It's a strange thing when both parties are sure they are right. I remember being in a pub in Kuala Lumpur when there was a prize at stake if you were first to answer a quiz question. I wanted the prize, which was a nice enough t-shirt and four free beers. The question was right up my street. I had to name three London-based Premier League football teams. Now, remember that at the time, my team, Charlton, were in the Premier League and that I was born in Charlton, so I ought to know. I shouted out Arsenal, Spurs and Charlton.

"Wrong", said the quizmaster, as another person offered Spurs, Arsenal and Chelsea. "Correct" shouted the quizmaster as my prize disappeared to the other side of the bar. I am pretty forgiving, but there's a limit, you know.

I talk to some philosophical Leiston fans after the game. "We were never really in the game", says one. "I'd bite your arm off for the player budget Bishop's Stortford probably have", says another. Curiously, a man wearing Bishop's Stortford colours with his arm in a sling walks past; I hope a Leiston fan didn't bite his arm. For Leiston fans, it's a 77-mile drive back to their ground, which, inappropriately after today's result, is Victory Road. If you are wondering where Leiston is, think of the somewhat better-known Sizewell Nuclear Power Station and travel westwards inland for three miles. Locally, there are many protests about the proposal to build Sizewell C, a two-reactor nuclear plant. The protesters have used the slogan, 'Chernobyl twinned with Sizewell'. One view from the Leiston fans is that the second-homers in the area are leading the protests about the building of Sizewell C. In contrast, locals see it as good for employment opportunities. It's only a straw poll but a fascinating insight. Sizewell also had significance in the Second World War. In 1941, Henri and Willem Peteri travelled 56 hours from Katwijk in Holland to land at Sizewell in a collapsible canoe. A monument was unveiled by Henri's widow in 2009. However, it was a dangerous means of escape as reportedly, only eight of 32 canoeists survived the trip. Meanwhile, if you don't know where Sizewell is, go to Leiston and head three miles eastwards towards the sea.

I am too early for my train back towards Rye, so I opt to have a swift pint at the Bridge House pub near the station. As I cross a road, my hat blows off in the persistently high wind. About fifteen cars narrowly miss my hat lying lifelessly in the middle of the road. As a bus approaches, I have just enough time to risk my life and rescue my hat. As you can tell from the fact that I am alive, I survived, as did my hat. On TV in the pub, Leeds play Brighton, wearing different shades of blue – I have no idea why Leeds needed to change to a colour closer to their opponents' shirts. A lad, who looks firmly set on his barstool, tells me that Newcastle beat Arsenal 5-1. I look mildly surprised. He then laughs and tells me he is joking. I can only assume that he thought I was an Arsenal supporter, and it would be fun to tease me. He looks crestfallen by my lack of interest.

The journey back to Rye is uneventful at first. I get to St Pancras to board the High-Speed train to Ashford. The train's conductor drip-feeds information about delays due to a fallen tree from the high winds. I take this in my stride like most other passengers. There's not much you can do when a tree blocks a line. The conductor updates us too frequently for my liking, telling us of a fifteen-minute delay, a 20-minute delay, a 27-minute delay and so on. Providing the delay is no longer than an hour or so, I will just take the following train from Ashford to Rye. We depart around 35 minutes late. On arriving at Ashford, life becomes slightly surreal. With a 40-odd minute gap between trains, I seek a final beer for the day. You might assume this is easy at an international station, but it's not on a Saturday evening. I can't find any signs of life on the station, except for a ticket and enquiries window. The man at the window is extremely helpful in my pursuit of a beer. He tells me there are two options, the BP garage or a bar called Hothouse, which is on the edge of the station car park. I opt for Hothouse. As I approach, I see that Hothouse is a large tin shed, more like a furniture store on an industrial estate. Music is coming from the venue. As I enter, I can tell it is not my sort of place, but I plough on and find a man at a desk selling bottles of beer with unusual names. I buy one and see a club of sorts and an elevated dancefloor. I'm a bit out of touch; maybe my description could be more emphatic. The average age of the customers seems to be about fifteen. I sit at a table outside the main hall and chat with a parent with children in the dance area. It's a friendly chat, but I leave to catch my train before we can get to know each other well.

It's a strange end to the day, but I'm glad to see my wife at Rye Station a little later when I finally return to my holiday. It's been an educational experience. I know how to pronounce Leiston and have thought more deeply about things on my bucket list. I have learned that I can't hire the Elsie Barrett Clubroom for a teenage party and discovered that almost every Football League team has 'ham' in its name. More importantly, however, my hat is safe and will be ready for Bishop's Stortford's 3rd Round Proper tie.

CHAPTER 6
ANTLERS

Saturday 18th December 2021 – Third Round Proper –
Cheshunt v Bishop's Stortford

*I*t's Friday morning, and I am returning to
Hertfordshire yet again. I don't know if the balls still
come out of a purple velvet bag when making the draw for a
Football Association cup competition. But, if they do, the
31st and 32nd teams out of the hat, er…bag, were Cheshunt
and Bishop's Stortford for the FA Trophy 3rd Round draw.
Come to think of it, the 3rd Round takes place on a
north/south regional basis, so the balls must go into two

purple bags. Regardless of the draw, I am heading back to Hertfordshire for a local derby. In the last round, I witnessed Bishop's Stortford brush aside Leiston by 5-1; I fancy the game at Cheshunt will be a more challenging test. Going into this game, Cheshunt have gone fourteen games unbeaten, and Bishop's Stortford have gone one better, playing fifteen games without defeat.

After travelling twice to Bishop's Stortford, the journey to Cheshunt seems familiar – a train from Kent to London, a trip across London, and thence northbound out of London. I am travelling to Theobalds Grove station. As I board my train from Tunbridge Wells, my mask causes my glasses to steam up. Mentally, I invent a combination of spectacles and a mask that does not steam up and present my idea to *Dragons' Den*. An unobtrusive demister button on the side of your glasses, working like the demister in a car, could be available in the deluxe version. I can hear Touker Suleyman changing to a high-pitched voice, saying, "You seriously want £50,000 for the Spectamask (my rather inventive brand name, don't you agree?) that has sold three units in your local pub at a profit margin of 40p per unit? To recoup my investment, you would need to sell…." His voice trails off in my head. Peter Jones picks up the Spectamask; it breaks in his hands before he speaks. I dismiss him as just plain clumsy. He makes gestures rather than saying what he thinks. Sara Davies gives me a straight "I'm out" in that northern tongue, and Deborah Meaden tells me flatly that my idea is nonsense. I pull out of the glasses and mask combo market, thinking those dragons have missed an opportunity.

It's a grey day outside as the train crosses the North Downs; a heavy mist hugs the top of the hills. A ticket inspector makes me jump as he arrives from the adjacent carriage. "Morning", he bellows in a cheerful voice. "Have your tickets ready", he commands in a Father Christmas ho-ho-ho voice; it is only eight days to Christmas. He will easily get a job at a Santa's Grotto if he wants extra income. Four women are deep in conversation about office politics. They disagree, albeit mildly, about many things, but they are united about their dislike for John. The oldest of the four women describes John as "up his own arse". On this topic, there is unanimous agreement. The ticket inspector has to ask them again for their tickets as they haven't reacted to his cheery greeting. They overreact when they notice the request and are apologetic, producing valid tickets. "Thank you, ladies", he yohohos as he gets on his sleigh to move to the far end of the carriage. The women take little notice of his unintended festive cheer and move on to Sadie, whose behaviour is now under the microscope. My mind wanders as I stare at the bleakness of an unpleasant English winter day. My mind winds back to the game at Chipstead against Whitehawk when all the forecasts predicted rain, rain and more rain. Yet, when I arrived in Chipstead, I dodged a bullet – or, more accurately and less dramatically, the 98%

chance of a downpour. Suddenly, there is hysteria amongst the four women. The only words I hear amid the hilarity are "he's just the same", which produces whatever the next level up from hysteria is. The youngest of the group is laughing so much that she is starting to snort. They settle down after this, and I settle down too. There are no further outbursts of laughter, and no character assassinations occur between Orpington and London Bridge, where I disembark.

I decide to walk from London Bridge to Liverpool Street. It is still very hazy in London, and I find it strange that two men take a selfie on London Bridge with an almost invisible Shard in the background. I guess it's not a selfie with two people. Indeed, a Google search informs me that it is an 'usie', but surely that means a selfie should be a 'meie'. More appropriately, I think a picture of two or more people ought to be a 'weie'. This is something that NATPOO (the National Association of Taking Pictures of Oneself) need to consider with some urgency. The photo in the haze reminds me of my visit to the Great Wall of China when I could not see more than ten feet in front of me due to fog. Still, the pictures in the Great Wall of China trip brochure were stunning. As I continue across London Bridge, I see a London Sightseeing Bus pass with one passenger on board, enjoying the hazy views from the open top of the bus. She appears to be Japanese and uses binoculars to see the haze in greater detail. After briefly pausing to look at my phone, I notice that the two men have overtaken me and are now taking a dualie (or whatever it's called) with Tower Bridge in the background. Fortunately, Tower Bridge is a distinctive edifice that will help the two gentlemen relive the memory.

As I approach Liverpool Street, I have the choice of running for a train to Theobalds Grove or taking my time. I choose a cup of tea and the next departure. The Soho Coffee shop is the nearest to hand. Even though a group of indecisive twenty-somethings in front of me take an age to decide how they want their coffee, I wait patiently. Brad, who places the order with an increasingly exasperated barista, finds the changes from macchiato to a latte and the oat milk to soya milk too much to reconcile. I want to help because I know what everyone wants better than he and the barista do. It's strange how coffee has become a generic term in my vocabulary for a hot drink. Indeed, you rarely see tea shops these days; if you want tea, you buy it at a coffee shop. Obvious, isn't it? The café is nothing like my memories of Soho, but I knew Soho better in the 1970s and 1980s. I expect Soho is full of bright, modern coffee shops these days rather than Chinese restaurants and strip joints. As I get to the front of the queue, there is a further delay as a man in front is unhappy about the mark-up on a cake if he eats it in the cafe. After much negotiation, he opts to drink his coffee inside but says he will take his cake away. As if we believe that. The lady on the till checks this with her immediate superior, who nods approvingly and without fuss. I make a mental note to check whether he eats his cake surreptitiously while drinking his coffee. I have never understood the expression "you can't have your cake and eat it". Perhaps, this is where it applies, except that he can have his cake and can't eat it. Well, not yet.

After my tea, I proceed to Platform 1 in good time for the train to Theobalds Grove. The carriage is sparsely populated, just a young woman opposite and an elderly lady a few seats away. As the train is about to depart, another elderly lady boards the train with two big bags brimming with Christmas presents. She carefully chooses a seat opposite the other older woman and announces that this is her first rail journey since the Covid lockdown in 2020. She explains she has "two years' worth of Christmas presents". It looks like more or, perhaps, she is visiting a big family.

The train looks more like an underground with long seats facing each other so that everyone is travelling sideways, as it were. The seats look brighter than they should be, given their dark orange, brown and light green colours. Two young men also join the train at the last minute and seem intent on not wearing masks, although we are reminded that some people are exempt from this ruling. I would put a fiver on these two men not being exempt. Judgmental, I know. I dutifully wear my mask, but annoyingly my glasses steam up. Touker, I told you I had a good idea. Peter, you clumsy so-and-so.

The lady with the Christmassy bags flits loudly from

topic to topic. Before we reach Cambridge Heath, two stops and five minutes into the journey, she has covered holidays in Whitby Bay, never enjoying pantomime, and route alternatives from Denmark Hill to most suburbs in Greater London. The listening lady does little more than listen, probably trying to keep up with the rapid flow of conversation. While still explaining the options for changing trains at Tottenham Hale, Mrs Christmassy Bags is now moving seamlessly into the dangers of Omnicor. She undoubtedly means the Omicron variant of Covid. She repeats Omnicor loudly enough times for me to exchange a slight smile with the young woman opposite. It's funny how you can tell someone is smiling even when wearing a mask. My fellow eavesdropper, bearing a SpaceNK Apothecary bag on her lap, is also very much tuned into the dialogue.

Mrs Christmassy Bags continues to change topics rapidly. Before we reach the fourth stop – and there are short distances between each stop on this line – I learn that Boris will be out within a week, fish has got expensive, she is the youngest of four children, and her mother lived through two World Wars and got bombed in both. The 'bombed homes' topic leads to youngsters moaning far too much these days – "youngsters have never had rationing, yet they moan if the internet is slow these days", she says. I feel a slight pang of guilt as I moaned quite a lot when my internet was slow earlier this week. I know more about this woman than acquaintances of over twenty years. If I believed heavily in conspiracy theories, I might conclude that someone had been planted in the carriage for my amusement. Admittedly, I am getting a slight feeling of Trumanshowitis. The listening woman is starting to look dazed and overwhelmed, but no one can rescue her. Mrs Christmassy Bags says she doesn't watch television because of all the 'doom and gloom', yet she almost immediately talks about Chris Packham and *Autumnwatch*. I missed the link to *Autumnwatch*, if there was one. Believe me; this woman can talk so much she is probably to blame if you see any donkeys without hind legs.

I am both disappointed and relieved when Mrs Christmassy Bags gets off the train at Edmonton Green to catch another train. I was not expecting her departure, and the listening woman is equally unprepared. She gets up and prepares to leave without warning. As a farewell to the listening woman, she merely says, "Lovely to have met you. Don't forget what I said". The command not to forget what she said is, of course, an impossible challenge. While tuning in, I have been writing copious notes, but I am the first to admit that there was so much information I have forgotten much of her output. I can assure you that you have just seen snapshots. I feel that the listening woman will remember none of it by the time she gets home tonight.

As the train slows to pull into Theobalds Grove, I notice that the SpaceNK Apothecary lady has left the train. I leave the station where there is no sign of an apostrophe. After my experience at Bishop's Stortford, I'm not losing sleep over apostrophes again. I come to a straight road that runs north to the centre of Cheshunt. A sign tells me I am about to enter Cheshunt within yards of the station. Below the sign, there is a reassuring arrow pointing to Cheshunt FC. I consider getting a cuppa in the Cross Coffee Shop, but their strange logo puts me off. I can only describe it as a haunted house sitting on top of a large cup. Soon, I come to the Roman Urn, cousin to the more famous Grecian Urn. I've heard the 'how much does a Grecian earn?' joke enough times (though not for a while), but the Roman Urn offers a possible variant. The Roman Urn is a pub where you would hope to get a Frascati or, perhaps, a Moretti beer. However, they do not look like they offer an Aperol Spritz cocktail.

As I plough on northwards, I do eventually find what I believe to be the town centre. Maybe, it's the sight of a Tesco store in the town in which Tesco gave birth to its empire. Tesco had its head office in Cheshunt until 2015. The name Tesco comes from the founder, Jack Cohen, buying a consignment of tea from Thomas Edward Stockwell. Stockwell's initials were supplemented with 'Co' to form Tesco. Just beyond Tesco, there are restaurants and an attractive bakery that will likely win my custom later. The Fishy Relishy restaurant catches my eye, mainly due to its name, but I don't feel that it rolls off the tongue; it seems a bit like naming a seaside café "She Sells Sea Shells on the Sea Shore". As I continue, a dentist claims to help the nation smile. I find its name, My Dentist, a little curious. I cannot understand why the 'My' part is enclosed in curly brackets. Perhaps the dentist wears braces. A nearby sign for Iron Man might lead you to believe this is the man you need for house removals or work with a high level of strength is needed. Or, perhaps, a body-building course, but he appears to be offering an ironing service. I pass Blooming Lovely, which is, more predictably, a florist. They are rightly trying to cash in on the Christmas shopping extravaganza by selling 'Santa stop here' signs. I hope they sell those signs before Christmas and don't leave them on display in the window; the children of Cheshunt would not want Santa to get grumpy by stopping at a closed shop.

I reach the Old English Gentleman, not a person, you understand, but a public house, which should be able to make a sale to me after my cup of tea at the bakery. As I get to the pub entrance, though, I am disappointed. A sign on the window says 'Regulars only'. Is this a Covid restriction? If not, how does someone who is not a regular ever become a regular? I ponder this conundrum but cross the Old English Gentleman off my list of potential lunchtime pubs for Saturday's pre-match pint. Nomophobia is the next establishment to catch my attention. It's a phone repair shop, and after a quick Google, I discover that nomophobia is the fear of not having a mobile phone. I amble back to the centre of Cheshunt and worry about my stomach. What food will I want this evening? I have not seen any pubs or restaurants that look good candidates for my custom. I think about a curry and spot an Indian restaurant across the road. It's called the Déjà Vu restaurant. I peer through the window and can just about read a menu on the nearest table. The menu looks familiar. Indeed, the tables and the tablecloths all look familiar too. The bar to one side looks like a bar I've seen before. I am beginning to think I have been here before.

Predictably, it will not surprise you that it's time for a cuppa and a sausage roll at Simmons bakery. They are most friendly when I arrive and fuss around me a little, ensuring I have a comfortable seat. I daydream a bit and then start googling possible pubs and restaurants for the evening. Mahek Indian looks a good candidate, but it's a fair distance from this part of town to my hotel at the other end of Cheshunt.

My next port of call is Lee Valley Park to see if it looks like a suitable place for a Saturday morning walk. Curiously, the River Lea (spelt l-e-a) runs through the Lee Valley (spelt l-e-e). There was a 50-50 split vote when the councillors voted on the name to adopt. The older name, River Ley, had already been squeezed out in the 19th century. My route to Lee Valley Country Park takes me past Cheshunt Station, with three pubs close together to tempt me in. One of these pubs will surely win my afternoon custom.

Windmill Lane, the road that leads down to the park, is unusual in that it is a mix of old, new and in-betweeny. Old and new sit side by side in Cheshunt, not always very comfortably. I pass the Laura Trott Leisure Centre, named after one of Cheshunt's most famous daughters. Laura Trott, now Laura Kenny, is married to Jason Kenny. Or, to be more precise, Dame Laura Kenny is married to Sir Jason Kenny. They famously won gold medals for cycling within minutes of each other at the 2012 Olympic Games and currently hold twelve Olympic gold medals between them. They are the most successful married couple in Olympian history. Extraordinarily, Laura took up sport to regulate her breathing after suffering from asthma.

While I am on the subject of famous people, let's not limit it to sporting prowess. Cheshunt has had more superstars in its midst. Cliff Richard may not have a singing school named after him, but he grew up in Cheshunt. As you may recall, he is known for singing in the rain at Wimbledon. And, when you learn that Victoria Beckham went to school at St Marks High School in Cheshunt, you might wonder why I am not walking around with an autograph album while I'm here. Other former residents include Glenn Hoddle, England's talented footballer and manager, and Linda Lusardi, who could be found with one turn of the page in *The Sun* in the 1970s and 1980s.

Walking along Windmill Lane, I am still thinking about an Indian meal tonight. I am now well past the Laura Trott Leisure Centre and reach the cluster of three pubs, all within spitting distance of each other. They all look candidates for an afternoon pint, but my first port of call is Lee Valley Country Park to see if it offers a potential morning pre-match walk. After passing the three pubs, I come to a level crossing next to Cheshunt Station; the gates are closed. There is an unusually large number of steps to cross the bridge over the track, and; as I am carrying a bag, I decide to be patient. A small group forms. There is an elderly couple, two women with pushchairs and children and someone who looks young enough to run up the steps, two at a time. A man on a motorbike drives right up to the gate, almost touching it; he wants to make a fast getaway when the barrier rises. A train bound for Stratford pulls into the station, followed by another train to Cambridge North. Now, slightly annoyingly, the gates remain unmoved. I have invested around four minutes of my life to avoid crossing by the footbridge, so I wait patiently like the rest of the group. A third, fourth, fifth and, unbelievably, sixth train pass before the barrier rises. The fifth train was too much for the cyclist. He caves in and struggles awkwardly across the bridge with his bicycle. Thankfully, the fifth train delivers the person the motorcyclist is picking up. Removing his helmet, he loudly shouts "Oi" to his newly-arrived friend and gesticulates to him. The male member of the elderly couple pulls a face at the shout of "Oi" and mockingly puts his hands over his ears. He shares a joke with me "you could have heard that shout two stations down the line". I laugh a little halfheartedly; his wife laughs with far more vigour. The wait is eleven minutes before the remaining pedestrians are clear to walk across without using the bridge. It is a ridiculous length of time to wait. "Better hurry up", says my new friend, "it might close again", he says as I clear the London-bound track. His wife chuckles.

Almost immediately, I am in the Lee Valley Country Park. The path splits, and the elderly couple chooses the opposite option to me. She says "goodbye" cheerily to me; it's the first time I've heard her speak; he carries on without acknowledging our separation. I worry that I should have guffawed more at his jokes. He did seem like the type who continuously tells unfunny jokes – quips, I think you might call them. I offer "enjoy your walk" in reply to the laughing lady, and we go our separate ways. I only walk as far as the River Lea, a distance of just over 200 yards. I quickly establish that it has a good towpath and, more importantly, is not muddy. The path will make a good route for my Saturday morning walk. With that established, I turn and return to the level crossing. It's open as I approach it, but I am in no doubt that I will use the bridge this time if it closes before I get there. Amazingly, it stays open, but as soon as I can see the track I can also see a train approaching in the distance. I move smartly. I shout to an oncoming pedestrian to run. He briefly looks startled by the command but then runs and gives an exaggerated wave as the alarm bell rings, red lights flash, and the barrier starts to come down again, maybe for hours for all I know.

After a strenuous couple of hours, it's time for a pint of beer at one of the three pubs close to the station. The first one, the Windmill, is closed, so my choice is reduced to two. Instead, I enter the Red Cow, only yards beyond the Windmill. It's unexpectedly busy in the Red Cow. I struggle to get anywhere near the bar. I can see the beer selection is not to my liking, so I battle my way to the exit. I cross the road with purpose and enter the more modern Maltsters pub. It is much quieter in the Maltsters, and my eye immediately spots a handpump offering McMullen Country Best Bitter. The landlady welcomes me as I indicate that I would like a pint of Country. "Pint of Country" seems a funny thing to say, but she does not doubt what I mean. I wonder if a weaker version of Country would be called County and a stronger version would be Continent. However, I imagine it would be inadvisable for anyone incontinent to drink too many of the stronger ones. I share a joke with the landlady and laugh at her retort. It is no funnier than the comedian's joke at the level crossing, and I feel slightly guilty again for not laughing at his comment a little more. Maybe, it's the pub atmosphere that makes me laugh. It is a nice pint and goes down well. In fact, it goes down so well that the glass is empty more quickly than I had intended. A younger woman arrives and takes over duties at the bar. She immediately notices my empty glass and asks whether I would like a refill. Noting my age, perhaps, she insists on bringing the new pint over to my chair, minimising my effort as I tap my card on her payment device. I finish my second pint. Despite the offer of a third,

I say that it is time I am on my way as darkness is not too far away.

Google Maps finds me a route through a housing estate via Russells Ride. I am curious why it is a ride, not a road or street. I intend to check this later. It brings me to the final leg of my walk to the Travelodge Hotel, which means crossing a busy dual carriageway, skirting a small industrial estate, passing some older houses, crossing the railway line and, finally, passing through more industrial units and past an extensive car showroom. It is not especially interesting, although I feel sorry for the child or children who live in a house with an illuminated sign reading ITA STOP HERE. I can't say whether Santa will appreciate that the first two letters and part of the third letter of Santa have an electrical fault of some kind. I'm no electrician, as I have already said, and it strikes me that someone called Rita is more likely to stop by. I cross the railway line again. This time, there are no gates; you use your judgement as to when it is safe. As I emerge from a wasteland, the shortest viable route to the Travelodge is over a small grass bank, which I scale with rather more effort than I had expected. I am soon at Reception and greeted by a friendly Travelodge representative, who informs me that the chef has Covid and no food is available this evening. I head to my room, needing some downtime before deciding where to eat this evening. The room has a panoramic view of the A10 dual carriageway. I hope the chef recovers quickly.

When evening comes, I opt for somewhere not too far away. The Vine is a fifteen-minute walk from my hotel, and as far as one can tell from my online research, it looks an ideal pub. There are two unattractive options within a fifteen-minute walk. One is back across the railway line; the other entails a brief walk alongside the A10 and then half a mile beside another dual carriageway. There is a perfectly safe path to walk along, but cars will whizz past in the darkness. I have no idea why the dual carriageway is called Winston Churchill Way. It starts to rain – well, drizzle – making the walk even more unpleasant. However, it's not so bad that I can reasonably quote Churchill on his dual carriageway "if you are going through hell, keep going."

I arrive at the Vine and wait to be seated, obeying a sign's instructions. I am warmly greeted and led to a table. "Is this table OK?" she asks. It looks the same as twenty other tables, so I nod approvingly. There is a Christmassy atmosphere, some of the tables have workers enjoying office parties, but these tables are far away from me. One group in an area I can only just see are wearing antlers. A waitress approaches and asks if there is anything she can get me. I baulk, as the first thing that comes into my head is antlers. She is very sweet but doesn't look ready for my perverse sense of humour, so I order a bottle of Rioja. "Yes, of course", she says. "Is that one glass or two?" she asks. I resist the urge to ask whether she sees an imaginary person in the opposite chair and stop myself from saying I would like four glasses. I wonder what the comedic duo I met at the level crossing would say in this situation. I fancy that to the question 'is this table OK?', the man would reply, 'well, it's made of wood and looks sturdy', while I am less sure how he would respond to the question 'can I get you anything?' All I know is that his wife would be rolling on the floor with laughter. I order a pizza which the Rioja washes down nicely. A woman at a nearby table invites her husband to finish a pie that she has been eating. She looks surprised when he dives in with his hands to retrieve the remaining pastry and mimics stabbing him with a fork. He looks like the sort of bloke with a whole string of small businesses and, appropriately, it would seem, with his finger in every pie.

A feeling of calm comes over me, although it borders on fatigue. Appropriately, Wham!'s *Wake Me Up Before You Go-Go* interrupts a string of Christmassy songs, but it is time to depart and have a reasonably early night; there's a big game tomorrow. As I get up to leave, a woman with antlers starts to dance in a vacant area in the bar; she may have had a glass or two too many. She is dancing exaggeratedly until her partner tries to lead her away, presumably to minimise his, rather than her, embarrassment. She will have none of it and wriggles away, runs a short distance and resumes dancing with arms raised above her head. He walks away, accepting defeat. I squeeze past the dancer, who, to be fair, needs a reasonable margin of error to pass safely. As I reach the exit, my plan to walk back along Winston Churchill

Way to my hotel feels like having to fight them on the beaches. I certainly do not have the energy that the dancer has. I use my phone to book Mr Uber's services, and a friendly man arrives in seconds.

Soon after I awake on Saturday morning, I check out my plans to walk alongside the River Lea for a couple of miles. I seek a route to leave the river near the level crossing. As Baldrick from *Black Adder* might say, this cunning plan means I can take the road towards the town and get a cuppa and a slice of Bakewell tart at the bakery. My walk means I head east back through the wasteland, across the uncontrolled rail crossing and onwards to Waltham Cross.

I didn't realise that Waltham Cross is just a stone's throw away. I am soon in the town itself, but this time I have no wish to encounter its centre. Waltham Cross has all the standard high street shops, but now my mission is to reach the point where the river crosses the A121 and follow the towpath along the river. When it comes to A-roads, the A121 has achieved higher, or more accurately lower, numeric status than it probably deserves. It heads east, crosses the M25 and, unusually, like the number seven, turns back on itself slightly in Epping Forest before heading to Loughton. Wikipedia describes its emergence from Waltham Cross at the intersection of four dual carriageways as 'interesting'. I suppose we all find different things interesting. I think it's rather ordinary compared to the A121 in Russia, a road that runs for over 500 kilometres. If you do pub quizzes, you might one day thank me for telling you that the A121 runs from St Petersburg to the R21 in the Republic of Karelia and is known as the Sortavala Highway.

At the roundabout where I join the A121 just outside Waltham Cross, I see an advert for the Flour & Soot Massacre on Boxing Day. I make a mental note not to be in Waltham Cross on Boxing Day. I then suffer a brief period of dyslexia. Another poster advertises the HH Muckers Concert; another offers a foot massage on 26 December. I can't imagine what the HH Muckers Concert is. Further, I can't imagine why someone would specifically provide a foot massage on Boxing Day, much as I am partial to a foot massage. I then realise it is yet another advert for the Flour & Soot Massacre. As I wonder if Elton John will be coming to Waltham Cross for the HH Muckers Concert, I manage to read the word 'concrete' instead of 'concert'. That makes more sense. If you are in Waltham Cross and want some concrete, HH Muckers seem to be the people you need to contact. I wonder if last night's Rioja has damaged me more than I thought.

As I continue along the A121, I am surprised to see a sign welcoming me to Essex and Waltham Abbey. I had never realised Waltham Cross and Waltham Abbey were in different counties and assumed that Waltham Abbey was part of Waltham Cross. As far as I can see, there is a divide between the Crossites and the Abbeyites. I soon learn that Waltham Abbey is the last resting place of King Harold II.

Now, if you found the stuff about the A121 interesting, this does eclipse it in every way, so read on. King Harold was the last Anglo-Saxon king and died in 1066 at the Battle of Hastings, only months after succeeding Edward the Confessor. There is a popular theory that Harold died from an arrow to the eye, but there is some dispute. The debate arises from an inscription in the Bayeux Tapestry, '*Hic Harold Rex Interfectus Est*'. As any good Latin scholar would know, this translates as 'Here, Harold is killed'. The controversy emanates from your interpretation of the Bayeux Tapestry. One school of thought believes a man is pointing at the man with an arrow in his eye; the other claims he is pointing at a man on his back. I must admit I feel neutral about the whole matter, but feel free to take whichever side you like; you won't offend me.

I walk towards the outskirts of Waltham Abbey's town centre. I see a man with a child carrying an inflatable Father Christmas. To be fair to Father Christmas, I probably should describe what I see as a slim Father Christmas carried by an inflated man. I take a photo of the Abbey and return to the A121 for a stroll along the River Lea.

The walk along the River Lea is a pleasant experience, with more swans per mile than I have ever seen. The path is not particularly wide in places, so passing people means turning sideways to avoid stepping on the muddy grass. Although I understand the unwritten rule of turning sideways to pass oncoming pedestrians, cyclists clearly have the right of way as I hop back onto the muddy grass to let one pass at speed. I mutter "arsehole", just loud enough for him to hear. When a group of five young lads approach on bicycles, I consider jumping into the river. However, they are a model of politeness as they all stop to ensure we pass each other tidily. As they cycle off, they share a joke, but I can't hear what they say. If they said, "look at that daft old git", it's fine by me, but they are far too polite – at least until I was out of earshot.

I leave the riverside track near Cheshunt Station and prepare myself for the thousand steps over the footbridge. I will not be waiting for six trains to pass again. As I approach, the gates close, and the bridge looks even higher than it did the previous day. A train flashes through without stopping at the station, and the gates rise. I pass the three pubs and move purposefully to the bakers for the cuppa and slice of Bakewell tart I had promised myself. The bakery is close to a roundabout on which two speakers are playing Christmas carols. *Hark the herald angels sing* comes from the speakers, sung by someone who sounds like Matt Monro. It's not particularly uplifting; I imagine that the local council have put the speakers there in place of a Covid-infested choir. As I think back, I realise that something has been missing this Christmas – there are no choirs in railway stations or outside shops; there is just a little piped music to make us feel Christmassy. Is this the first year I haven't heard Slade's *Merry Christmas Everybody*? I'm not too bothered, you understand; it's just an observation.

Nonetheless, antlered staff provide tea and Bakewell tart, leaving me to think ahead to the afternoon. Or, more accurately, switch right off. Antlers are undoubtedly *de rigeur* in Cheshunt, if only at Christmas. I wonder whether Laura Trott wears antlers at Christmas. However, it doesn't feel Christmassy, even with only seven days to go to the big day. Maybe, the 18th of December is a big day in some households. For example, Billie Ellish, Brad Pitt, Steven Spielberg, Keith Richards and Christina Aguillera are probably enjoying birthday parties today. Further, Joseph Stalin would have been 144 years old today if he were still alive. And who knows? - Cheshunt v Bishop's Stortford may turn out to be the most famous event to take place on 18th December in years to come. Frankly, it hasn't got much competition unless you include the first performance of Tchaikovsky's *The Nutcracker* or the announcement in 1912 that Piltdown Man was an extinct human species at the Royal Geological Society. And, of course, Piltdown Man proved to be a hoax.

After leaving the bakers, a Christmas song that I recognise but cannot name emanates from the speakers on the roundabout. It doesn't appear to be making the locals festive, or me for that matter. Maybe, I should buy some antlers. It's time to set off for Cheshunt's Theobalds Lane ground for a pint and to feel part of the pre-match build-up. I avoid the high street and take the lesser-travelled route alongside Cheshunt Community Sports Centre, which backs onto Cheshunt FC's ground. I stroll along Albury Ride and The Ride, both eminently rideable, and down a track that runs the length of the Community Sports Centre. Frustratingly, I can hear people playing football, but the pitches are on a raised level, leaving me to listen and stare at a high grass bank. I hear a young man shout "wide" repeatedly, but from the tone of his voice, I imagine the pass to his wide position never happens. I'll never know for sure.

It's not long before I find my way to a side entrance to Cheshunt's ground. No one is surprised at my 1.50pm arrival for a 3pm kick-off even though there is no one around the pitch. When I arrive at the bar, I understand why; several others have come through the turnstile already. After ordering a pint of Guinness, I ask someone who looks official if they know Jim Tuite, Cheshunt's historian. I introduce myself to Jim, who soon gently chides me for pronouncing Cheshunt as 'chess hunt'. "It has a 'z' in the middle", explains Jim as I desperately retrain my brain to say 'Chezunt'. Having thought 'chess hunt' all week, it is hard to undertake such retraining at such short notice. Jim is very friendly and one of those who seems to know anything and everything about Cheshunt FC. Jim reminds me of Tony Kempster, who was the non-League statistician extraordinaire. His website, tonykemspter.co.uk, still exists in a frozen state in his memory following his premature death in 2009. His encyclopaedic website was many years ahead of its time. As for Jim, you feel as if you could ask him about a game in 2003 and he would know the score, the scorers, the attendance, and the referee's name. As a lifelong Charlton supporter, I drop into the conversation that I seem to recall Charlton playing Cheshunt (pronounced Chezunt) in the Aetolian League back in the 1960s. He looks ever so slightly impressed. I reckon he is awarding me a Grade 2 historian status, although I have a long way to go to reach his Grade 10 status.

The Aetolian League only lasted for five seasons. Charlton 'A' and Cheshunt played in the League for the first three years before Cheshunt departed to the Spartan League, and Charlton' A' withdrew. I vaguely recall seeing Charlton draw 6-6 with Snowdown Colliery Welfare in the Aetolian League, but my memories are sketchy as I was only eight or nine. Jim laughs at these memories and relates how Cheshunt ended up in a league with teams in deepest Kent. Cray Wanderers apparently persuaded Cheshunt to jump ship from the London League in 1959 after the clubs met at the end of the 1958-59 season. Jim has to depart for official duties, and by the time I finish my second pint, I am ready to take my place pitchside.

The seated area nearest the bar is already busy, so bearing in mind the need to keep socially distanced close to Christmas, I proceed to the stand on the opposite side of the pitch. This stand is almost empty as I take a seat. However, it is as though the stand itself is socially distanced, as it is set back several yards from the pitch and has a view obstructed by the dugouts. I opt to stand and lean on the railings around the edge. By this time, forty seconds have elapsed, and Cheshunt's Enock Ekongo has been the victim of a heavy challenge, which finishes his part in the game. It is not a good start to the day for the Ambers as, due to Covid, they can only field two substitutes. Apart from Mr Ekongo's forcible removal, the game starts cagily. Indeed, I comment to a nearby spectator that there won't be more than one goal in this game. She smiles as if to humour me, seemingly preparing to remind me of my assertion if the match ends as a 4-4 draw. After fifteen minutes, we see the first real goalmouth action. Cheshunt's dangerous number nine, Rowan Liburd, holds the ball up well and drives it across the box. It only needs a touch from the outstretched leg of Reece Beckles-Richards, and Cheshunt will be one up; the ball carries on its path for a goal kick.

In these early exchanges, Cheshunt show a stronger and more physical side than Bishop's Stortford's previous two FA Trophy opponents, Chipstead and Leiston. They are not getting a lot of time on the ball but match Stortford's powerful midfield. Football pundits talk of teams cancelling each other out; the first half-hour of the game exemplifies this. Bishop's Stortford's best move of this period comes when a well-worked move down the right flank requires an astute catch from George Marsh in Cheshunt's goal. At the 30-minute mark, Ben Marlow, Bishop's Stortford's strong midfielder, latches on to a loose ball, but his shot is just wide. There is no question that anyone has much time on the ball as the game occasionally threatens to boil over. Jonny Giles of Bishop's Stortford, who had a lot of time on the ball in the previous FA Trophy games, looks rushed today. The closest to a goal comes just before half-time when Cheshunt's Beckles-Richards figures again. He finds Zack Newton, who battles well in the box, before firing a shot at a tight angle towards the inside of the near post. Jack Giddens in Stortford's goal gets down smartly and manages to keep the effort out with the aid of the post. It's 0-0 at half-time, and no one can argue with that scoreline. However, I am enjoying the game immensely; it's highly competitive, albeit at this modest standard compared with the likes of Manchester City and Liverpool.

The second half starts the same way, although early in the half a tangle on the edge of Cheshunt's penalty area results in a free-kick to the Blues of Stortford. Jonny Giles' free kick is well-struck but is safely collected by Marsh. Cheshunt's Zack Newton continues to be all over the pitch and is arguably the most dangerous player on either side. A long, hanging cross evades Marsh on the hour. As the ball drops loose, a snatched volley goes well wide. As the game wears on, you feel that Bishop's Stortford are starting to gain more possession. However, they are not creating any chances as they rely too often on the long ball. Cheshunt's defence never looks troubled, and a tie decided on penalties becomes increasingly likely.

It suddenly occurs to me that I have not checked my phone once for the scores of the Premier League and EFL games that are taking place at the same time. This is a fundamental change of routine; this FA Trophy journey is absorbing more of my attention than many other important elements of my life. I know that I can irritate others by checking the latest scores of games while watching television in the evening. I can give the appearance that I am bored with a film or some other entertainment, but it is just my obsession with knowing the latest scores. In my defence, I never waste my time on things like Farcebook, but football and cricket scores can mean that my phone is never far from my hands. Actually, on the train to Cheshunt earlier, I had made a list of reasons why I like non-League football. I have so far made five notes, although one is illegible and looks like 'clarinets'. I wonder what the hell I was thinking; bad handwriting and cryptic notes to myself are a bad combination. For what it is worth, the other four were: nicer fans, more honest players, camaraderie amongst all involved (players, supporters, club officials, even match officials) and fewer people getting in my way. I had forgotten better beer and more modestly-priced beer. I spend a short time wondering what clarinets could mean to reflect better and cheaper beer without success.

Giles curls another dangerous ball into the box, but no one can get close enough to make it anything more than dangerous. Cheshunt make a rare attack after 70 minutes when they move well down the right side. A good cross from Anthony Church finds Liburd, whose flick header brings a good save from Jack Giddens. Bishop's Stortford have two penalty appeals, one for a push and one for handball, but Mr Mackey looks right to wave play on both times from my vantage point. There are a couple of oohs and aahs in the dying minutes as both defences find the ball ricocheting around their boxes. Cheshunt come closer to scoring as a bobbling shot needs someone on the line to keep the scores at 0-0. The whistle for full-time comes, and I am about to witness my second tie involving penalties in this season's FA Trophy. By the way, did I tell you that I could tell this would be a low-scoring game?

Bishop's Stortford choose to take penalties at the end their travelling fans occupy. The first four penalties all result in goals, but the fifth produces the first miss as the usually sure-footed Giles hits the Cheshunt crossbar. Cheshunt convert the next two, leaving Jenville Renee the unenviable task of scoring for Stortford to make Cheshunt take their fifth penalty. George Marsh guesses right by diving right, and amber shirts flood onto the penalty area to congratulate their keeper. There are celebrations and groans, depending on which team you support.

I make my way to the bar to hear what everyone thinks. On the way to the bar, a youngster asks his Dad why Cheshunt didn't take their fifth penalty as they could have won by a bigger margin – 5-3, instead of 4-3 on penalties. Dad tells him that Cheshunt didn't care once they had won. The young lad asks the unanswerable question, "Why?" When I reach the bar, I join a trainee groundhopper for a beer. I meet Luke Burford, who is a referee. It transpires his mentor is today's referee, Oliver Mackey. I think Mr Mackey did a pretty good job in a tense and occasionally fiery game. I learned later that in the period between full-time and taking penalties, Mr Mackey sent off Bishop's Stortford's Mark Haines, presumably for persisting with protestations about the claimed penalties. Luke has travelled from Leicester to see this game; I think it's fair to call him a groundhopper. You could argue that he is more of a refereehopper, but that sounds weird. Luke is almost certainly a sharp-eyed referee himself. He was quick to spot the offer of a free beer to any groundhoppers on my *fatrophyhound* Twitter post. Luke wins his free beer. I then meet Jim Tuite again, who is enjoying a beer with friends. I am delighted to receive a free signed copy of Jim's history of Cheshunt FC as a souvenir.

I leave Cheshunt's Theobalds Lane ground. I'm not wearing antlers, and I have no birthday celebrations to attend. However, Cheshunt's win has become the most famous event ever to occur on the 18th of December. At least, it has for me.

CHAPTER 7

SHOTS

Saturday 15th January 2022 – Fourth Round Proper –
St Albans City v Cheshunt

A week before setting off for St Albans, I had allocated three periods of ten minutes each day to practise pronouncing Cheshunt as 'Chezunt'. By looking into a mirror, I learned that my pronunciation would be acceptable if I didn't allow my jaw to move and forced 'Chezunt' to come from the upper chest. Every time I let my jaw move, I stuck a sharp pin in my finger to remind me. It might have been an old-fashioned way to educate myself; it seemed to work. "Have a good time at the Cheshunt match", my wife trills as she drops me at the station on Friday. "Chezunt", I reply as I take my bag from the car. She looks at me blankly as though she may have misheard me say "cheerio".

After overcoming their local rivals, Bishop's Stortford, in the last round, Cheshunt are staying within the bounds of Hertfordshire for a trip to St Albans City. I could hear the groan at my home in Kent from Cheshunt's players when their ball came out of the bag after St Albans City's. A friend has told me I am stuck in the Hertfordshire Triangle; it has a ring to it. St Albans are riding high in the National League South, one level above their Isthmian Premier opponents.

The morning of Friday 14th January 2022 is a cold day in Tunbridge Wells when I board the train en route to St Albans. The sky is bright blue with a few puffy clouds, similar to clouds that a reasonably talented nine-year-old child might paint. A woman boards the train with me and sits opposite, reading her morning paper. In a carriage with 100% Covid mask-wearing compliance, it is hard to understand how she keeps reading with steamed-up glasses.

The passengers on my train are a quiet bunch; even those travelling together are generally uncommunicative. At Hildenborough station, a young woman, probably aged around twenty, boards the train, wearing what I would refer to, possibly wrongly, as clubbing attire. I can't imagine why you would want to have a bare midriff at 10am on a Friday when the temperature is sub-zero. My mother's voice jumps into my head, telling me I will 'catch the death of me' going out with wet hair. I conclude that she has either misjudged the temperature on this sunny day or that she is going out with her mates straight from work. Probably, the latter, I fancy. I stop thinking about it in more depth; I just know I wouldn't want to be that cold – for any reason. "Chezunt, Chezunt", I repeat to myself in my head to keep up the practice. Two businessmen sit in front of me. After a lengthy silence, they moan about a difficult meeting they have to attend. "We'll need a beer afterwards", says one, chortling. The other agrees as they consider possible pubs around Covent Garden. They revert to silence.

A woman breaks the monotony by boarding with two bulging sacks of party balloons, the silvery type on sticks, but without the sticks. There are probably five or six balloons in each giant bag, causing her to wobble along. They hamper her progress into the carriage and subsequently to a seat. It looks as though this is the first time she has considered the logistics of travelling with such an awkward load. She wisely decides to stand with her encumbrances, as passing between the seats is impossible. After a long silence, the businessmen retrace their plans for the 'needed' beer after their meeting. It's almost the same conversation word for word. They appear to be putting more effort into their beer preparations than the bumpy meeting ahead.

After getting off the train at London Bridge, the hazards of travelling by train surface for me. My connecting train to St Albans has a delay of fifteen minutes. Fifteen minutes soon becomes twenty minutes and eventually thirty minutes. Fortunately, the sun is reaching Platform 5 of London Bridge station, and it's not as cold as I feared. Due to the delays, Thameslink has decided, quite reasonably, to cancel the train that is due to run thirty minutes later on the same route. Their messaging, though, is confused. Station announcements repeatedly apologise for the cancellation, but not the delayed train. Passengers aiming for the late train are privileged to receive an apology despite not suffering any delay as the previous train is arriving at the time they wished. At the same time, I suffer without a hint of regret from Thameslink. A woman asks me if it's the same train. My first thought is to give a Smart Alec reply, but I hold back in time to confirm that she will be fine on the delayed train. She smiles at me and says, "thank you so much", as though I have made her day. Perhaps, I have.

The train hacks through the centre of London, stopping at Blackfriars, City Thameslink, Farringdon and London St Pancras before heading northwards to Hertfordshire. I can't stop myself from checking what happened to Holborn Viaduct on Google, as that used to be the station after Blackfriars. I find it hard to believe that Holborn Viaduct closed in 1990. I would have gambled £100 on Holborn Viaduct still being in use ten years ago. This train route connects Brighton on the South Coast to Luton and Bedford. It would be an easy trip to Brighton for

Luton fans if they find themselves in the same division. And, of course, if Whitehawk drew Bedford Town in the FA Trophy.

After Hampstead Thameslink station, the driver puts his foot down, or maybe it's a lever he pulls, as we speed towards St Albans. I nip to the nearby toilet on the train and hit the jackpot – the soap, water and dryer all work as you would hope, a real rarity. As I stand there peeing, I try to read the graffiti. The closest I can get to reading one of the daubings is 'WWF', but I cannot imagine why World Wide Fund For Nature members would use spray cans in a toilet. I press the button to open the door, and nothing happens. I briefly imagine ending up in Bedford, but two firmer pushes on the button do the trick.

I return to my seat as we pass metal constructions that probably house many of the things we have delivered to our homes these days. We pass through Borehamwood, and I remember that one team I would like the winners of tomorrow's tie to avoid is Boreham Wood. I need to escape from the Hertfordshire Triangle! The puzzle of why Boreham Wood (two words) play at Borehamwood (one word) bothers me slightly, but it is not something I care to research right now. Boreham Wood recently ended St Albans City's FA Cup progress this season. After getting through three rounds of the FA Cup, each requiring a replay, St Albans City faced League Two's Forest Green Rovers at home in the First Round Proper of the FA Cup.

They beat Forest Green 3-2 in front of an impressive home crowd of 4100. Their reward was an away draw in Hertfordshire against Boreham Wood, which they lost by a 4-0 margin to end their dreams of facing a big name in the 3rd Round. The attendance for the Boreham Wood game was 4101, one more than the previous tie. Was someone unwell for the Forest Green game?

While St Albans City's FA Cup exploits may not have hit too many high spots over the years, one game that does stand in the record books is a 7-8 defeat to Dulwich Hamlet. While the scoreline is one I cannot recall seeing in any other football game, it was especially notable as Wilfred 'Billy' Minter scored all seven St Albans' goals. I hope St Albans will celebrate this game's hundredth anniversary in 2022. Wilfred remains a legend, scoring 356 goals in his 362 appearances for the Saints. If you like obscure football quiz questions, try this one. What connects St Albans to Crystal Palace? Well, it's a bit of a trick question, in fairness. The answer is that the first headquarters of St Albans Football Club was the Crystal Palace public house on London Road in St Albans. The pub was demolished in the mid-1980s.

I head from the station towards St Albans' town centre – or, more accurately, city centre. I have visited St Albans before, recalling that it was flat. But even small hills seem much steeper when carrying a bag. Before I reach the reception desk at the Travelodge, a cardboard cutout receptionist greets me, smiling warmly. As my eyes meet the cardboard receptionist's unflinching eyes and her fixed smile, I realise I need to walk another ten yards to find a human being. I receive a warm greeting from the actual receptionist, who is there in the flesh. She takes my bag so I can pace the streets of St Albans unburdened; it's far too early to check in to the hotel.

I leave the hotel and look at the menu of the closest restaurant to my hotel. It's called the Alban's Well, which sounds remarkably like 'all is well'. My mind races back to the Bishop's Stortford wrangle over apostrophes. Frankly, I don't understand why St Albans has no apostrophe. There was a person called St Alban, so logically this city is St Alban's. Curiously, the restaurant is on St Peter's Street, which proudly displays its apostrophe. There are too many issues to worry about, though. Should Saint be abbreviated? Should St have a full stop after it? And does St Peter St make sense? As I peruse the menu, I notice they have adopted a modern policy of having no pound signs for the prices. Also each item has a price rounded to a whole number of pounds. Under extras, I spot British Kimchi 1 Olives & Samphire 2. It sounds like an exotic football result, like Hashtag United 1 Dagenham & Redbridge 2 but posher.

Before exploring St Albans, I decide I need something to sustain me. There are so many cafes and restaurants that I panic and opt for Pret as it's a safe bet. I sit down with a cup of tea and a wrap and notice that everyone else seems to have more purpose than me. Mothers with their toddlers are chatting animatedly. Businesspeople are typing away on laptops. Two students compare notes. A man laughs at a magazine he is reading. I do little more than stare into space. I realise that I am a strange mix. I am happy doing nothing, yet too much nothing is not right for me. On this occasion, the brainless fifteen minutes do me a power of good, and I feel revitalised. As I re-enter the street, a busker appropriately launches into The Carpenters' *Top of the World*.

St Albans is a nice enough city. Maybe, a bit too nice for me. I am sure it has a rougher edge somewhere, but I've not seen it yet. I see why TV football personalities Jimmy Hill and John Motson chose to live here. And now, amongst its residents, the ordinary-sounding Stacey Dooley has made not-so-ordinary St Albans her home.

In the pedestrianised area, there is a place where shops selling beauty products surround you. Molton Brown, Champneys and Jo Malone compete for my attention – well, not my attention, but those looking for beauty products. Inadvertently, in my notes, I noted Farrow & Ball competing in this enclave, but I later learned that they specialise in paint and paper – altogether a different sort of painting and papering over the cracks, I fancy. I come to Flying Tiger, Copenhagen, in French Row (a narrow street, not a Gallic oarsman). Flying Tiger claims to design products "to make you feel good" – if they could sell me a pint of Harveys Bitter in more or less any glass vessel, they would achieve their claim. There is a TV series called Flying Tiger, but it seems unrelated, as it is about a gang called the Black Snake Gang. I don't imagine there is a Black Snake Gang in St Albans. As I move away from Flying Tigers, I get a strong whiff of cannabis from a man's rollup. He may be moving closer to flying tigers as I move away.

I have had enough of high street shops, trendy cafes, bars, and restaurants. It's time for some culture. I walk to St Albans Abbey, and, to be fair, it is hard not to be impressed. Having visited Waltham Abbey on my previous round trip to Cheshunt, I can say that St Albans Abbey knocks Waltham Abbey into a cocked hat. If tomorrow's game reflects the difference in abbeys, Cheshunt are in for a drubbing. I take a path to get closer to the Abbey but find I am trapped in a loop of tracks with no escape. There are building works all around the Abbey. I retrace my steps and find a long-winded route back to Verulamium Park and the Abbey. As I leave the trap of tracks, I pass schoolboys eating their lunch or just hanging about – or, more likely these days, hanging out, which somehow sounds wrong. One boy I walk past says to his pal, "a healthy body is a healthy mind". I can't imagine saying anything like that in my schoolboy days – or, probably, since. I google the expression to see if it is a famous quote, but Google responds with an overwhelming selection of alternatives, ranging from vegan diets to TED talks and weight-loss programmes. One contributor to a website claims that 'a healthy person can think normally and act instantly according to the given situation'. I'll leave you to debate that one with your friends.

Finding the entrance back into the park from a different direction proves more difficult than imagined. I pass an entrance that claims that "these gates are in constant use, please do not obstruct". I suspect I could have waited for two hours, and no one would have wanted to use the gates. They aren't in constant use. Eventually, I spot someone leaving what appears to be the park via another gate. Being the perfect gentleman, I allow her to come out first and assume she will hold the gate open for me in return. As it happens, she slams it purposefully to stop me from entering. Surprised, I try to push the gate and find it has a push-button security entry system. I now realise why she slammed the gate. It is a side entrance to a school. She was worried that I was, at best, trying to gain access without permission or, at worst, a dangerous paedophile. Realising my mistake, I continue down the road while she sits in her car and eyes me suspiciously. The road towards the entrance I want is another 100 yards down the road.

Before exploring the park, I arrive at Ye Olde Fighting Cocks, the oldest pub in St Albans. Indeed, amongst others, it claims to be the oldest pub in England. A sign outside invites me to a Wednesday Quiz with generous prizes available. Unfortunately, I cannot join the merry quizzers. I wonder whether Oliver Cromwell, when passing here, was tempted by the quiz on the night he slept at the pub before returning to the Civil War the following day. If there was a quiz when Cromwell visited, you wonder how he reacted when it was the history round. 'I hate history', he may have said, 'I am better at current affairs'. We'll never know.

I decide to enter. It's rather dark inside as my glasses try to readjust from the sunlight. The barman is delighted to inform me the pub has been re-awarded its Cask Marque accreditation today, which means I can drink my pint with even greater confidence. After consuming one pint, I get up to leave and try to find my way back to the main entrance. I am, for some reason, disoriented and ask for help. I am sure the barman thinks I am on a pub crawl and visiting pub nine of ten. He points me to the exit, still basking in the glory of his renewed accreditation.

I enter Verulamium Park. Verulamium, as any historian or Latin scholar would know, is the Roman name for St Albans. I find saying and typing Verulamium about equally troublesome; in my head, I hear Americans saying aluminum instead of aluminium to add to the confusion. I see a party of schoolchildren on their way to a visit to the Abbey; at least, I assume so. I overhear the teacher telling the class to stop. "Remember, Year 4", the teacher says, "you are representing the school today, so please be extra calm". She makes further announcements as I move out of earshot, but the words use the same script I heard on trips when I was at school. Maybe, they still use the same manual. I don't know what these schoolchildren will learn. They may learn that it is probably the oldest place of worship in the country, although they may not hear about its use as a place of persecution and executions. Amazingly, some of the bricks in the tower are Roman bricks. Robert Runcie, who later became Archbishop of Canterbury, was Bishop of St Albans from 1970 to 1980. Indeed, he was buried in 2000 in the churchyard at St Albans Abbey.

I cross the River Ver, which seems an afterthought of a name for a river in St Albans. I decide to walk around the lake, which takes in remnants of the Roman Wall. It is remarkable how parts of the wall have remained, but it doesn't do much for me. I feel more elated when I approach a man with a basset hound. As a former basset owner, I almost always ask current owners whether their basset is stubborn. It's a silly question because the answer is always in the affirmative. My wife and I have had several dogs in our years together, but Betty, our basset, was the only one who was constantly able to outsmart me. If I wanted to put her back on her lead at the end of a walk, I had two options: - catch her when she wasn't expecting it or pretend I was very pleased with her. However, if I overplayed my hand and showed that I was too pleased with her, she would become suspicious and increase the distance between us. Her escape into congested rush-hour traffic in Tonbridge High Street while I had control of two other dogs on leads was arguably the most stressful ten minutes of my life. On another occasion, Betty decided to have a poo on a pedestrian crossing as cars waited for us to cross. This was one of the funnier moments, particularly as the waiting drivers found it so amusing. The basset in Verulamium Park watches as I chat with the owner but, in true basset fashion, decides this has gone on too long and starts to wander off. "I need to go", explains the owner unnecessarily, "I am supposed to meet my wife shortly". However, he didn't need to blame his wife for the rushed departure. I am fully aware that life is easier if you allow the basset to be the boss.

The path around the lake took me past six or seven football pitches, where, I assume, the likes of British Kimchi and Olives & Samphire contest exciting encounters. Who knows? Perhaps, they played an early form of football in Roman times. Given their road-building techniques, we can assume they used 'route one' tactics. Just before I come to the end of the path, a woman on a bicycle rings her bell three times. Rather than being a warning of her presence, it is a command to get out of the bloody way. I have nowhere to go as pedestrians are coming toward me. "I'm coming past", she announces as several pedestrians take hasty refuge. I mutter, "old bat"; I am unsure how audibly and wonder where the expression 'old bat' came from; I can't remember using it since I was at school. I come to the Roman Museum at the other end of the long, thin lake. I almost decide to enter, but something stops me. I am not sure what. Instead, I visit the Park Café.

The cafe has an elaborate one-way system with a pick-up point for purchases. It is to help us avoid getting Covid. There are two roped-off columns for queuing; I choose the wrong one. As a group enters, my lack of appreciation of the traffic flow means that I drop from third to fifth in the queue. It's a painful mistake as one of those jumping in front of me orders eight beverages. The two-person team working in the café has a rigorous system in place. One takes the order, the money and then makes the drinks; the other does nothing. Although I have already paid, I almost decide to give up as the hard worker of the team struggles to deliver the mounting backlog of orders. When my tea arrives, I go to a table covered in crumbs and brush them on the floor. As four o'clock comes, it appears to be closing time. Suddenly, the lazy one livens up, moving tables and belatedly wiping dirty ones. I hate that question, "Is everything alright?" when it's not, but I play my British role and say it is. I won't be back even if St Albans City are at home for the next three rounds. As I prepare to leave, a man with a yellow and blue bobble hat asks if they are still open. I miss the reply as I focus on the badge on his hat to see if he is a St Albans City supporter. I think he wonders what I am looking at until I realise it's a badge for a cycling club that shares the same colours as St Albans City FC.

I walk the length of the lake, pass St Albans Abbey and find what would have yielded a more accessible entry to the park. I leave through the Great Gateway of the Monastery, dating back to 1360. A sign informs me that from 1553 to

1869, the building at the Great Gateway was a prison before becoming part of St Albans School. A sign outside warns everyone that 'Bikes chained to these railings will be removed and disposed of'. I can't help thinking that the English teacher at the school was not consulted about the sign, as he wouldn't have ended the sentence in a preposition. And, yes, I am sure there are sentences in this book that have a preposition to end with. Oops.

I wander into an area of narrow streets that are pleasant enough but samey. I decide it is time to return to my hotel. In the narrow streets, I am slightly confused about where the town centre is. I ask a passing lady, who appears to be marching slowly rather than walking, which road I need to take to get back to the town centre. "City centre", she corrects me as she continues her march without telling me where the city centre is. I use my directional instinct, which is right on this occasion. I cross a street called Romeland, which sounds more like a theme park with gladiators and baths. As I turn a corner, I almost bump into a scary-looking man with a big dog, who is more Hannibal Lector than Hannibal with an elephant, despite the size of his Newfoundland dog. I consider a quick trim in Alternative Barbering, but the name puts me off. Perhaps, they are barbarians in keeping with the Romeland theme.

I feel in need of refreshment or, more precisely, a late afternoon pint. I pass the Old Bell, which offers "bottomless bubbles". I stride on, assured that I don't need bottomless bubbles, although they're preferable to a bubbly bottom. I walk the length of the high street in the town, er, city, and come to a roundabout with three pubs dotted around it. Just as I enter the Cock Inn, I realise I have been in this pub before – maybe, ten years ago when I was staying in St Albans on business. An England international match I watched on the television in the pub comes back to mind. However, I have no idea about the opposition or the score.

I have to wait at the bar while the barman serves an excitable young man next to me.

He orders a shot, which prompts the friendly and patient barman to ask, "Which one?"

"The strongest one", he replies. The barman is more hesitant now and suggests several alternatives. The young man turns to me, appearing to seek advice. I am no expert in shots and offer no help. Fortified by a couple of drinks, he excitedly tells me that he is getting a date with a young lady if he drinks eight shots in two hours. He gestures to the young lady, who is talking to another man while glancing back at the shot drinker. The shot drinker mutters something about showing how strong he is, but I can't help thinking he will be flat on his back in an hour. Let's hope he doesn't complete the bet and take her out this evening for the bottomless bubbles; he would be legless, never mind bottomless.

I drink my pint and exchange a joke with a couple sitting next to my table, losing interest in the date bet. I am in text communication with my daughter, Charlotte, as I sit with my pint and tell her the story of the shot drinker. "Fair play to him", she texts, secretly wishing she could witness the event. The shot drinker, his friend (I assume), and the young lady leave, presumably to resume the challenge in another pub. I don't feel any need to follow and discover the outcome.

There is an air of peace in the Cock Inn as Friday afternoon drinkers prepare for a leisurely weekend. As I am about to leave, *Brown Eyed Girl* by Van Morrison comes over the speakers, prompting a man in his forties or even fifties to dance flamboyantly for four or five seconds before resuming a normal pose. It's a brief moment of lunacy, although he looks awkward as he rejoins his party. I leave. It's time to go back to my hotel to read or do something mundane for a couple of hours. As I approach the hotel reception, I smile at the cardboard receptionist and almost speak to her before remembering I need to walk another ten yards.

Friday evening comes and goes. The choice of restaurants in St Albans overwhelms me. I am somewhat indecisive and wander up and down two or three streets. In an otherwise empty street, a car travelling slowly alongside the kerb sounds its horn, and the driver waves frantically at me. I return an involuntary half-wave until, out of the corner of my eye, I notice a young woman lurking in front of a shop. She runs to the car, which is now stationary. I feel a bit stupid as she walks past me. Why on earth did my arm start to raise itself before breaking into a wave?

In the evening, I opt for a pub, the Peahen, selling decent but reasonably standard pub food. After some further indecision, I have a yearning for a steak and ale pie until the waitress tells me that the steak and ale pie is off. I assume she means 'off the menu' rather than past its sell-by date. She tries to press me to have a 'tasty' chicken and leek pie, but I feel fussy; it's not what I want. Fortunately, the glasses of Rioja are going down well and taking my mind off the lack of pie alternatives. The fish and chips meal I have as an alternative is above average and satisfies my hunger. There's an awkward moment when I go to the loo and return to find four vultures circling my table as I return. If you are a solo drinker or eater, there is no easy way to indicate you 'own' a particular space. I return just in time to be able to shoulder-charge a middle-aged woman about to take my seat. Of course, quite reasonably, I hold back on the shoulder charge and politely tell her that the table is mine. The waitress returns and offers me dessert, but I opt for another glass of Rioja as my dessert. It's soon time to go to bed as I don't fancy eight shots tonight. In fact, I never fancy any shots, but I am worried about the young man seeking a date with the young lady.

Two things strike me when I pull back the curtains of my room on Saturday morning. First, there's a heavy mist in St Albans. Secondly, outside my window, a street market has appeared. It is already bursting into life as traders prepare for their early customers. Below my window is a massive display of vegetables. I take breakfast but check out soon afterwards to explore further. As I leave my room, a hotel worker almost walks into me, possibly checking another room. "Sorry, sweetheart", she says, as I narrowly avoid crashing into her with my bag. I am not sure when was the last time someone called me 'sweetheart'. I have noticed a few women call me 'my lovely', presumably in recognition of my advancing years. I pass reception and smile back at the cardboard receptionist before leaving the hotel.

Outside in the misty high street, there is a queue of twelve people waiting to buy vegetables. Have the national newspapers declared a shortage of vegetables, causing panic-buying? A seller asks a potential customer, "How many do you want? One? Two? Four? Eight? Sixteen?" The customer, slightly flustered by the doubling-up sales technique, opts for four.

It puts me in mind of a situation when, as a much younger man in Bangkok, doubling up nearly got me into trouble. I was walking through a red light area of Bangkok when a young man approached me with pictures of attractive scantily-dressed women. Yes, I know walking through a red light district sounds suspicious, but it was the shortest route between a bar and my hotel. "Like pretty lady?" he asked. I walked on, giving the globally-accepted palm of the hand gesture to indicate a lack of interest, but he still saw me as a potential customer. His rationale was, not unreasonably, that any single man in Bangkok is a potential customer. "You like two pretty ladies?" he offered. I continued to walk on, saying "no thank you", but he was keen to make a sale. "You like four pretty ladies?" Now, bear in mind that I had had a few beers; the doubling-up sales technique had managed to stop me in my tracks. You could sense that his hopes of a sale had leapt as I stood still. Now, something triggered in my brain that I had no control over. The words that came out of my mouth without a moment's thought were: "Can you do eight pretty ladies?" I had involuntarily joined in his doubling-up game. Why? I can't explain. The question was whether he could supply eight pretty ladies. What do you think? You bet he could. "Come, come, come", he commanded. I am fairly sure he was referring to the direction I should follow him rather than my sexual capabilities. I didn't find out. Just as fast as I had uttered the words, 'eight pretty ladies', extra energy poured into my legs and I moved away quickly. He followed me patiently for some distance until he realised that I was a lost cause. Perhaps I am a lost cause.

I walk through the market stalls and shops of St Albans, but my heart is not in the hustle and bustle of a shopping centre on a Saturday morning. I don't feel the need to buy a cushion, even at £4 each. The residents of St Albans, while keen to snap up their vegetables, are also less excited by the prospect of the £4 cushions. I pass a shop called

Anthropologie. It sounds more like an apology for studying human behaviour, particularly as it seems to limit itself to flogging women's clothes. I am more curious about a stall that sells momo food. What the heck is momo? There are chicken, pork and vegetarian options but no indication of what momo is. Fortunately, I am not hungry, but I can hear Lord Sugar say, "it should do what it says on the tin". The last stall I look at, and almost the last one in the market is *www.chilternproducts.co.uk*. I expect to find local beers, cheeses and other produce. Instead, I find that they sell buffalo tails, beef tendons and, more mysteriously, pizzle sticks. A woman asks for beef tendons, which causes the vendor to check on the size. It's time to leave the market; I am sure I don't want any pizzle sticks. Shots and pizzle sticks. Is this what brought Stacey Dooley and John Motson to St Albans?

I feel a bit aimless today. St Albans seems to stand for shops, excellent restaurants and Roman paraphernalia. I am sure these things make it a pleasant place to live, but I am struggling to find any desire to explore. I decide on a zigzag route to Clarence Park, the home of St Albans City FC. My path to Clarence Park passes the St. Villa restaurant, which offers British and European cuisine. I suppose Brexit means that you must now spell out that the British part still has European connections, although I am more intrigued by the full stop after the St in 'St. Villa', a strange decision in St (no full stop) Albans. More worryingly, I pass MD Tattoo, whose logo is in a wiggly font. The thought of a tattooist with a shaky hand does not seem like a good advert for their skills. To make matters worse, the 'MD' is indistinct and looks like 'NO'. Maybe no tattoo is a good decision.

I reach the vicinity of Clarence Park, but I cannot find any signs for an entrance. A gentleman of a similar age joins my road from a side street, so I ask him for directions to the ground. "Follow me", he replies chirpily, "I'm going right past it". My choice is a bad one. Although he is as friendly as he looks, he strides off at a pace that would leave Usain Bolt gasping for breath. He notices that he has quickly opened up a three or four-yard gap on me, so he waits before bursting ahead again. "Up here on the left, then right", he says, losing patience with my lack of speed. As he disappears into the distance, I raise my arm high in the air to acknowledge his help, but it's too late as he is already overtaking more pedestrians and becoming a dot in the distance. I make a mental note to look for someone with a limp the next time I need directions.

I reach Clarence Park, a proper park, not just a football ground. St Albans City have played here since their formation in 1908. The ground dates back to 1894, originally used by St Albans FC and St Albans Amateurs. One of the most famous players to wear the yellow and blue of St Albans City is Dean Austin, who went on to make over 100 appearances for both Tottenham Hotspur and Crystal Palace.

In the park, there are swings, roundabouts and dogs hurtling about as madly as my three labradors. The football ground sits alongside the railway track and looks nice enough from the few vantage points where you can see beyond the fences. I pass the public toilets, grandly named Ornamental Park Public Toilets; you wonder if there was a big opening ceremony with dignitaries. Maybe, even a royal flush. I come to a tea shop about two-thirds of my way around this modestly-sized park. It is an entirely different experience from Verulamium Park – I wish aluminum would not ring in my ears. Inside the café, they are friendly, smiling and efficient. They encourage me to have breakfast, unaware I have already eaten a substantial repast. A pleasant fifteen minutes pass as I think ahead to the afternoon's game, taking place a few hundred yards away. As I leave, the owner asks if I am in Clarence Park for the football and tells me I must have breakfast next time. "You won't be disappointed", she promises me. I explain that returning to the café depends on St Albans City's form this afternoon and whether their ball comes out of the bag as another home tie, but I assure her that, subject to those criteria, I will come back for breakfast.

At one o'clock, it's time to find my way to the railway station where I will meet my friend, Jon. He is travelling across London to be a part of my Hashtag United to Wembley trail. I've known Jon a long while and, as a young man, used to play football at the same club as him. Although

Jon may not have been the most talented footballer, he did have an extraordinary ability to commit murderous fouls that looked entirely accidental. I sometimes used to wonder if Jon needed a ball when playing. His amiable manner also helped, as he would apologise profusely and help the unlucky victim to his feet or the nearest hospital. Referees were left to think the foul couldn't have been as bad as it first appeared.

Jon arrived promptly at St Albans station. I suggested we head to the Robin Hood pub to meet the Cheshunt Ultras, a bunch of their loyal fans, for a pre-match pint. There was no need to twist Jon's arm. En route to the pub, I explain that the Cheshunt Ultras have become Twitter pen-friends of sorts. Sure enough, on arrival, I meet a friendly group of fifteen or so Cheshunt supporters. They are supping their pints while watching two heavyweights of the English Premier League, Chelsea and Manchester City, slug out a goalless first half. There's a good atmosphere, yet there are mixed reactions when I ask if they fancy their chances. The most positive reply is "anything can happen".

We drink our pints slowly before leaving for the ground. After entering Clarence Park, we ask for directions to the bar. A St Albans official is kind enough to escort us to the bar to ensure we get a pint of Camden Ale in comfort. I cannot ask for better service. It's quiet there initially, but traffic at the bar builds swiftly as kick-off approaches. Man City score, and it ends 1-0. In the cocoon of the bar, kick-off creeps up on us quickly. We hastily drain our Camden Ale and make our way to the coldish terraces of Clarence Park. We decide to park ourselves at a crush barrier in line with the edge of the penalty area St Albans are attacking. The theory is that we can expect National League South St Albans City to exert their superiority over their Isthmian Premier opponents, Cheshunt. I predict a 2-0 or 3-0 win in the Saints' favour. However, in the first minute, Zack Newton posts a warning by getting behind the St Albans' defence. The threat comes to nothing as St Albans dominate the early exchanges. National League South leading scorer, Shaun Jeffers, shows the danger he is, both down the middle and cutting in and taking on defenders from the left. I tell Jon that my prediction is a safe bet.

It's home favourite, Johnny Goddard, who proves to be the more significant danger as the half wears on. After his low free-kick to the near post is scrambled away by Preston Edwards in the Cheshunt goal, he proves a constant threat. As I check my electronic teamsheet, the name, Preston Edwards, jumps out at me. Edwards appears in a wonderful YouTube video in which he is sent off after about ten seconds while playing for Ebbsfleet United. Soon after this save, Goddard's curling shot flies across the Cheshunt goal and is just wide. However, arguably his best chance arrives after Mitchell Weiss cuts in dangerously from the wing. The ball falls to Goddard, a little higher than he might like, as he rifles his shot over the bar. Anywhere under the bar, it would be a certain goal.

In between, a shot-cum-cross by Newton is pushed away by Michael Johnson in the Saints' goal. After twenty minutes, Goddard weaves his way to the byline and pulls the ball back through a sea of legs. No one connects, and the ball rolls harmlessly away. Despite St Albans looking more likely to score in the early stages, Cheshunt are quick on the break and win a succession of corners – seven in a fifteen-minute period. As the half progresses, chances become less frequent, with Cheshunt looking comfortable in defence. McKenzie and Gardiner in the middle of Cheshunt's defence look solid, and Chevron McLean at left-back is always ready to help the attack. When the whistle goes for half-time, it's hard for either side to complain about the scoreline. If there's a doubt, it's whether Cheshunt can maintain their impressively high work rate for another 45 minutes.

A more than decent half-time chicken wrap with chilli sauce helps warm us up, after which Jon and I decide to take the weight off our feet and watch from the halfway line in the stand. Just four minutes into the second half, I am lucky enough to witness what must be the goal of the season. Cheshunt's Newton scampers down the right side of the field and crosses, seemingly harmlessly, to Reece Beckles-Richards, the Antigua & Barbudan international. Under pressure, Beckles-Richards exchanges a one-two with the hard-working Giuseppe Re. From the moment, Beckles-Richards receives the return pass, it is pure magic as his shot from outside the box sails beyond the desperate dive of Johnson and into the top corner of the goal. I'm in the fortunate position to be right behind the shot as it curls unstoppably into the net. I note that it is the goal of the season; I recall doing that when Tom Annetts scored for Chipstead at Hashtag United. If I have to pass judgment, Reece scored eleven out of ten, whereas Tom only scored ten out of ten. Needless to say, the travelling Cheshunt fans behind the goal leap up and down and rush to congratulate their hero.

I am expecting a St Albans onslaught from this point. But within ten minutes, St Albans' task becomes far more difficult. Beckles-Richards takes on and beats the left side of the home defence and sends in a looping cross beyond the keeper's reach. The one player St Albans would not want on the end of the cross is Rowan Liburd, the Saint Kitts and Nevis international. The 6' 2" striker charges in to make it 2-0. It looks as though he bundles the ball over the line, but when I later inspect the video replay, he not only gets in position well, but his deft header ensures that a defender on the line has no chance to block his effort.

Cheshunt's players are now covering every inch of the pitch and look confident they can win this one. Giuseppe Re epitomises the team's effort, competing for every ball in midfield and trying to set up another threat for the forwards. A badly misplaced pass by a St Albans player produces a sarcastic comment from someone two rows behind me. "Oh, that's brilliant", says the St Albans fan as the pass finds a Cheshunt defender. I hope there is an irony-challenged American in the crowd who wouldn't be able to resist asking why a fan shouted "that's brilliant" when it was such a bad pass. To be fair to St Albans, around the 70-minute mark they raise their game, arguably for the first time since the early exchanges. A shot from outside the penalty area by Mitchell Weiss arrives at the right place for Edwards to save comfortably. Goddard briefly threatens the Cheshunt goal, and a free-kick shortly afterwards brings a punch to safety by Edwards. It doesn't look enough though. A young lad in front of us asks his Grandad, a home fan, what the score is. "2-0 to them", Grandad dejectedly replies.

In the 73rd minute, it's a case of 'They Think It's All Over'. Rowan Liburd picks up a ball that comes loose on the edge of the box and sweeps it into the corner of St Albans' net. I don't need to describe the response from the players or the Cheshunt fans behind the goal. Think ecstatic and add a bit on. Only Cheshunt pessimists will recall a game eight years ago when Cheshunt led St Albans 3-0 but still lost 5-3. I am not expecting a St Albans onslaught from this point or any repeat of that game. "Is it still 2-0?" asks the young lad. "3-0 now", Grandad mumbles. I wonder if people from Mumbles mumble.

The last part of the game plays out uneventfully. Everyone in the ground knows which team will be in the hat for the FA Trophy 5th Round. Weiss goes close for St

Albans with a near-post shot. In added time, Beckles-Richards hits the bar for Cheshunt after a neat ball into the box from Re, but it doesn't matter. The final whistle goes, and Cheshunt have achieved an impressive 3-0 win.

As I enjoy a post-match pint in the bar, there's a marked difference between the lively Cheshunt supporters, the swaggering Cheshunt players and the shell-shocked St Albans' fans. I'm told that it is 30 years since Cheshunt have beaten St Albans City. There is no sign of the St Albans players. I later learn why. The manager wanted a quiet chat with them all for thirty minutes afterwards. On the day, the better team won. Jon and I decide to investigate the culinary delights offered by the Chilli Raj.

CHAPTER 8

HATS *(again)*

Saturday 12th February 2022 – Fifth Round Proper –
Stockport County v Cheshunt

I am boarding a bus to Edenbridge to start my journey to Stockport. Following Cheshunt's impressive 3-0 win at St Albans City in the last round, the Hertfordshire part-timers will be facing the current leaders of the National League, Stockport County. It will be the farthest north I have travelled on my FA Trophy trail from Hashtag United to Wembley. It is more than two degrees of latitude north of where I live, which is probably enough to ensure I will be heading into plenty of rain. I am not a regular passenger on buses. Two people get off the bus; it looks like I shall be the only passenger. As I climb the first step onto the bus, I stumble as it is steeper than I had expected. As I grasp for a rail to steady myself, I am not ready for the driver's question, "are you tapping?". I look vacantly at him. As I start to proffer a fiver and some coins, he smiles and asks, "cash or card?" The question is redundant. I simultaneously put £5.70 into his little tray, saying, "Edenbridge Town, please". He looks surprised that I know the correct fare, imagining, perhaps, I am too old to work out the machinations of the internet, where you can check bus timetables and fares. "Perfect", he says, giving me a welcoming look. I might add that, as the only passenger, I hope I am making his life that bit more rewarding. I find there is overuse of the word 'perfect' these days, but, on this occasion, the money I have tendered is perfect.

As we approach every potential stop, there is an automatic announcement loudly announcing its identity. It would be better if the driver muted these, to be honest. Perhaps, it helps his day pass more quickly. There is a major flurry of activity at Four Elms, a small village on the route. Two men travelling alone, a woman also travelling alone and a couple board the bus. They are all of retirement age. One of the men looks anxious to catch my attention. I look up.

He nods, smiles and says, "Good morning". I return the greeting but do not encourage further discourse. The woman travelling alone has already engaged with the couple at the bus stop. "What about Charles?" she begins. "He's got Covid, and he saw the Queen two days ago". The accompanied woman briefly replies in a low mumble, but the solo traveller has plenty more to offer. "It would be terrible if the Queen caught Covid too. Of course, Charles will need to isolate now for ten days unless his literal flow test is alright". Yes, I am sure she said 'literal' and not 'lateral'.

I decide to tune out, but when I tune back in, she is still talking about how Charles might be affected by Covid. Christ, is this all people have got to talk about? I try to ignore the conversation, but the words 'Charles' and 'Queen', for inexplicable reasons, jar my brain. The dialogue between the two women switches to journey purpose. "I'm getting off at Lidl", says the one who's worried about Charles. "Oh, we're going to Waitrose", replies the other woman with a slight air of superiority. Thankfully, my stop comes before these mundanities make me lose my will to live. As I leave the bus, the man who wanted to catch my attention, wishes me "good luck". I nod and say "cheerio", but immediately have to face the driver, who offers "take care". "Thank you", I reply. I am unsure whether he is suggesting that I take care of the step I stumbled over earlier or, like the passenger who said "good luck", he may know of some danger that awaits me. I hope it's just a general throwaway comment. I let it go and walk the few hundred yards to the station.

I have a fifteen-minute wait at the station, which is

mostly uneventful. A woman in her forties appears to be explaining to her teenage son how to wash a pair of jeans in the machine. The step-by-step guide goes into great detail as she tells him to press the button next to the mauve one. The conversation goes on and on. Perhaps, the person on the phone is not her teenage son after all. Maybe, it's a blindfolded five-year-old taking part in a modern version of pin the tail on the donkey. The train to East Croydon arrives on time, despite the signs warning of a five-minute delay. As I join the busy train, the only obvious spare seat is next to a huge man already occupying one and a half. Despite my own girth, I let my fattist tendencies reveal themselves. I turn tail and go in the opposite direction and eventually find a seat next to a young woman.

At East Croydon, I have to change platforms, which briefly becomes a challenge as platform alterations confuse fellow travellers. I take the lift. The lift announcement is "plat" with an almost silent 't' as I arrive at platform level. I have a short wait for my train to St Pancras, which will be followed by a short walk to Euston for the train to Stockport. A train pulls in alongside the adjacent platform. It is red and bears the words 'Gatwick Express' on the side. The station announcer tells us that the big red train on the platform is not the Gatwick Express but a "normal" service stopping at Streatham and London Bridge. He announces this information repeatedly, confirming that it is a big red train. It is certainly red, but it is no bigger than any other train. It wouldn't fit on the track if it were bigger than any other train. It bothers me, but this train is just a regular train, painted in a very bright colour. The big red train departs, and my small grey train arrives.

I'm looking forward to my visit to Stockport. I know the region quite well through business connections, but I do not remember visiting the town centre. I have always thought of Stockport as being in Cheshire, but I learn that the northern parts of the town fall into Lancashire. The rest of Stockport falls within Greater Manchester, about seven miles from Manchester city centre. If you associate Liverpool and Everton with the River Mersey, you should note that Stockport County's ground is nearer to the Mersey than either of the Liverpudlian teams. If you're lucky, you might win a pound off someone in a pub if you frame the question carefully. The Mersey disappears in central Stockport under a shopping centre before re-emerging near County's ground. And to finish your geography lesson, the Mersey starts in Stockport as the rivers Tame and Goyt join on the north-eastern edge of the town to form the Mersey. I hope you've been paying attention to all this information; there may be a quiz with a big prize at the end of the book. Spoiler alert: there isn't.

I board the train at Euston. I am on an earlier train than planned; consequently, I have no seat reservation. The train looks busy. I overhear two studenty types speaking positively about the availability of seats from Stoke. I am not standing all the way to bloody Stoke. I cannot find an unreserved seat. Therefore, I have to play Russian roulette and choose a reserved seat, hoping that the intended occupants have also opted for a different train. OK, so it's hardly Russian roulette, but I see others turfed out of their seats as late arrivals with reserved seats claim their places. As the train pulls slowly out of Euston, no one has asked me to vacate my seat, but I feel a sense of doom as a small group, who have joined at the last minute, move down the carriage, looking for their seats. I stare at the seat in front, hoping that they will not notice I am occupying one of their seats. They stop and check the seat numbers on their tickets as they reach me. I stare even harder at the back of the seat in front. I feel an overwhelming sense of relief as they pass and continue a couple of rows further down the train, asking a group of four young people to relocate. Maybe, there is a God.

The conductor introduces himself as the train picks up from a snail's pace. "You can buy snacks and drinks from Coach C", he explains. He continues, "There is no trolley service on this train as all our staff are inactive". I have no care for the trolley service, but the warning that all their staff are "inactive" catches my attention. I know nothing about driving a train, but I assume it involves pulling a few levers and hitting the brakes when necessary. I hope the driver is as active as he needs to be.

On the train, I take the opportunity to read Jim Tuite's

amazing book on the history of Cheshunt Football Club, entitled, using an admirable pun, *Look Back in Amber*. The print font is microscopic, but so is the detail within the book. I learn that the 1949-50 season was the season that Cheshunt raced to fifty goals in eleven games after beating Hastings United 11-1. A section on Cheshunt's all-time greats starts with Don Archer, a post-war keeper, pictured wearing the finest baggy shorts of his day. Don recalls getting to the ground on a trolleybus. I'm suddenly feeling old; I remember trolleybuses, with their roof-mounted twin trolley poles and overhead electric wires.

Cheshunt's history has been full of ups and downs. However, reaching their upcoming 5th round tie at Stockport County comfortably exceeds their previous performances in the FA Trophy, a competition in which Cheshunt have tended to flop.

Cheshunt have had close connections with Tottenham Hotspur over the years. Terry Medwin, an FA Cup winner with Spurs, was manager of Cheshunt when they were runners-up in the Athenian League in 1964 and Mike Dillon of Spurs featured in the amber shirts. Tottenham have used Cheshunt as a training ground, and it seems several Cheshunt supporters have an affection for Spurs. Iain Dowie, who represented Northern Ireland 59 times, is one of Cheshunt's most famous former players, although I will refrain from commenting on his brief tenure as Charlton's manager. Many say that Cheshunt's most famous day was when they beat FA Amateur Cup holders Bromley by a 2-1 margin in front of 6,000 spectators in the 1949/50 season. However, a win tomorrow for the Ambers would mean that the upcoming Stockport game would replace the Bromley game as the club's finest hour – or, hour and a half, to be more exact.

The driver appears active enough as we arrive at Stockport safely around two hours later. My hotel, the Holiday Inn Express, is just across the road from the station. A young, friendly, nervous lad checks me in; I wonder if I am the first person he has ever checked in. Maybe, I look scary; my wife tells me I can look scary sometimes. I head to my room, sort out my luggage and prepare to set off. I want to explore the area around Stockport County's ground and the town centre before it gets dark. The two areas are roughly equidistant on either side of the railway line.

My trip to Stockport has taken me to the biggest town I have visited on my Wembley trail. Stockport County have a rich history, competing in the Football League every year from 1900 until 2011, except for one: 1904, when they failed to get re-elected to the League. In 2011, they fell through the trapdoor to non-League football and have only just started clawing their way back to the edge of where they aim to be: in League Two. As recently as the 1996/97 season, they reached the semi-finals of the League Cup, eliminating three Premier League teams before losing 2-1 to Middlesbrough. Stockport County fans are keen to remind you that between 1997 and 2003, they faced Manchester City six times, winning three times and only losing once. Tomorrow, Cheshunt players will play on the same pitch as Manchester City did.

I set off on foot towards Edgeley Park, Stockport County's home in - surprise, surprise - Edgeley, a Stockport suburb. I note down pubs on the way to the ground as I will meet an old friend of mine, Chris, before the match tomorrow. He will be gamely travelling across the Pennines from Yorkshire to see this 5th Round tie. I notice a pub called the Armoury on a roundabout about halfway to the ground. I cross the roundabout to peer through the window to see if it sells beer on handpumps. It gets a tick on my checksheet as an approved pub. I continue towards Edgeley Park, avoiding the temptation to sample the beer in the Armoury.

As I near Stockport's ground, I immediately feel that this is quite different from the non-League grounds I have visited on my Wembley trail so far. Stockport County's home looks and feels like a League One stadium. There is a club shop that is open on a Friday, there are staff working here full-time, and the stand behind one of the goals looks enormous. It is a different world from the venue of Hashtag United's 1st Round Qualifying tie. I suspect this will be the biggest ground that most of the Cheshunt team have ever played football in. I wander round to the main entrance and enter the club shop. I try to buy a scarf and learn that scarves are about the only thing out of stock. They sold a load of them last Tuesday before the game against Chesterfield when over 10,000 packed in to see the top two sides in the National League contest a 2-2 draw.

I walk back towards the station, crossing Arnold Street. "If only it had been named Arnold Lane", I think, but then realise that not everyone would recognise Pink Floyd's debut single. I start humming *Arnold Layne* to myself. I want to peer through a gap in the fence to get a better view of the stadium that will stage tomorrow's contest, but two lads in their twenties are already looking through the gap, so I have to wait my turn. They are impressed by the ground and ask me when the next game takes place. I provide them with a detailed description of the combatants, my Wembley trail, and the FA Trophy history. I get the feeling they wanted a one-sentence answer. "Thanks, brother", says one of them as they start to walk away. I take a hard, long look at the lad, but there is no way he can be a long-lost brother. It would mean that my mother had a child in her sixties or seventies without me knowing. I dismiss the idea as ridiculous. I find myself humming *He ain't heavy, he's my brother*. Have I just become aware of a previously unnoticed habit of humming songs relevant to my current circumstances? I resist the urge to hum *Singing in the rain* as I look up at some threatening clouds.

A poster advertising a dinner at Edgeley Park with Frank Bruno catches my eye. £60 to see Frank Bruno feels like a punch below the belt; I'm not sure I would particularly want to hear Bruno say, "Know what I mean, 'Arry" for £60. Whether Cheshunt can deliver a knock-out blow this weekend remains to be seen. I walk away from the ground and notice a new housing development in a new road called Bergara Close. Now, Danny Bergara is revered by the good people of Stockport – and, quite possibly, the bad people too. I suspect that he ranks above other famous sons and daughters of Stockport, such as Fred Perry, Michelle Keegan, Joan Bakewell, Jason Manford and Ricky Hatton, to name but a few and who comprise an interestingly mixed bunch. Oh, and let's not forget Tess Daly from *Strictly Come Dancing*. I have always hoped Keira Knightley would appear on *Strictly Come Dancing* so Daly could introduce Knightley. Anyway, Danny Bergara was a Uruguayan who played for Racing Club and three Spanish clubs; he was a useful striker. Danny managed Stockport County between 1989 and 1995. He saved Stockport County from relegation from the Football League and led County to three unsuccessful playoff Finals. He was also the first foreign manager to lead a club side out at Wembley. Stockport County named a stand after their hero and still fly the Uruguayan flag at the ground. I find myself humming the Uruguayan national anthem as I leave Bergara Close. Actually, I don't. Does anyone know the Uruguayan national anthem? One assumes Danny Bergara knew the Uruguayan national anthem before sadly dying at the age of just 65.

I decide to take a slightly circuitous route back to my

hotel. I pass the Armoury and head down a road that looks as if it may become more interesting as I continue. It doesn't. I see a sign for something called Last Revolution. It sounds like a trendy bar. As I near the place, I realise it's a beauty salon. I try to imagine why anyone would name a beauty salon Last Revolution, but maybe that's what the clientele in Stockport wants. Only at the last moment do I realise that it's called Lash Revolution. Seemingly, the clientele in Stockport wants to revolutionise their lashes. I reach the main A6 road that passes through the centre of Stockport. It has plenty of rush hour traffic with buses and lorries pumping out noxious smells. The Town Hall, though, stands grandly in its Edwardian elegance. You can take tours of the building I learn and, if it takes your fancy, you can participate in ballroom and sequence dancing throughout the year. I think we can assume this is periodically throughout the year rather than some marathon of sequence dancing.

I continue down the A6, passing its assortment of pubs, cafes and small shops without stopping in my quest to reach St Petersgate, the main entertainment area of Stockport. Someone decided long ago to make Petersgate one word to avoid difficult decisions about apostrophes. I rather think they copped out. I pass Sandwich Corner, which sounds like a place that would sell a frustratingly inadequate snack. Why would they just sell a corner? What do they do with the rest of the sandwich? Throw it away? I pass Inkclosure, a tattoo parlour. I seem to have an obsession with noting tattoo parlours. The name Inkclosure doesn't work as a pun, but the place looks as though it may have closed down, in which case the owners had some foresight.

I am soon in St Peter's Square; there is no question here that this is the square of St Peter as an apostrophe is there for all to see. St Peter's Square looks as though it could be a nice square, but someone put a church in one corner, which is nice enough in itself but breaks up the squareness of the square. To ensure that it can't be turned into a pleasant spot to enjoy a beer, coffee or even some tacos, youngsters are performing rollerskating tricks on the equipment provided in the middle of the unsquare square. A statue of Richard Cobden stands on one corner. Cobden was a Liberal politician in the 1800s who is most famous for leading the Anti-Corn Law League. What he would make of skateboarding and the rollerblading taking place under his nose is anyone's guess.

Upon leaving the square, you soon come to the Hand of Hope Tattoo parlour, which further nourishes my obsession. What is it with these tattoo parlour entrepreneurs? I have never had the slightest inclination to have a tattoo, but I would want more than a hand of hope performing the inking if I change my mind. Maybe, they should name it Steady Hand.

I come to the nicer part of Stockport now. I can tell. Appropriately, a casino sits on the corner of a road called

High Bankside as I approach a bridge. I expect to see a river, stream or canal below, but below is just a road. Here, I learn that this end of Stockport has higher and lower parts with steep hills that are hard to avoid – making you gather speed as you descend and gasp for breath when going upwards. Fortunately, the hills are short and sweet – or, more accurately, short and harsh.

I come to the Market Hall in Market Place. Market Hall is on a proper square, although upon checking Google Maps, it gets more complicated. The square with the church and skateboarding is not a named square, and the market square is called Market Place. If you're still with me, St Peter's Square is a straight road between the two squares, not a square at all. If you're confused, so was I. The Market Hall is quietening down for the day, but it looks like an interesting place to shop. I am more in need of a beer, and opposite the market is Produce Hall. Produce Hall has a handful of outlets selling everything - beer, tacos, coffee, cake, snacks, pizza, you name it - which all share the same vast seating area in its centre. The place has a nice vibe and is popular with afternoon visitors. I can't help thinking that Produce Hall is like one of those places where the contestants of *The Apprentice* compete. Someone who looks faintly like Karen Brady is raising her eyebrows in that Bradyesque way as someone serves tea and cake. A young lady offers me tacos. To encourage me to make a purchase, she uses the sales line "mixed tacos are the same price." I am not sure what they are the same price as.

I head to the one that focuses on craft beer and craft wine. I buy an overpriced pint of Camden Ale, which has followed me from North London. Or, more accurately, I have followed it from North London. The place has a nice buzz, and there's plenty of people-watching to do.

I spot a man with a tatts sleeve – at least I think that's what I've heard it called – if he went to Hand of Hope, he is presumably reassured by now. He is a big burly man with a wild beard and looks as though he should have a foaming pint in each hand. Instead, he has a small glass of red wine as he focuses on his phone. He looks away from his phone, appearing deep in thought as though he is thinking up a poem's first lines. I nickname him The Poet. A woman struggles womanfully (see, I can be politically correct) to get through the entrance with a pushchair and three children as others leave. I belatedly move to help her, but she signals that she is quite capable of coping. Being a gentleman, I arrive at the door in time to hold it back when she is almost through the door with her family. She thanks me. She makes her way to a counter to buy snacks for her kids. Five minutes later, she buys a pint of Camden and sits at the adjacent table to me. She smiles and thanks me for my help.

"I need this", she says. "Do you think I can have another before I get them home?" she asks. I don't feel qualified to answer this question, but I respond conspiratorially as drinkers do. "Oh yes, I would", I offer. She laughs but is soon distracted by the demands of one of her children, who is drawing dinosaurs. "Does a dimorphodon have wings?" the child asks her.

She asks me if I know. I have no idea, but my mobile phone has the answers. Yes, it does. I finish my pint and leave better educated, exchanging farewells as I leave without a mixed taco, or any other taco, in my stomach.

I wander around the square before heading back to my hotel. As I hesitate outside a pub, considering the establishment for my evening entertainment, Dave introduces himself to me. He has had a few beers. He correctly identifies me as a Southerner and asks me why I am in Stockport. "Football", I answer. He immediately concludes that I am in town to see Manchester United play Southampton the following day. Dave is a Manchester United fan but doesn't get to see them often these days. I explain my interest, and he is fascinated. He asks me if I'm a journalist or a writer. I try to explain my status as a writer, but he no longer listens and is embarrassingly over-impressed with my supposed writing credentials. Almost without warning and fuelled by the several ales he has had, he wishes to commission me to write his life story. He tells me he started by growing cannabis at home (quality stuff, he assures me) before becoming a full-scale drug dealer importing from the Netherlands and Central America. He keeps telling me he has some great stories, including someone holding a gun to his head. He tells me how he played in a band, recording two albums before leaving. He separated from his wife after "she shagged a Scouser". He finds that funny, but it confirms my knowledge of the Manchester-Liverpool rivalry. He laughs when I suggest that a Brummie would have been OK, but a Scouser was a step too far. "You're good", he says, putting his arm around me. I'm not sure what he is referring to. His partner joins us outside the pub as we share football stories, after which he gives me his email address to consider the proposition of writing his autobiography. In practice, I am unclear about what the offer is. We go our separate ways, and I suspect that I look dazed. In fact, I am dazed. Dave gave me so much information within the space of five minutes I am already wondering how long the book would be. Hang on. I'm not writing a book about a former drug dealer whose wife ran off with a Scouser.

I return to my hotel, where there is a liberal sprinkling of Manchester United supporters getting ready for the match against Southampton on Saturday lunchtime. When I say 'getting ready', I mean that they are drinking beer as though it is going out of fashion. I decide to retire to my room for some rest before hitting the hotspots of Stockport on a Friday evening.

I opt to return to Produce Hall for my evening entertainment. On the way, I have a quick beer in the Petersgate Tap, a small bar with a good range of ales. There is a party atmosphere there, and I feel a bit of a lost soul in a small bar where everyone else is in groups, laughing and chatting. The beer is good, and I proceed to Produce Hall. As I open the door, it is immediately apparent that there is no room at the inn. No matter what price I am willing to pay for mixed tacos, I will not be getting them tonight. I browse a few nearby pubs but my plans are in ruins; they all cater solely to drinking rather than offering food and drink. Maybe the people of Stockport see no reason to eat on a Friday night. I am starving and settle for Zizzi as Google Maps offers sparse options that take my fancy. Zizzi is quiet but functional. A couple sits down at the table next to me. "Let's push the boat out tonight", she says. As I chomp away at my meal and sip my glass of wine, I am aware of lots of food arriving at the next table. The boat is clearly out. If I didn't know better, I would say they were expecting two friends to join them, given the food they ordered. It reminds me of when I was in Johor Bahru in Malaysia on my own at a restaurant by the river. Each dish on the menu was so cheap that I assumed it was like a tapas with small plates, so I ordered four dishes. The waitress gladly took the order and delivered four full meals to my table a little later without reacting. I did my best to make an impact on the vast amount of food but failed miserably.

Having stuffed myself with a spicy calzone in Zizzi, I walk towards the hotel. Something drags me into the Wellington pub on the way back despite my determination to return to the hotel a few minutes previously. It is moderately busy in the Wellington, but nothing exceptional for a Friday night. After buying a pint, I quickly spot a Stockport County shirt. At least, it is the right colour and looks to have the right shade of blue. I have to get unnecessarily close to the man wearing the shirt to check but decide I can't identify the badge without making it obvious.

I ask him straight, "Are you a Stockport County fan?" "Aye, I am", he replies in that rounded Mancunian accent. "You're not from here", he correctly observes. I explain that I have come up from Kent to watch the game against Cheshunt and that I am following my FA Trophy trail wherever it takes me. "Long road up here", he says, laughing. "Did you drive?" I explain that I arrived earlier by train and have been researching Stockport. "Best to explore all the pubs", he says, laughing again. "Not much else here", he chuckles into his beard. Everything he says seems to make him laugh. It is time to check that he is going to the game tomorrow and get him to predict the score. However, before I finish my query, he jumps in. "No", he drawls. "I wear two hats, I do. I support United and County". "You mean Manchester United, I take it?", asking an unnecessary question. "Is there another United?" he says through a chuckle. He gives me a look as though I am stupid. His face changes, and he becomes more serious; the laughter has gone. "Aye, I wear two hats. United and County. I like to share out my support evenly, but tomorrow I'm going to see United play Southampton. I could get back for second half of County game, but I'll probably stay for a beer in Manchester, like. Got season tickets for both, so I can do what I like". I privately suspect Manchester United trumps Stockport County mostly.

I am about to ask for his prediction, but he is now on a roll; the beer makes him talk more randomly. Nay, philosophically. He's back to the hats. "Like I wear two hats, like, but we all wear lots of hats, don't we, like? (I may have added an extra 'like' there). I have a husband hat, a daddy hat and a teacher hat". I look at his head. He is bare-headed, and there is no hat to be seen. So, he's a teacher, which is mildly surprising, but I would not have expected him to refer to himself as a daddy or having a daddy hat. "That's three hats, then", I quip. "A sort of hat trick". He ignores what I consider an OK pun. It's not a laughing matter now, though, as he tucks his beard closer into his County shirt. "We all have to wear many hats in this life", presumably not in other lives. He continues, "and, sometimes we have to wear more than one hat at the same time". My mind is now racing. I am not sure I have seen many people wearing two hats simultaneously. It conjures up a strange picture as I try to imagine two hats that would work together; a dunce's cap would fit on top of a fez, possibly. I'm not listening to him anymore. Our combined beer intake and the obsession with hats are too much for me. And then, the penny drops. Stockport County are nicknamed the Hatters because of Stockport's history of hat-making. I want to get back to my room and write this all down before I forget a word of the dialogue (I may not have succeeded wholly).

Relief washes over me when he says, "Right, I'm off to the Turdlytotten for a pint. Good luck." And, in a moment, he is out of the door. I am sure he didn't say Turdlytotten, but he was putting on his coat (but no hat) and turning slightly away from me as he said it.

Someone who had been drinking with him comes over and says, "you were lucky he was so talkative tonight". "It's all about finding common ground. Just talk about hats, and he is a fine raconteur", I reply. I google frantically as I feel a burning need to know his destination pub's name. Two nearby options come up – the Town Hall Tavern and the Nelson Tavern. Make your own choice. I decide it is more likely to be the Town Hall Tavern; it kind of sounds like Turdlytotten. I realise belatedly that I should have asked him if he expected Manchester United to win and whether he would eat his hat if they lost. But maybe not. It may have been a hat too far. The man in the Wellington feels like my first real scoop - a Hatters fan obsessed with hats.

After the Mad Hatter departs, I drift into a discussion with someone talking about music. I overhear them mention Joy Division, a band I loved before Ian Curtis, the lead singer, sadly committed suicide. I only saw Joy Division once, but their energy and effect on my brain were more potent than any other band I have seen. Dave, the second Dave of the day, tells me Joy Division used to record their music at Strawberry Studios in Stockport. Dave tells me Strawberry Studios closed "years ago", adding that it was "very unique", but I forget why or what made it very unique instead of just unique; there must have been a damn good reason, I guess. He reels off a list of artists who have recorded there, noting that 10cc owned the place before selling it. He lists artists memorable to various age groups – The Smiths, Neil Sedaka, Barclay James Harvest, The Moody Blues and Cliff Richard. "Not to mention Paul McCartney", he adds. So, I won't mention Paul McCartney. After more musical memories, Dave and his friends move on to talking about people I don't know. I feel something of an interloper suddenly and drift away from them. It feels like it is time to move on.

My euphoria about the hat scoop is brief. On the way back to the Holiday Inn Express, I decide to use my Gold Member free drink voucher for a quick nightcap. The bar is busy and full of Manchester United scarves and red shirts with Ronaldo, Fernandes or Pogba on the back. I have never felt the need to wear a football shirt with someone else's name on the back. I could wear a Manchester United shirt with Fred on the back out of respect for my father. Probably not. As I approach the bar, the barmaid tells a man who can barely speak that he cannot have another drink. At length, struggling to complete a sentence coherently, he asks if he can take his pizza to his room to eat. She confirms that he can. I compliment her on the diplomatic way she handled the customer. She smiles and says how much she hates having to do that.

I'm up early on Saturday and ready for whatever tourism Stockport offers. In third place after the Robinson Brewery tour and Etherow Country Park, Tripadvisor tells me that the Air Raid Museum is the place to go. An advert offering me a Peaky Blinders Day Tour with a cream tea at Tommy's Church for £75 is outside my budget, highly tempting though it is. Instead, I visit the Air Raid Museum. The cashier at the entrance shares a joke or two as I pay a concession rate. When I ask for the concession rate, he quips, "is that as a student?".

"Of course", I reply, extending the humorous exchange, "never too old to learn". "Too true, sir", he replies light-heartedly.

The tour is unaccompanied as I wander around an underground rectangle of tunnels. The headset gives you some interesting facts, with some old artefacts on view. It's impressive and boring in equal measure. As I reach the exit, having completed the four sides of the rectangle, the cashier asks me if I have any questions. I can't think of one for the life of me and feel with some guilt that I have made his day a little less enjoyable. I suspect he knows the answer to every question you might ask. I leave and imagine I am the only guest so far today, and maybe for a while yet.

I tour the shopping area, but it is like many other shopping centres. I head up Lower Hillgate. It is a steep climb from Lower Hillgate to Middle Hillgate and on to Higher Hillgate. I suppose I should have expected a steep hill if I had thought about it. I pass several pubs. They may not sell food, but every pub seems to offer 'a friendly welcome' or something similar on a board outside. The residents of Stockport must demand a friendly welcome even if they are willing to stay hungry. I start to feel that I am leaving Stockport and turn sharp right, back towards the A6 and towards the heart of the town. I pass Mansion House, Guildhall, and Covent Garden and wonder if I have been teleported to London. As I return to the centre of Stockport, I find the Ardern Arms, a pub with food. Not only that, they advertise real ale and real food. The Ardern Arms is not where you go if you want imaginary food. I wonder if you order imaginary fish and chips whether the barperson asks whether you prefer imaginary mushy peas or imaginary ordinary peas with it. I decide to grab a cup of tea and a cake near St Peter's Square, the square with the church in it. The first place I see offers a breakfast barm. I am not sure what a barm is. Is it something members of cricket's Barmy Army have for breakfast? However, I don't want breakfast with or without a barm. A friendly young man serves me a pot of tea and a millionaire's shortbread at a bargain price. I use Google some more to find out what a barm is. It sounds like a northern concoction with eggs and black pudding in a sandwich. Google reveals that I am close, although it appears to be anything breakfasty in what I would call a bap.

I return to the Holiday Inn Express as I have thirty minutes to kill before my friend, Chris, arrives on a train from Yorkshire to join me for today's big clash. I meet Chris at Stockport Station, the train arriving bang on time. We march towards the Armoury, where we catch up on news as I've not seen Chris for a few months. A text arrives from my friends at Cheshunt, suggesting that we meet for a pre-match pint in the Jolly Crofter. Having finished a good pint in the Armoury, we set off to meet the Amber Army in the Jolly Crofter. As we approach the pub, I notice two things. First, another text telling me that the Cheshunt supporters had moved on to the Prince Albert and, secondly, a mutual feeling that we didn't want to be in the Jolly Crofter. I've no idea how jolly the crofter used to be, but I can only assume he died years ago. Enough said. The Prince Albert is a short walk and close to Stockport County's ground. The pub is busy with Cheshunt and Stockport supporters mixing freely and chatting amicably. We find ourselves in a small circle of fans from both camps; you just don't get this atmosphere in pubs before Premier League games. Why is it that non-League opposing fans can comfortably stand side-by-side, enjoying a beer?

The Cheshunt fans in the Prince Albert pub are here to enjoy their day. They would love to win at Stockport today, but enjoying the day is what it is all about. Seeing their team play at Stockport County makes it a special day. Having seen Cheshunt twice already, I know that they will not give up and not let their fans down. The spirit amongst the players, officials and supporters is there for all to see. Stockport County fans have been long-suffering. Since they slipped out of the Football League, it's been a long road back. They fell to the National League North Division in 2013, but they have subsequently been on an upward trajectory, particularly since local businessman, Mark Stott, bought the Club in January 2020. After years in the doldrums, the good times are within touching distance. I remind a Stockport fan that reaching the Football League marks the end of taking part in the FA Trophy and the introduction of the turgid Papa John Pizza Cup. He groans.

Another Stockport fan tells me there are three famous records that County hold. They recorded the highest score for a Football League match – a 13-0 win over Halifax Town in 1934. It was, apparently, only 2-0 at half-time, but it may have been 3-0 or 4-0; my informant is a little shaky on detail. The second record is that Stockport played in front of the lowest crowd ever of thirteen. There's some complication to this fascinating fact due to another game taking place beforehand. This fact might be even shakier. Thirdly, Stockport County took part in the longest game ever. Why and how? I have no idea. I prefer the fact that the club plays nearer to the River Mersey than Liverpool or Everton.

Stories abound in the Prince Albert. Another supporter is keen to tell me about Stockport County's game against Tiger Star in China. He can't remember the score, but the match drew a crowd of 22,000, and Tiger Star allegedly renamed the club Stockport Tiger Star after the game. At a post-match banquet, the players enjoyed, if that's the right word, sea slugs and pigeon heads, so the story goes.

We leave the pub and approach the turnstiles, which are only a minute or so away. As you enter Stockport County's ground, it feels like a Football League club. The Club Shop is busy, supporters move purposefully, decked out in their blue scarves and hats, and there is a general buzz. The Cheadle End stand is two tiers and vast compared to the grounds I have visited in previous rounds. I quickly realise that we are in the block next to the noisy travelling Cheshunt supporters. It is Cheshunt's big day out. It is the furthest they have ever been in the FA Trophy by three rounds, plus they are more used to crowds of a few hundred rather than over 3,000. They have been singing non-stop for half an hour before the game and show no signs of flagging when kick-off arrives. In the first minute, Stockport threaten. A neat drag back in the first minute by Cody Johnson, an amazingly promising sixteen-year-old, sends Cheshunt a warning that the hosts are capable of making space. Seconds later, skipper Sam Minihan closes in on the visitors' penalty area, setting up a chance for Myles Hippolyte, which a defender fortuitously deflects for a corner. I mutter to Chris that this will be a long, tough afternoon for Cheshunt. The Cheshunt fans keep singing. As usual, I am wrong. In the third minute, Rowan Liburd,

Cheshunt's tall, dangerous number 9, times his run well to receive a ball in the inside right channel. Ross's outstretched arm just about saves his goalbound shot. After fifteen minutes, Liburd threatens again as he intercepts a misplaced pass, but Ross meets the challenge again. Maybe, this won't be as one-sided as I thought. Still, the Cheshunt fans sing; this time, they tell the world that "Hertfordshire is wonderful".

As the game settles down, the most significant danger comes from Minihan's marauding runs down the right flank. But, to be fair, Cheshunt gradually tighten up on this means of attack. On twenty minutes, Stockport almost take the lead. After the ball flashes back and forth across the penalty area, Connor Jennings has a close-range chance to hit on the turn. His shot hits the outside of the post and rebounds to safety. It's Cheshunt's first let-off. The Cheshunt fans continue to sing. Chances become few and far between, although young Josh Edwards fluffs an opportunity to volley the Hatters of Stockport ahead after another good run from Minihan. Leading up to half-time, Jennings has a shot well saved by George Marsh in the Ambers' goal. Hero at St Albans, Reece Beckles-Richards, has a half-chance after Stockport dither in defence, and Jennings forces Marsh into another good save. However, it is 0-0 at half-time, and Cheshunt fully deserve to be level on their big day out at Stockport.

At half-time, it's the usual routine of having a pee, but

I am reminded that we are now approaching the more serious rounds of the FA Trophy. There is crowd segregation, albeit with security set at the lowest levels. However, when I try to use a gents toilet in the Cheshunt part of the ground, a young steward considers me a security risk and tells me to walk 200 yards through the Stockport fans. Weirdly, I can leave the ground and join a queue for pies, teas and the like with supporters from either club, but I am not allowed to have a pee with people from Hertfordshire apparently. It's a slightly sad moment as I note that this will become the norm as I get closer to Wembley. I know it's something that John Stoneman laments in his book, *The Road From Wembley*. John started a similar FA Cup trail to me, starting at Wembley FC and returning to Wembley at the end of his journey. I think he got to the 2nd Round Proper before being in a segregated area, unable to move from the block where he was seated and finding queues for everything. I think I chose the right cup to follow.

Things start evenly in the second half, but Stockport move up a gear after ten minutes. Mark Kitching attacks down the left side and pulls the ball back from the byline. Alex Reid looks sure to score from close range, but somehow Cheshunt's Adam Crowther, who has performed steadily throughout, is on the line to save the day. The Cheshunt supporters continue to sing. Will the travelling army last the whole 90 minutes? The goal-line stop fails to keep Stockport

County at bay for long. Moments later, an innocuous-looking exchange of passes leads to substitute Ben Whitfield finding Hippolyte with enough space to shoot confidently into the corner to give County a 1-0 lead. Still, the Ambers' fans sing.

Stockport dominate following the goal, but Cheshunt battle hard to stay in contention, giving their hosts from two divisions above no easy passes. Marsh saves well again as County threaten, but the Cheshunt fans don't only sing when they're winning. Daniel Ojo leads a rare attack for Cheshunt from left-back. He twists and turns, but this final twist upsets his balance, causing him to fire wide. It is beginning to look as though Stockport have enough to see this game out. Things take a surprise turn with just over ten minutes left. First, Ross has to come out of his goal to head clear a dangerous long ball and then, two minutes later, he handles outside his area to prevent a good goalscoring opportunity. The referee dismisses Ross immediately, and we wonder whether this game has a final twist. Now, the Cheshunt fans find even more voice. The resultant free-kick is arguably too close to the penalty area, but Liburd makes a decent attempt to dip it under the bar. The red card has a slightly surreal effect on the game as Stockport play out the dying minutes, running down the clock. Stockport survive and deservedly win 1-0, but it has been a fantastic effort by the part-timers from Hertfordshire. The players and manager come over to salute the fans, who surely will lose their voices this evening.

I could not have complained if that was the end of the day. I witnessed a fantastic effort against a top-notch non-League side. However, Stockport County have generously arranged a lounge for the Cheshunt supporters to use after the game. I manage to gatecrash the event without anyone questioning my presence – Stockport officials or Cheshunt fans. There's no doubt that the Cheshunt supporters have welcomed me; I will miss them in the last three rounds of the competition. There is an almost carnival atmosphere as the travelling fans salute their heroes and the management team. Chris departs to catch a train back to Yorkshire, which it transpires, becomes a bus to Manchester due to a fatality on the track. I soak up the atmosphere until the players and supporters leave to head back south – or, in some cases, enjoy Manchester's nightlife. I take a slow walk back to my hotel and realise I need a quiet evening to reflect on my day. The day epitomises what non-League football is about for me. The game has been well-contested and enjoyable to watch. The Cheshunt supporters have had a day they will never forget. I've had a day I will never forget.

Back at my hotel, I search for an Indian restaurant and find the Last Monsoon. Although it is away from Stockport's centre, it has a good rating and it's not too far to walk. It looks ideal. When I arrive, it immediately feels ideal as well; I am welcomed by the staff and get a table in comfortable surroundings. The Last Monsoon provides an extremely friendly atmosphere and serves excellent food.

I chat with a young couple at the adjacent table in the restaurant. Mark has striking blond hair, and Lena has jet black hair. They seem to speak in alternate sentences, as though they are well-practised. They are instantly likeable as they come across as decent, honest people but with a dash of quirkiness. Mark reveals that they only met at work ten months ago and have lived together for six months. I quickly learn that they both like to keep fit, going to the gym at least four times weekly. I ask Mark and Lena if they ever watch Stockport County.

"I've been twice", replies Mark. "But they lost both times," he says, giving the impression it was his fault that they lost. Lena claims that she almost went a year or so ago. I figure they won't go to Wembley if Stockport County reach the FA Trophy final.

If I ever become a restaurant critic, I promise to award Last Monsoon my five-star rating. I was lucky to find a good restaurant serving good food. It's bedtime for me. It's been a long day. I wander back to my hotel humming, "Hertfordshire is wonderful". I suspect it won't be for the last time. No energy remains for a brief diversion to the Turdlytotten or elsewhere tonight. After reaching my hotel room, I am in bed within minutes. "Hertfordshire is wonderful" won't go out of my head until I consciously try to choose an alternative song. I'm still full after my curry as I climb into bed. It's no coincidence that *He ain't heavy, he's my brother* becomes an unwelcome alternative before I finally fall asleep.

CHAPTER 9

HOLES

Saturday 12th March 2022 – Quarter Final – Needham Market v Stockport County

My train leaves Tunbridge Wells station; I am looking forward to my trip to Suffolk. Except that I am looking backwards as my seat is facing the rear of the train. A lady in a blue hat complains to her husband that all the seats face the wrong way. I empathise with her. It's not enough for her to think of the joy passengers on the return journey will get facing the right way. I must admit that I prefer to travel forwards on public transport. In my view, travelling backwards is slightly better than travelling sideways as you sometimes do on Tube trains. The Goons' song, *I'm walking backwards for Christmas*, from the 1950s, comes to mind. I rack my brains to remember the other silly Goons' song of that era. I can't get *Hole in the Ground* by Bernard Cribbins out of my head, but The Goons' *The Ying Tong Song* pops into my head just as frustration starts to creep in. *The Ying Tong Song*, which contained the highly creative lyrics, *Ying tong iddle I po*, was the B-side of a less remembered song called *Bloodnok's Rock and Roll Call*. And if you don't recall 'Spotty' Minnie Bannister, you are probably under 70. You can't get lunacy like that anymore.

Although I have had holidays on Suffolk's beautiful and not-too-overcrowded coast, I have never been to Needham Market. It's closer to Ipswich than I realised. In my research for the game, a truly amazing fact reveals itself. June Brown, who plays the part of Dot Cotton in EastEnders, was born in Needham Market. But, here's the big thing. She lives in Chipstead. (Note, sadly, June Brown died subsequently on 3rd April 2022, the day after the FA Trophy semi-finals.) June, however, takes second place, I think it is fair to say, to Joseph Priestley, who discovered oxygen, or dephlogisticated air as he preferred to call it. And, we all need oxygen, so it is, arguably, more important than an EastEnders star. Joseph has been referred to as a dissenter, combining theism, materialism and determinism, a nice combination, I think you would agree. He worked on his theories for years; he didn't just pluck them out of thin air. You would be wrong if you think I am an expert in everything connected with Joseph Priestley. In reality, I know more about June Brown, even though I never watch EastEnders.

Facing backwards, I gaze out of the window at the Kent countryside we have already passed; I observe a drab day. Clouds sit on the hills of the North Downs, looking as though they have taken up residence there for the rest of the day. A dash of humour brightens my morning. I notice a poster on the train encouraging travellers to pursue a Met Police career. There is a friendly, smiling policeman on the poster, who happens to be black, presumably to reassure the public that there is no inherent racism in the police. The poster's slogan is 'Search Met Police careers'. 'Out of control' has been added to the slogan by a wag, using a black felt tip pen. It is signed by "Damn Cressida Dick" using the same pen. We can assume that it is highly unlikely that it is Dame Cressida's actual signature. The writer of the joke may have stolen the joke from Tim Vine, although the joke is often mistakenly credited to Tommy Cooper. The joke goes like this: "So I was in my car, and I was driving along, and my boss rang up, and he said 'You've been promoted.' And I swerved. And then he rang up a second time and said, 'You've been promoted again'. And I swerved again. He rang up a third time and said, 'You're managing director.' And I went into a tree. And a policeman came up and said, 'What happened to you?' And I said, 'I careered off the road.'" We leave Sevenoaks station with drizzle in the air.

The journey to Needham Market takes me north, east and south. Well, southish. I have to take a train northwards to Cambridge or Ely and then travel east and south to Needham Market. There is a further complication because there are no hotels in Needham Market, so I am staying in Bury St Edmunds, around twenty minutes on the train from my desired destination. The Limes Hotel used to serve as a town centre hotel in Needham Market, but the owners allegedly upped sticks and left without warning in 2017. It left tourists and even wedding parties in distress as the hotel management never thought to inform booked guests. There is a Travelodge hotel close to Needham Market, but it is on the wrong side of the busy A14 dual carriageway, over half an hour's walk from the town centre. When booking, I didn't fancy a view of the A14, which runs across England from Rugby to Harwich on the east coast. Instead, I chose the Premier Inn at Bury St Edmunds North as my base, which boasts a fine view of a drive-through Starbucks.

At London Bridge, I change trains to join an almost empty train bound for Cambridge, where it will terminate, as the guard puts it. There are worse places to die. At Potters Bar, I am aware that I am firmly in Hertfordshire. The Cheshunt fans' chant of "Hertfordshire is wonderful" rings through my head as though it was a couple of hours ago. Potters Bar sits equidistant between St Albans and Cheshunt, the combatants on my FA Trophy trail two rounds ago. As we halt at Welwyn Garden City, I wonder what constitutes a garden city. Welwyn Garden is not a city, and, from my train window, it bears little resemblance to a garden.

At Hitchin, four young lads join the train, chatting excitedly. They are all wearing lanyards, which don't look right over their casual attire of t-shirts and jeans. Maybe, I've participated in too many conferences wearing business attire. I consider what event they have been attending. To me, they look like online gamers, which may be a convenient pigeonhole to shove them in. Secretly I hope that they work in the high-flying world of international finance. However, I fancy there might be an online gamers jamboree in Hitchin today; it seems unlikely that a major international finance conference is taking place in Hitchin. We are soon arriving at Letchworth Garden City, which has also achieved the same illustrious status as Welwyn. A sign on the station platform rejoices in the fact that Letchworth Garden City was the first garden city, presumably a dig at their neighbours. Sir Ebenezer Howard was responsible for garden cities as far back as 1903. Great work, Sir Ebenezer, although, if I am honest, I am still unsure what constitutes a garden city. Is there a quango that monitors the worthiness of towns to become garden cities? In 1902, Sir Eb, as he may have been known, released an update to a book called *Garden Cities of To-Morrow*. Of course, he did not have access to spell-checkers to correct the word tomorrow in his title. He proposed that garden cities should be developed on municipal land for which "men of probity" would act as trustees. So, there you have it. Sir Eb exported the concept around the world as far afield as Poland, Pakistan, Brazil and Indonesia. There are eighteen garden cities in the United Kingdom. However, only Welwyn Garden City and Letchworth Garden City have the words 'Garden City' in their name. Others merely have 'Garden'. Hampstead Garden Suburb is, perhaps, the best known of these poor relations, at least, to me. Others with 'Garden' in their name include Glyn Cory Garden Village in Glamorgan, The Garden Village in Kingston-upon-Hull and Penkhull Garden Village in Stoke-on-Trent.

The train moves briefly onto a single track, a sure sign that this will be a slow journey. My attention switches to a young man speaking, I assume, to a friend. I can't help noticing that he generally uses the same three responses to everything his friend says. 'Truth', 'no way', and 'wicked' cover the required response to whatever his friend says. I interpret these as "yes", "no", and "great", respectively. Although "no way" has a different meaning when it ends with a high-noted inflexion. It seems to be a way of expressing surprise. Actually, he has a fourth response that he used at least three times. That is, "LOL". By this, I mean that he spells out L-O-L. Less effort than laughing, doubtless. Do young people not laugh anymore? I chuckle to myself at the thought, although I immediately stop it and say 'LOL' to myself.

As you pass into Cambridgeshire, you get bigger skies and flatter fields, although some flatter to deceive. Mostly, if there is a slope, the incline is so gentle that you could run up the gradient without effort. This assumes you can run on completely flat ground without losing your breath, which I am not prepared to test these days. It's so flat in parts that the radio masts for phones are not much taller than an average basketball player.

Coming into Cambridge on this line is a weird experience as buildings of three or four storeys encircle the city, many in bright colours. This is its final destination, and as the train slows we pass Homerton College, Abbey College and the Laboratory of Molecular Biology, where, I assume, they study moles. As the train stops just outside the station for two or three minutes, the passengers are in various stages of preparation for disembarkation. As I collect my bag from the rack, a man flicks his coat sleeve in my face. He gives me a strange smile when an apology would have averted my scowl. We shuffle off the train, and I congratulate myself on being more patient than most of my fellow travellers as a woman struggles to round up her three young children. As I leave the train and seek the platform for my train to Bury St Edmunds, I realise that the platforms are not in a logical numeric order. With eight minutes for my transfer, I feel slightly aggravated by the platform numbering, but maybe the sleeve in my face has made me irritable. I take the lift to cross platforms and share it with a friendly lady.

As the lift rises to the bridge level, she forcefully says, "you get what you deserve". What have I done now? She quickly apologises and explains that she has a condition that often makes her say whatever is on her mind. She laughs and tells me that it can cause some "right old problems". She is one of those people who is instantly likeable. "It isn't a problem", I assure her. And, to be frank, it's not. As we leave the lift going down, she barks, "you could tidy this up", to no one in particular. "The thing is", I assure her, "you are right". An old tin can with the remains of its contents spilling out clatters around the lift, and a ripped-up newspaper gets under our shoes. She is right; it could do with a tidy-up.

The train to Bury St Edmunds leaves on time. It is refreshingly more modern and comfortable than the train to Cambridge. The train makes its first stop at Dullingham, which looks, as it sounds, dull and lifeless, although quite pleasant through another lens. As we approach Dullingham, I spot a hare in a field or, maybe, it's a giant rabbit. A man, who appears to be texting, walks his two dogs in the field. I try to think of a pun based around the hare of the dog, but nothing comes to mind. The train pulls into Dullingham station on the 'wrong' platform, by which I mean that our trains usually drive on the left, but this one doesn't. I'm trying to remember if trains on the continent typically pass and stop on the right. I can't recall.

We are soon in Newmarket. A man, wearing a flat cap, boards the train. He looks like he has just participated in *One Man and His Dog*. In a role reversal, the man with the flat cap is barking. He is barking commands at his wife as she nervously puts one bag in the luggage rack but not another. He orders her to switch the bags around with a pained look, which she does nervously. I worry that in the privacy of their own home, he uses a whistle to give her commands like the dogs - one short blast on the whistle for tea and a long blast followed by a quick blast for a cheese sandwich. I don't like him at all. And, yes, perhaps my imagination has run away a bit too far.

As the train approaches Bury St Edmunds, the countryside changes from almost complete flatness to gently rolling slopes. I get off the train and leave it before it makes its way to Ipswich. Google Maps offers me alternative routes to my hotel as I leave Bury St Edmunds station. Both options are relatively short and look equidistant. I thoughtlessly choose the one that goes up a fairly steep hill and back down again when you turn the corner. I won't make that mistake again. I cross the car park of the Premier Inn, Bury St Edmunds (North) and try to check in. I arrive fifteen minutes before check-in time and find no one at reception. I need to get checked in quickly as I want to catch the next train to Needham Market so that I can start my exploration of tomorrow's host town. I wait patiently for a couple of minutes and then spot a self-check-in tablet device on the reception desk, but soon realise that it is only for checking in your car. I then notice a sign which tells me to press a buzzer if no one is at reception. I press the buzzer and wait. About two seconds later, a pager on the check-in desk starts to buzz and dances merrily about the receptionist's desk. It stops after a few buzzes. I wait and then press the buzzer again in case it activates more than one pager. This time, the pager buzzes and dances towards the edge of the desk, which means I have to rush to the staff side of the desk to prevent it from falling on the floor. Just as I am starting to feel some frustration, a lady appears and gushes a welcome at me. "Let me see if I can check you in early. It depends if any rooms are ready", she says. It's ten minutes before the permissible check-in time. I bite my tongue as she gushes that she has managed to find me a room that is ready. I pretend to be ever so grateful.

I go to my room and have a rapid cup of tea before setting off to Bury St Edmunds station again to catch the train to Needham Market. Impulsively, I buy a Twix from a vending machine in the hotel lobby. I press the right buttons, but then the event turns into more of an amusement arcade game. As the coil holding the Twix in the machine winds back, the corner of the Twix remains hanging by a thread. I walk to reception, which has a younger employee there now.

"We don't do the vending machines here", she says

unhelpfully, returning to whatever she is reading. I briefly wish I was the lady in the lift at Cambridge, saying, "how about getting off your backside and worrying about a customer" but, in reality, I can't get excited over the loss of 80p. I decide to give up. Just as I do, she looks up from her desk and says, "you could try bashing it". Once I am told that I can bash it, I bash it. I give a hefty thump. The machine shudders at my second attempt, and the Twix falls into the collection bin. "You all right?", she asks, as I catch her sending a text. I am not sure whether I grunt or don't say anything.

I take the train to Needham Market, which is very quiet until many schoolgirls board the train at Thurston. Although many schoolgirls are likely to make a fair amount of noise, these are all polite and well-mannered. Two of the four girls sitting on the opposite side of the train discuss homework. One of them does look rather swotty. She is talking about a book character's motives and emotions. I don't recall making such analyses on my way from school. She talks about her intensive homework schedule for the next two weeks. I'm impressed. I tune out until I hear the swotty-looking one talking about partying. As I tune in again, they discuss a party or some sort of get-together they are all attending tomorrow evening. I feel faintly embarrassed that I am eavesdropping when the conversation moves on to Luke, whom he is shagging, and how the swotty one would shag him any time. Well, I misjudged the swotty one, it seems. As an old man, I feel awkward and try to shut my ears to their youthful conversation, which occasionally drops to a whisper behind a hand followed by a giggle. But, it's harder not to do some things than do them. Thankfully, I manage to tune out, and Luke disappears from my mind. Nonetheless, I am still shocked that the swotty girl is not just a swotty girl. I wonder if her parents know that she's more than swotty.

As the train pulls into Needham Market station, I wait at the door alongside the guard. It is starting to rain, and the sky looks ominous. "I've got to cycle home, so I hope it stops", says the guard in an overly jolly way. With my immediate plan to scour Needham Market, the rain and dark sky don't fill me with the same merriment. "I hope it doesn't last long", I say in a downbeat way. "You never know", says the guard with the same excessive cheeriness as I walk off to the station exit. By the time I have used the subway to leave the station, the rain has stepped up a gear. There is no real option except to take refuge in one of the two pubs conveniently close to the station. As I pass the Rampant Horse pub, I note that it looks like an excellent place to get something to eat later, but I opt for the Swan now, which is across the main road that runs through Needham Market.

Waiting at the bar in the Swan, a gentleman, who has decided to start celebrating the weekend early, engages me. He wears a checked jacket and a white shirt, which go well with his ruddy cheeks. I find it hard to comprehend what he is saying. Coming nearer to me and saying it louder helps marginally. I eventually work out what he finds funny and needs to share with me. He is telling me that it's best to get wet on the inside when it's wet on the outside. I think he means it's best to go inside a pub and pour beer into your innards when it rains. I can see his point, although I never feel the need to wait until it rains. Upon seeing me fully understand his observation, he laughs uproariously. It's a good enough quip but not uproariously funny. No one comes to serve me at my end of the bar, so my newly-found acquaintance tells me to leave it to him. He stumbles back to the bar, almost knocking over a stool and shouts across the bar at the barmaid serving in the other bar. I feel faintly embarrassed. She looks attentive and plans to attend to me when she has finished serving the other customer. When my beer arrives, I escape to a corner of the pub to enjoy my drink, primarily to avoid my new acquaintance. I vaguely regret moving to a quiet corner because it's too quiet. I watch the rain falling into the puddles that quickly form outside. Time drags, particularly as I am keen to start exploring Needham Market. When the rain fades to drizzle, I finish my pint and prepare to leave. I have forgotten about my friend, who calls across to me as I depart. I wave back exaggeratedly, causing two pool players to look up from their tense battle.

My first impression of Needham Market is that it is a

pleasant town. On one side, it is hemmed in by the railway line. On the other side, it is a mixture of old and new. The main road through Needham Market is almost straight, and most things to see are on this main thoroughfare. I pass the Curious Fox, which has enough things to make humans as well as foxes curious. Curiously, though, it is closed on a Friday afternoon. I pass a small road called The Pightle; I have no idea how you pronounce this strangely-named road. My favourite is 'pigtail' or, maybe, 'pie'. Alternatively, it could rhyme with 'turtle' with a pig on the front. A pig with a turtle on the front conjures up a strange image in my head. However you pronounce it, it doesn't roll off the tongue. Living on this road could mean much explanation when giving your name and address if you have an unusual name or a name with multiple spellings. I see a sign pointing to The Creetings and wish I could buy a postcard saying 'Greetings from The Creetings'. There are few people about; the drizzle has convinced most locals to stay dry on the outside and the inside. An advert in a window for brass tuba lessons makes me wonder how high the demand in Needham Market is for tuba training. I continue northwards, passing the Christchurch, which advertises coffee, books and puzzles from 10am the next day. I make a mental note to see what puzzles are on offer. As I continue northwards, town centre things gradually fade. I decide to head back as the sky looks more ominous again. The rain returns and starts dampening my spirits and jacket; I march quickly back to the Rampant Horse after a brief excursion off the main road.

Once inside, I notice that I am wetter than I imagined. I decide it is time to get something to eat, but there is a lack of spare tables. Somehow, the friendly bar staff manage to find a table for me. It's not long before a generous portion of fish and chips accompanies my glass of beer. My exploration of Needham Market has ended for the day. When I have finished, I offer to sit at the bar so the staff can accommodate other customers arriving. I am led to a stool at the bar and meet some friendly locals. I share stories with a man who is a big Ska fan and still attends gigs in Southend and around the area. I try to remember the top Ska bands and quickly remember The Specials, Toots and the Maytals and The Selecter. I recall that Selecter is misspelt. After that, I struggle. I tell him I am still young enough to enjoy live music regularly. I feel he has pigeonholed me into the wrong genre of music, so I tell him about my exploits seeing British Sea Power, Big Thief, Wolf Alice and Porridge Radio in the last week or so. He nods approvingly and appears equally surprised and impressed. We then share tales of Thailand and Malaysia, countries where we have both spent a fair amount of time. He gives me a copy of the Bury Bummer to read about Needham Market's game against Stockport County. He explains that the Bury Bummer is the nickname for the *Bury Free Press*, a local paper. Upon learning that locals generally refer to Bury St Edmunds as Bury, I ask him what locals call Needham Market. "Needham Market", he replies, as though I have asked a stupid question. I suppose it was a stupid question.

My attention drifts to another man fascinated by my FA Trophy trail; I explain that serendipity has brought me to Needham Market. He claims to support Needham Market but confesses that he will watch Ipswich play Portsmouth at Portman Road instead tomorrow. "It's a big game", he says apologetically. He soon leaves, having "to see a man about a dog". Call me distrusting, but I fancy he has no intention of discussing dogs with another man this evening.

As I order another pint, I meet Gus, a larger-than-life character. Not only is he going to the game between Needham Market and Stockport County, but he used to play for Needham Market in his day. Our conversation flits from Ronnie Kray to the government and non-League football. I agree to meet him for a pre-match pint tomorrow. As I drain my pint, I decide to take a reasonably early train back to Bury St Edmunds. I need my rest to prepare for the next day's big game.

On Saturday morning, I eat far too much of the eat-all-you-want breakfast at the Premier Inn. I may have misread the sign as eat-all-you-can. A woman, sitting alone at the next table, shares joke after joke with a couple at another table. She has a jolly hockey sticks manner and, judging by her empty plate, looks full of beans, metaphorically and literally. I leave my table as the hockey-type and the couple burst into loud laughter; it sounds like the type of laugh after a rude joke. It's time to set off for Needham Market.

I arrive at Bury St Edmunds station with over ten minutes to spare. Those minutes pass quickly as a man in his twenties fiddles around unendingly at the only ticket machine. He seems to be checking the fares to a range of destinations. Moreover, he is careful to hide these destinations from my view. Perhaps, he thinks I am a private detective. I imagine he is choosing which of his 'other women' he is deciding to visit today. He eventually comes to a decision. He inadvertently allows me just enough sight of the machine's display to see his destination; it appears that the lucky or unlucky lady lives in Chelmsford.

Sitting by the window on the train, there is bright sunshine outside; yesterday's clouds have disappeared. At Stowmarket, the stop before Needham Market, I stir from my breakfast-induced stupor when someone with a dog greets me. I look up and take two seconds to realise it's the Ska fan who is familiar with Thailand and Malaysia. My first thought turns to Ska again. "Prince Buster", I think and then wonder if I got the Ska star's name wrong. He thinks it is a fantastic coincidence to meet again; I've eaten too many sausages to react. We leave the train together, and he kindly points me to the Cattle Tunnel that leads under the railway line to Needham Lakes, my next port of call. We part company, sharing jokes about fate ensuring we will meet again soon. I am doubtful. Before entering the tunnel, I notice that Needham Market has a tattoo parlour. I have been obsessed with noting tattoo parlours on my FA Trophy trail to Wembley. Frankly, I am surprised Needham Market has a demand for a tattooist, but I don't know much about the tattoo industry. Sacred Kraken is the parlour's name. Kraken is a legendary sea monster that lurked off the coast of Norway, enveloping passing boats. Maybe, I misread the sign. Perhaps, it said Scared, Kraken.

Before taking the Cattle Tunnel, I arrive promptly at 10am for the opening at Christchurch for the coffee, books and puzzles get-together. I am about to investigate, but the two women at the door look too scary - not scary in a Kraken way, but they look as if they might envelop me in religion. Cowardice and common sense prevail as I head back to the Cattle Tunnel. The Cattle Tunnel unsurprisingly accommodates cattle well, but humans over five feet tall must stoop as it passes under the two rail tracks. As I emerge from the tunnel, I continue around the pleasant countryside surrounding Needham Lakes. Signs provide information about nature's offerings for March. Swans and great crested grebes abound for birdwatchers, while lepidopterists can admire butterflies such as brimstone, comma, peacock and red admiral. If you're wondering whether I use voice-recognition software to write this book, be assured that I type it all, and the comma is a butterfly.

I pass dog walkers and exchange brief conversations,

particularly with a couple who, like me, have three Labradors. The oldest Labrador wanders off, finding our conversation too dull. Another dog owner trains their smaller dog to jump between several tree stumps arranged in a line. I cross the River Gipping and find myself drawn by crowds walking towards a hidden corner of the parkland. As I approach, I realise it is a car boot sale. I turn tail. As I near the completion of my lap around the lake, I was expecting a café that could provide me with a cup of tea, but there is no café, so I head back towards the town along the road. I pass a road sign indicating that elderly people are in the vicinity. The sign has the silhouette of a man with a stick and a woman holding his arm. As I peer into the sun's glare, I see the same couple in real life. Perhaps, their silhouette was used for the road sign.

I walk through the town centre to grab a mid-morning cuppa in the Angel Café. It's busy. As a solo visitor, a staff member sends me upstairs where it is empty. I am joined upstairs by an elderly couple shortly afterwards. The man makes a joke about running up and down the treacherous stairs. He tells me they have lived in Needham Market for over 35 years and "absolutely love it". "It's not the same as it was", the woman offers to counterbalance her husband's enthusiasm for the town. "Too much new housing", she complains. I see her point; some of the housing doesn't seem to be in keeping with the town's history. "We call it avoidable housing, not affordable housing". He is, I suspect, half-joking, half-complaining.

The Angel Café is in an old building with rickety floors. As I depart, I decide to use their toilet, a long, thin room with a significant downward slope. As I walk towards the toilet, I unexpectedly gather speed, causing my knees to clatter into the porcelain. When I leave the Angel, I cut through some back streets to the farmers market, which happens to be operational this weekend. On my way, I pass what the coffee shop customer designated 'avoidable housing'. There is building work taking place in several places. As I tour the farmers relatively small market, I can't help thinking that most goods on offer have nothing to do with farms. A chocolate brownie is my only purchase, but it's a definite ten out of ten chocolate brownie.

I return to the main road through Needham Market and sit in the sunshine on a bench in a small area commemorating the Golden Jubilee of Her Majesty. I enjoy the sun and bright blue skies until a few spots of rain come from nowhere. The rain disappears as quickly as it unexpectedly arrived. I walk past a knick-knack shop called YesTodays. I like a pun (as you may have noticed), but this pun doesn't seem to work. As I pass another church, the St John the Baptist church, I am invited to come inside and pray for Ukrainians. Another passer-by starts a minor argument by saying that we should pray for Russians too. It's a point, but the lady replies, "Yes, but the Ukrainians have no choice". I decide to keep out of the debate and move towards a blackboard where children can use chalk to place messages for Ukrainians. Most children have used yellow and light blue chalk, confirming that the nation's awareness of Ukraine's colours has leapt in recent days. I can't help noticing two messages. One begins "Dear Holly Father", the other "I pray for UK rain". It's either a jolly good, if inappropriate, pun or a simple spelling error. I can only assume the child wrote the message the previous day. If so, God certainly answered that prayer about rain yesterday. As I am about to carry on my walk, a lady invites me in for a Lent soup lunch. However, my poor hearing makes me wonder whether it is a Lent soup lunch or a lentil soup lunch - or, less likely, a Lent soup launch. I decline. I walk away and notice a sign that sends a clear message, "No more gifts for Ukraine". It's not a pro-Russian slogan, though. It qualifies this message by stating that they already have too many gifts to handle. In keeping with the theme of ambiguity and misspellings, there is a notice for a toddler session to see "butterfly's and bugs". I think someone needs to be sent to Bishop's Stortford to learn about apostrophes.

Needham Market is a compact town, and there is little more to explore. I decide to make an early appearance in the Swan and sip my pint slowly; it should ensure that I get a seat. Also, I remember that the Brighton v. Liverpool game is on television to provide entertainment. As I enter the pub, I see the first blue scarves of the day; northern accents are everywhere. I look for a seat and discover that the pub opens into a large area with plenty of seating. I sit at a table with a good view of the big TV screen. A man with a bald head immediately stands in my line of vision; the reflection of the TV screen on his bald head is not distinct enough to view the game this way. He notices that he is obstructing my view and slightly overreacts by waving his arms and moving more than he needs to one side. I overreact in turn by giving the hand signal used when a driver gives way to you. The bald man smiles and pretends to move back in front of the screen; he's laughing. As the Brighton v. Liverpool game kicks off, the players take the knee. "Taking the knee meant something different in my playing days", quips a Stockport supporter at an adjoining table. "If I couldn't take the knee, I would go second-best by taking an ankle". The pun has occurred to me; I feel slightly aggrieved as though it has been stolen from me.

A group of four Stockport supporters arrive and take seats at an empty table. Only two of them seem to have a drink. A few minutes later, a fifth person joins the table, ferrying back and forth to the bar with two trays of shots. I would estimate that there are 24 shots on the two trays. They disappear in about five minutes, leaving the two beer drinkers to return to their beers before leaving soon afterwards. On the tables, I notice that there is a Football Special Menu. It offers far less than the menu I looked at the previous day and seems to have special prices. I'll say no more.

I talk to a Needham Market supporter who is also watching the Liverpool game. We discuss non-League football and how different it is from Football League games. My newly-found friend summarises it succinctly – cheaper, friendlier, more honest. He asks me if I ever go to watch Ipswich. It dawns on me that he thinks I am a Needham Market fan. A local, perhaps. I explain my reasons for being at the game. He appears mildly interested, but I am aware I am going into far too much detail and with far too much enthusiasm. Even though I can see that he is switching off, I can't stop words coming out of my mouth, reminiscing about Hashtag United, Chipstead and Aylesbury. He looks relieved as he spots his friend arriving. I can't quite explain why I went into boring mode then.

Ten minutes later, I remember that I had promised to meet Gus and take a walk around the bar, which is rapidly filling up. Sure enough, he is at the bar with a group of friends. He introduces me to two people with the same name as me. One of the Phils notes that we all look alike – thinning hair and glasses – I just need to grow a beard. Is it possible that we were cloned as children? One of the Phils was Gus's manager at Needham Market when they played in the Suffolk & Ipswich League in the 1980s and 1990s. There's some debate over Gus's abilities as a footballer, mostly derogatory. And, then, a big moment. A man joins the party who has a big claim to fame. Not only did he hitchhike around Mexico for the 1986 World Cup Finals, but he managed to get on the pitch for a photograph with Maradona, holding the cup aloft. Impressive. Time passes quickly, and it is soon time to leave for Bloomfields, the home ground of Needham Market. There is some discussion about a venue for post-match beers. Someone mentions "Rumps", which I mistakenly take as the unlikely name of a nightclub in Needham Market. "Ramps, Rampant Horse", someone explains to me. Its time to go to the match, I think.

Bloomfields is a neat ground with a full-size training pitch alongside the main stadium. Needham Market FC have been on the up since their days in the Suffolk & Ipswich League. The club spent the early 2000s in the Eastern Counties League, progressing to the Premier Division in 2005. In 2010, they were champions of the Premier Division and advanced to the Isthmian League. They made their way to the Isthmian League Premier Division five years later, where they play now. It's been a steady rise over 25 years, and the club and its facilities are impressive. Kevin Hurlock currently manages the club; he played for seven league clubs, including 206 appearances for Manchester City between 1997 and 2003, and 32 appearances for Northern Ireland in a similar period. He finished his career at Needham Market and took over the reins as manager in 2020.

Soon after kick-off, it becomes apparent that this will be a tough gig for Needham Market. Stockport County's players pass the ball confidently, look stronger in the challenge and are very fit. It's hard to match a full-time professional club, but Needham Market's players cover the ground to give the visitors as little space as possible. As early as the fifth minute, Antoni Sarcevic threatens the Marketmen's goal with a shot that flies just wide after the ball comes loose from a corner. Three minutes later, Marcus Garnham in the Needham Market goal smothers a shot from Scott Quigley after a bout of head tennis.

Playing against a strong wind, Needham Market need to hold on until half-time if possible. Their first serious attack comes after twenty minutes when a long ball has the visitors' defence struggling to clear. Playing alone upfront for Needham Market, Luke Ingram works hard to take some pressure off the overworked midfield and defence, but Stockport keep up the pressure. A timely block denies Stockport's Quigley when he makes a good run in the inside right channel. Stockport undo the defence when a long bouncing ball finds Quigley again. His accurate cross to the middle of the goal finds Alex Reid, who heads home comfortably. It's a deserved 1-0 lead to the National League leaders.

The goal subdues the home crowd as Stockport continue to threaten. Three minutes later, a move down the left flank is blocked. Stockport move the ball back and across the park to central defender Jordan Keane. He moves forward purposefully, unchallenged, before unleashing a vicious shot that flies into the top corner of the net, assisted, one suspects, by the strong wind at his back. 2-0. It's my third FA Trophy 'goal of the season'; I will need to think hard about which goal gets the nod for first place. A rare break from Needham Market puts Stockport under pressure, but County are soon at the other end of the pitch as a quick free-kick sees the talented Quigley drag his shot across the face of the goal. Moments later, a dangerous free-kick from Josh Edwards almost has the home side conceding an own goal, but the ball flashes past the post for a corner. The last thing Needham Market want before half-time is to concede a third, but a long ball on the stroke of the interval finds Alex Reid, who takes his chance well to make it 3-0.

At half-time, I chat to the locals and then carelessly manage to drop my phone over the barrier at the edge of the pitch. Fortunately, I am standing next to an agile teenager, who, without asking, leaps impressively over the railing with ease to retrieve it. It would, at minimum, have been a major operation for me. The home supporters around me predict final scores ranging from 0-4 to 0-8. What a pessimistic bunch! The eight-goal pessimist, after some thought, adds, "or maybe more".

The second half begins at a more relaxed pace, although it is not long before Garnham in the Needham Market goal makes a good save from Quigley. There is an inevitability about the game which prevents it from being exciting. While Stockport County's players stroll around, Needham Market are doing their best to keep the floodgates shut. They are doing a reasonably good job of it but rarely threaten. After 55 minutes, however, Stockport have a rare panic when skipper Sam Minihan's backpass brings a miskick out of keeper Ashby-Hammond, which results in a corner rather than a freak goal. At the other end, Edwards and Quigley work a good opening, the latter hitting a dangerous shot on the turn that is well saved. Cody Johnson, who has been impressing throughout, continues to control the ball and spray it around like an experienced midfielder rather than a teenager. He looks to be one for the future. With less than ten minutes to play, Jennings and Whitfield combine well to force another good save from the home keeper. Luke Ingram gets a late half-chance for Needham Market, and Jennings almost adds a fourth, but the second half produces no goals as Stockport settle for a 3-0 victory. A crowd of 1526, Needham Market's second-highest ever, leaves the ground, reflecting on what might have been, but Stockport showed their class over the 90 minutes and never gave the hard-working Marketmen a real chance.

As I leave the terraces slowly with the crowd, I chat to a local from Needham Market. He and his wife are pretty philosophical about the game. "Men against boys", I offer, feeling that I am on safe ground. "You can say that again", she replies. I don't say it again. "Giants against minnows", he says, laughing, widening the gulf between the teams. I'm left imagining eleven fish playing any sort of team at football, let alone giants. I conclude that a game between boys and fish would be more one-sided than men against boys. Which begs the question: why are small teams in cup tournaments referred to as minnows?

After a quick beer, I return to Bury St Edmunds. The train from Needham Market is packed with Ipswich Town supporters travelling home from Portman Road. "A proper boring game", says one supporter with the resigned look of a fan who has witnessed such disappointment many times before. "If you don't try to score, you'll never score", he tells me. It's impossible to fault his profound words.

At Bury St Edmunds, I return to my hotel before setting off for what is becoming my regular post-match curry. I find a couple of pubs to have a pint. I sink a frothy beer in the Nutshell, which, in a nutshell, is by far the smallest pub in Bury. The pub is busy when I arrive, with two people inside. When a group of three and another two arrive, it is packed to the rafters. After my pint, I depart for the Spice Garden Indian restaurant; I am starving as I haven't eaten since breakfast. The waiter offers me a table in a corner next to two friendly guys, who have had plenty of beer, I suspect. They drag me into their conversation, ranging from air travel to things you need most in life. It's all a bit deep for me at this time of night, but their top five were mobile phones, money, beer, a good woman and intelligence. They try to press me for my top five, but they are drunk enough to forget as they veer off and onto the topic of clothes shops. They are nice enough chaps, but I feel a sense of relief as they uproot and seek another unneeded beer. I briefly wonder what their next topic would be, but I slip into a more soporific state, reflecting on my day at Bloomfields.

On Sunday morning, I return home soon after breakfast. The train journey takes me back through Cambridge, but the outspoken lady is nowhere to be seen. My route home takes me through Bishop's Stortford and Cheshunt, two teams I saw in earlier rounds. I cross London, failing to notice warnings about Tube closures, but eventually arrive at London Bridge, where I shall meet my wife and her friend. They happen to be in the area. I text her to say I will meet in a café in Toilet Street, unaware that autocorrect has changed Tooley Street to Toilet Street for me. Her reply, "What are you talking about? Is it a joke." confuses me. I am aware she knows Tooley Street well. We eventually meet, and I reassure her that, although the chaps in the Indian restaurant put a good woman fourth, I put a good woman first. She always looks to the heavens when I say things like that. I may be digging a hole for myself if I pursue this topic. Indeed, a *Hole in the Ground*, big and sort of round, as Bernard Cribbins would say.

CHAPTER 10
MAGIC

Saturday 2nd April 2022 – Semi-final – Wrexham v
Stockport County

*A*h, the magic of the FA Trophy. I know some people
still refer to the magic of the FA Cup, but, for me,
following the FA Trophy to this semi-final stage has been
magical. I am heading to Wrexham for the second time in
my life. The first occasion was over thirty years ago when I
attended a conference at a country hotel not too far away; I
can't remember where. As far as I recall, the conference
organisers had arranged a fun and games evening for

entertainment. A small group decided that curry in Wrexham would be a better idea, so off we went to see the bright lights of this Welsh market town. In truth, the curry was poor, and the pre-curry pub was, at best, ordinary. Maybe, a fun and games night would have been the better option. However, on this occasion, I am heading to Wrexham full of optimism; thirty years is a long time.

As I wait for my train at Tunbridge Wells station, sleet starts to fall. I realise that the weather has been kind to me on my FA Trophy trail to Wembley. Besides getting wet when Bishop's Stortford played Chipstead, the weather has been OK. My journey to Wrexham is tortuous, requiring me to take five trains – one to London, a Tube across London, then trains to Birmingham, Shrewsbury, and finally Wrexham. But, it's an adventure and I am looking forward to whatever may lie ahead. Besides, my destination is one of four candidates for the UK's City of Culture in 2025. I hope to discover whether Wrexham can at least match whatever the other three candidates, Bradford, Southampton and Durham, can offer. I am travelling on the Thursday before the semi-final tie between Wrexham and Stockport County. In non-League terms, it's the equivalent of Manchester City versus Liverpool. Both clubs enjoy sizeable attendances, often approaching or exceeding 10,000 paying customers, and are on golden streaks of form. Stockport have won twenty of their last twenty-one games, the only minor disappointment being a 2-2 with Chesterfield in the League.

Wrexham are also on a run of back-to-back wins, which means something must give when the two face each other on Saturday lunchtime.

The train pulls into Tunbridge Wells station and is quite busy; I choose a seat where the train is emptiest. Diagonally opposite, I can see a woman wearing what I would call the full monty Covid mask; it looks as though she is ready to do some spot welding at first glance. She is one of a handful of passengers wearing any kind of mask, but I respect her choices. As we pull into Sevenoaks, she gets fidgety, and I realise that she is looking for someone who is joining the train. As her friend, wearing a cheapo, standard mask, moves through the carriage, they exchange waves and, I infer from their eyes, beaming smiles. As they meet, Ms Full Monty Mask removes her mask and hugs her friend, who tries to whip off her cheapo, standard mask mid-hug. They share a joke and sit down unmasked, seemingly unaware that they may be about to infect each other. As the train gathers speed, they become even more reckless as the previously-masked friend produces some face cream, which they both use. It seems an unusual thing to share. Ms Full Monty then tells a funny story, which has them both laughing conspiratorially. They look like old school friends who would laugh at anything and everything. One story ends with the raconteuse lying back slightly and simulating sleep. It is time that I tuned out, although I can't help wondering if they will catch Covid from each other, having thrown caution to the wind.

I succeed in tuning out of the two friends' conversation after a busy-looking man joins the train. He smiles at me, and I nod back. He pulls out his laptop and multi-tasks as he looks at his computer while sending texts on his phone and checking an old-fashioned paper diary. A phone call interrupts his endeavours. It is business-related, and he is friendly but to the point. "Send it over", he tells the caller just a little brusquely before showing his gratitude for the work and bidding farewell. He comes off the call and smiles at me again, saying, "It's non-stop", through a smile. If he is testing to see if I am eavesdropping, he gets his answer.

"I can tell", I found myself saying with a chuckle. I try to write a comment in my notepad inconspicuously.

The two now unmasked women are sharing more amusing things. One is showing the other pictures on her phone. "Oh, that's disgusting", says the other woman as they both laugh, one hysterically and one with a slight snort. I don't really want to know what they find disgusting; on second thoughts there is unquestionably a part of me that wants to know.

As the train approaches its final destination, Charing Cross, I suddenly realise that the two unmasked women have escaped without me noticing. I will never know if the welding kit was donned. The ensuing Tube journey across London to Euston is as pleasant as Tube journeys can be; Tubes are one of my least favourite forms of travel. At

Euston station, human ants teem around, although this may be unfair to ants as ants always look far more purposeful. A child drops a packet of sweets in my path, and I squish one with my left foot. The child's mother looks at me as though it was deliberate. I buy a luxury sausage roll and a bottle of water and hasten to platform five as minutes have slipped away without me being aware. It looks meatier, chunkier and less healthy than a common-or-garden sausage roll.

The train to Birmingham is busy. I'm thankful I have a seat reservation, as the thought of standing feels as bad as life can get. I find my seat with about five minutes to spare. My window seat is in a block of four, occupied by two women, a child and several bags. I gently point out that my seat is reserved, but my civil approach brings a slightly hostile look and sighs. I won't feel so reserved if they make this difficult. They grudgingly start to move, at which point I notice a small dog appearing from under the table. One of the women places the bags in the rack above the seat and barks, "I hope you like dogs". There's nothing like having a dog and barking yourself. I break the ice a bit by saying that I love dogs and that it's not a problem – the dog, that is. As I shuffle into my window seat, the woman, like a practised conjurer, produces a second small dog from her basket. I half-expect her to go "ta-da" or say, "abracadabra". "How many have you got in there?" I joke while doing my best to look a friendly, cheerful chap. "Just two", she replies, looking more approachable. My comment breaks the ice, and we are on course to getting on like a house on fire, an expression I've never fully understood. I get out my phone to respond to a message and hit the wrong button. "Bollocks", I say aloud, which has my fellow travellers laughing.

We have moved from thawing to fully defrosted. I open my sausage roll bag to eat the contents while it's hot. This act prompts the child to ask for his sausage roll, which one of the women coincidentally has up her sleeve; at least, it seems so. The pig and pastry magician passes the young lad his sausage roll, which is cold and distinctly inferior in quality to my luxury version. "I prefer them hot", he says while enviously looking at mine. "They only had cold ones", says the woman. I eat my warm luxury sausage roll in silence.

My newfound friends leave the train at Coventry and leave me in peace for the last stop to Birmingham International, where I change for a train to Shrewsbury. As they leave the train at Coventry, one of the women decides that I warrant a 50% farewell. She mumbles "bye", half-waves, half-smiles and half-nods. I tell her to "take care"; it sounds like a warning rather than a friendly parting remark.

The Shrewsbury train is empty and a bit of a chugger, looking capable of speeds of no greater than 30 mph. As we approach Birmingham New Street, a building with different shades of pink stars catches my eye. I notice graffiti on another building where the word 'CRUTS' is sprayed in big letters. I wonder if this is the work of a dyslexic dog owner attending the annual dog show at the National Exhibition Centre. I google "CRUTS", and all is revealed. It stands for Charitable Remainder Unitrusts. I learn that they should not be confused with CRATs, CLATs or CLUTs. As the train travels towards Wolverhampton, intense sleet replaces bright blue skies with no more than 30 seconds' warning.

As we approach Telford, I am treated to some truly magical countryside and notice the cricket ground at Shifnal, which looks idyllic. A man with long hair sitting opposite, and watching a cartoon, misses the view. He then falls asleep with his head on top of the iPad. It reminds me of my first days at school when the teacher tells you all to rest your head on the desk for fifteen minutes. I guess it was a way of quelling a noisy bunch of five year-olds; it seemed to work. As the train stops at Telford, he wakes with a start, hastily shutting his iPad and making his way to the door. He does look worryingly tired; I hope he's not driving from the station.

At Shrewsbury, I shall make my last change for the train to Wrexham. Five minutes before we are due to arrive at the station, my mind suddenly thinks about Shrewsbury Town's departure from the Football League. I have an impulse to check the year they became a non-League club. I search on my phone, and it is with some surprise that I find it was as long ago as 2000. The distraction causes me a mild panic for two reasons. First, I need to pack my things away hastily as the train slows to a halt. Secondly, and more importantly, it's a tight connection with a penalty of one hour's wait if I miss it. I scramble around and check that I haven't forgotten anything in my haste. The train to Wrexham has a total route, which I shall only be sampling, taking six hours and four minutes. The complete track weaves slowly through Wales and the English borders, starting at Maesteg in the south of Wales and heading to Holyhead in the northwest corner of the country. I see a two-coach train sitting at the adjacent platform and I march along purposefully.

Shrewsbury station has its curiosities. The main station building was the creation of the impressively-named architect Thomas Mainwaring Penson. If anyone sounds like an interesting architect, Thomas Mainwaring Penson does. The building is listed and has a mixture of turrets, chimneys and towers in a mock Tudor style, supposedly to match the style of the former Shrewsbury School, which is on the opposite side of the road. The school is now repurposed as a library. From what I can see, it reminds me of a poor man's St Pancras Station in terms of architecture. The station is also on two levels with platforms numbered from 3 to 7. Alas, there is neither a Platform 1 nor a Platform 2. Oh, and by the way, Shrewsbury returned to the League in 2004. I found that detail as I was disembarking from the last train.

The journey from Shrewsbury to Wrexham is mainly picturesque. Chirk is a good stopping-off point on this route if you like castles, canals, and aqueducts. Don't be fooled by Chirk's Welsh name, Y Waun, which may unfairly make you think of the word yawn. Maybe, Chirk is a sleepy place. Soon after leaving the yawny place, you pass the Dee Valley. I read a Wrexham tourist guidebook informing me that Wrexham nestles between the Dee Valley and the Welsh mountains. The guide makes Wrexham sound rather nice until you read the second paragraph, which outlines how easily you can escape Wrexham if you find yourself there. I'll make my own judgements when I arrive. Bathed in bright sunshine, the Dee Valley looks like an excellent stopping point, but I have urgent business in Wrexham, so it will have to be another time.

As I leave the train at my destination, two disappointments strike me simultaneously. First, the route from the station to my nearby hotel means I have to cross a bridge and turn back on myself, walking at least 500 yards to gain some 200 as the crow flies. Second, and more importantly, the sunshine has given way to a blizzard. It is only a short distance to the Premier Inn where I am staying, but my clothes are soon white. As the automatic doors of the hotel zip back, the receptionist smiles as she greets an abominable snowman. Everything improves quickly. Check-in is friendly and unfussy, and I soon have a kettle boiling in my room. I look out of the window, and there is bright sunshine and the floodlights of The Racecourse Ground, Wrexham's home patch, in view. Did I imagine the blizzard?

Things are on the up at Wrexham Football Club. At the end of 2020, actors Ryan Reynolds and Rob McElhenney bought the club. Since their arrival, there has been an upturn in results, having signed some talented players considering their National League level. An April Fool joke caused some amusement earlier in the year when Ryan Reynolds was supposedly intending to play in goal for Wrexham. Thankfully for Wrexham fans, he didn't. Wrexham left the Football League in 2008 after 87 years. Their cup performances are arguably more memorable than their league efforts. Representing Wales in the European Cup Winners Cup, they famously beat Porto 1-0 in 1984. They even reached the Quarter Finals before losing to eventual winners Anderlecht in 1976. Wrexham's best FA Cup run came in the 1973-74 season when they defeated Rotherham United, Middlesbrough, Crystal Palace and Southampton before bowing out to Burnley. For the Burnley game, they took 20,000 fans to Turf Moor. Finally, I can still picture a 37-year-old Mickey Thomas scoring a spectacular free kick to beat David Seaman in the Arsenal goal in the 1991/92 FA Cup. That goal levelled the scores with eight minutes to play; Steve Watkin finished the job for lowly Wrexham two minutes later. Arsenal and Wrexham were 91 places apart at the time.

Although it's late afternoon, I decide to make an initial exploration of Wrexham's town centre. The first notable establishment I come to is Jane Smellie's. I bet she was the butt of much humour at school. Jane offers optician services and ear wax removal, but, significantly, there's nothing connected to one's sense of smell. I notice the intriguingly-named Wrexham Lager Club on the right side of the road. Wrexham Lager was the first lager sold in Britain, introduced to us Brits by two Germans, Ivan Levinstein and Otto Isler, in 1881. Wrexham Lager was served on *The Titanic*. Indeed, there is a story that Wrexham Lager was the last drink served on *The Titanic* before it sank. I suppose the captain and his first-class passengers would have abandoned their sherry glasses well before the last drink was served.

Wrexham Lager lasted until 2002 but was resurrected in 2012 by Mark and Vaughan Roberts, two locals. I'm not a great lager drinker, but I make a mental note to have a pint before leaving town. I pass Papa John's Pizza and appreciate how lucky non-League teams are that they are not forced into playing in the meaningless Papa John's Pizza Cup, the competition for teams in the lower reaches of the Football League. I suppose if your club wins it, it ceases to be meaningless, but does anyone remember the runners-up? If Wrexham make it to the Football League, one of their punishments will be having to participate in the Papa John's Pizza Cup. The 'four seasons' joke comes to mind and won't go away. In the window of the pizza outlet, there is a sign that informs the world: 'better ingredients, better pizza'.

This information doesn't mean that John and his Dad use better ingredients; it's just a truism, assuming all other conditions are equal. This rant might seem pedantic, but a pizza with vastly superior ingredients baked for six hours will be inedible as it will be burnt to a frazzle. It simply is not necessarily true.

I pass a billboard reminding me that Wrexham is a candidate for the 2025 UK City of Culture. Almost every sign in Wrexham is in English and Welsh, which means the video on the billboard gives the same message about Wrexham and Wrecsam. I realise I am now becoming acutely aware of the Welshness about me. A road sign for Mold has the Welsh translation of Yr Wyddgrug. I may have made mistakes with the pronunciation of Cheshunt in earlier FA Trophy rounds, but I refuse even to attempt Yr Wyddgrug, much as I like the 'grug' ending of the name. It's probably pronounced quite differently from what I imagine.

The City of Culture bid is a serious business and gives Wrexham a chance to elevate its status in the eyes of the world. Local poet and writer, Evrah Rose, explains:

"Can't deny how much I adore Wrexham, from our traders, sporting legends and savvy local businesses to our musicians, wordsmiths and artists – spanning our green spaces, Chirk, Caia Park, to the Republic of Rhos. The brilliance of Wrexham is unquestionable. As a people and community, we're proper mint!! I won't apologise for banging our mighty drum, not sorry."

So, there you have it, the people here are proper mint.

And, it's no good saying, "bah, humbug" to that. According to the bid's website, one of the more curious reasons for making Wrexham the City of Culture in 2025 is:

From taking a quiet stroll along our UNESCO World Heritage Site to crowd-surfing at a gig, we've got a lot going on.

It's an interesting take, and we will find out in May if crowd-surfing impresses the judges.

I reach the pedestrianised town centre of Wrexham, and it looks like a million other town centres; well, a hundred, perhaps. Besides orientation, my main goal is to find somewhere to enjoy a curry in the evening. I realise judging an Indian restaurant from the outside or looking at the menu in the window may be a poor way to make an assessment, but I make my first stop at the Ijazz restaurant. It's about one hundred yards down an unmemorable road off the main high street. The Ijazz restaurant looks reasonably upmarket and spacious with an imposing frontage. I don't especially like its name; I've never liked jazz, but, as they regularly say on *Escape to the Country*, it ticks all the boxes. As I was considering booking a table, a staff member unexpectedly opens the front door for me. Slightly startled, I ask him if I need to book a table for the evening. He smiles without answering. I take this to mean that I don't. We smile some more, and I turn and leave with nothing else to discuss.

I return to the town centre via a circuitous route, which coincidentally brings me to the area where most of

Wrexham's pubs are. I cross two roads to enter the Fat Boar, a pub I have already identified as an excellent place to eat on Friday evening. I enter, and a friendly face welcomes me and finds me a good pint of beer. The pub has a pleasant atmosphere, and the lady with the friendly face recommends that I book a table for the next day. I overhear two men talking about football and can't resist asking if they will be attending the FA Trophy game. One laughs. "He will be, I won't", the taller one replies. The other man takes up the explanation: "He expects Ronaldo to be playing at Wrexham. I love seeing Wrexham play. I don't want to see overpaid prima donnas prancing about". Actually, I am sure he said, "prime donors", but I can't imagine prime donors prancing about. The laughing man laughs again. The conversation fizzles out.

On Friday morning, I wake up early – around 5am. My curry at Ijazz was average plus; nothing outstanding, but good enough. I turned down the Kingfisher and Cobra beers favouring the local delight, Wrexham Lager; it was very drinkable as lagers go. My average plus rating has redeemed Wrexham's reputation for curries. I'm not one to bear a grudge, but thirty-odd years ago, I did eat one of the worst curries of my life in Wrexham. An average minus mark would be an overly generous grade. It reminds me of a restaurant I saw in Chiang Mai in Thailand, where they had a sign in the window that read, 'our food is very average'. I can only assume something got lost in translation after they had typed a Thai phrase into Google Translate. However, nothing beats a restaurant in China that, I imagine, fed a Chinese slogan into Google Translate. They must have got a 404 response, and proudly placed a banner outside their restaurant proclaiming: Server Translation Error. Anyway, if my experience of curries is reflected in the quality of the competing football teams in tomorrow's game, Stockport will win comfortably.

Sitting in bed with a cup of tea, I plot my route for the day. It's a punishing schedule, including a walk around Wrexham's ground before walking south to Erddig Country Park. The walk to Wrexham's ground takes me three or four minutes. I note that my seat is on the nearer side of the stadium. And, a stadium, it is. With all respect to Needham Market, Cheshunt, Bishop's Stortford and others, this is a different level. Next to Wrexham's ground is Prifysol University. I think it was the commentator, John Motson, who used to talk about players with an educated left foot. Sometimes, it was a cultured left foot. If Wrexham have a good left-footed player, it might help their City of Culture bid. I never understood why he thought a talented left-footed player had an educated left foot, whereas right-footed players were never referred to in the same way. Note, though, that I am left-footed. However, I am sure Mr Motson would never refer to my left foot as educated or cultured.

I continue on my lap around Wrexham's ground and

pass the Centre for Creative Industries. Something that resembles a smashed-up park bench sits on the lawn in front, looking decidedly uncreative to my eye. But there is a creative cow on a sloping grassed roof. Not a real cow, I should add. I continue my lap using Google to find out more about the university that sounds like a profiterole. I am disappointed to discover that 'prifyssol' is Welsh for university. University University then. Thinking about it, I cannot recall seeing Prifyssol University on *University Challenge*.

Wrexham may be ordinary, but I feel comfortable here for reasons I can't explain. I grab a quick tea and croissant in Nero and am ready to head towards Erddig Country Park and Erddig Hall. I pass a bar called Defected, which offers craft and tails. I can only deduce that this means craft beer and cocktails rather than witchcraft and rabbits' tails. I don't plan to find out. Interesting establishments abound even if the area looks more unkempt than the kempt city centre. I pass Wrexrent, which claims to be a leader in the local home rental market. It's only a rumour, but their offshoot business selling second-hand cars under the trading name Carwrex is not doing so well. A Chinese takeaway further down the main road to Erddig calls itself China China. I wonder why they felt the need to repeat the word China. As I wander along, my brain recognises that there are many everyday words or sayings with duplicated words or letters – tom-tom, can-can, beriberi, bye-bye, hush-hush, mama and haha quickly come to mind. Then, there are people such as Eric Djemba-Djemba, the Cameroonian footballer, and Neville Neville, Gary and Phil's Dad. Mind you, Neville Neville takes the biscuit, which may explain why he is overweight. All these wandering thoughts leave me wandering in the wrong direction. It's easy-peasy to go off course with all this jiggery-pokery in the hurly-burly of getting to Erddig, but that's veering into reduplicative words, of course. There is no more time to dilly-dally; it's time to go in the right direction for Erddig Country Park.

Having left a small recreation ground behind, I pass by some modern houses and arrive at a track that leads straight into the Erddig Country Park. As soon as I enter, I meet a dog-walker and pass the time of day, talking about dogs, Wales and non-League football. When I tell him I am writing a book about the FA Trophy, he replies, "Oh, very good". I think he sounds convincing, but there's a nagging doubt. I wonder if he thinks I am a bit crazy, coming all this way for what he might consider such a trivial event. But I like him, and we return to the safer ground of dogs and Wales. We part company as his basset hound walks in an incredibly slow waddling way, far slower than my incredibly slow waddling way.

Erddig Country Park is beautiful. Dogs chase balls, sheep potter around aimlessly and streams babble away – or is it only brooks that babble? The tranquillity breaks for me when a small child cycling down a gentle slope looks out of control and, more alarmingly, heads straight for me. His face resembles a gremlin's, doused in water, while his mother appears to freeze, hoping her child doesn't plough through me. I also freeze and adopt the pose of a goalkeeper hoping to save a penalty. At the last moment, the child veers to his left and brings the bike to a standstill.

I come to a sign for the Cup and Saucer in Erddig Country Park and wonder if it is a cafe that can provide a cup of tea and a piece of cake. It transpires that it is, to quote blipfoot.com, *the inflow to an hydraulic ram that uses a small drop in the river to raise a small proportion of it to a greater height.* Built in 1899, this feat of engineering still powers the fountains today. Personally, I would rather it made tea. After a steepish climb, I arrive at Errdig House. A passer-by had told me about the 'wonderful tea shop' next to Erddig House but failed to mention that it wasn't open today. It looks like I will be thirsty for a while.

I retrace my steps and return to the centre of Wrexham. The return walk is more downhill than uphill, although I find walking uphill easier than downhill. A specialist has explained why my arthritic knees find walking downhill harder than uphill. Unfortunately, I glazed over when a doctor hit me with an avalanche of jargon and technical terms. I resolve to look this up on Google later. After leaving the park, I make the two-mile walk through housing estates old and modern in the direction of the city centre. I walk towards an inebriated man. Approaching him is a merry dance as he staggers from one side to the other of the narrow path. He does a double stagger to his right at the last moment, opening up an escape route for me to his left. He narrowly avoids colliding with a tree carelessly parked on the pavement.

As I approach the city centre, I get a splendid view of St Giles Church, which dates back to the eleventh century. It looks more imposing as I approach from the south. When viewed from any other direction it gets lost in the city centre's shops, offices, and restaurants. I pass the Fat Boar, where I will eat later in the day, noting next door's Star Café is closed. A sign on the door tells the world that Star Café is, curiously, also known as Grays Electrical, which might shock some people. In desperate need of tea and a snack, I walk down Chester Street, passing a dentist called Talking Teeth. Who wants teeth that talk? Next door is Green World, a store purporting to be a 'certified cyco retailer'. An image of a person with horns in the window leaves me none the wiser about what they offer. I then spot Kristina's café and feel relieved to find somewhere that fits my needs perfectly. Outside the café, someone has dropped a sliced loaf, which looks quite mouldy. It's certainly a different spin on the City of Culture.

I decide to have a mid-afternoon pint in the Royal Oak before returning to my hotel for a rest, having covered around eight miles. I order a pint of Slumbering Monk, which is probably a poor choice at this time of the day. *Reach out, I'll be there* is playing on the jukebox as I join a conversation with three ardent Wrexham fans. They are talking about last Saturday's sensational win over Dover Athletic when they bounced back from 5-2 down to win 6-5 in the 98th minute. It doesn't match Charlton Athletic's 5-1 half-time deficit against Huddersfield Town in 1957, when Charlton eventually won 7-6. However, I have no wish to dampen their spirits or spoil their moment of joy. Sadly, it's one of Charlton's more recent moments of joy.

I notice a man in a jacket and tie, also wearing what my father used to call a pair of slacks. It seems he is taking sole responsibility for the music on the jukebox. I watch as he chooses songs by Barry White, The Animals, *Ring of Fire* by Love Affair and James Brown. He asks how old I am and calls me 'a youngster'. I laugh. He sips his lager, which has a whiskey chaser alongside it, gets up and adds two songs by Abba to the queue. I'm not trying to give the impression that I am young at heart, but my music tastes have kept up with modern and often obscure bands and artists. However, his choices suit a lazy Friday afternoon. I can't remember the last time I chose a record on a jukebox myself; it must be forty years ago. I do recall, however, a game we used to play in pubs in my younger days. A group of my friends used to find the worst B side possible and play it repeatedly. What a waste of money that was.

The landlady, Stacey, engages me in conversation when I order a second Slumbering Monk. I explain that I am writing a book and that fate has brought me to Wrexham. She is fascinated, or at least, appears to be, and is keen to see her pub gain prominence in the book. She succeeds, as you can see. She suggests I try the Magic Dragon pub as she notices I like real ale. I make a mental note to have a pint there later.

My friend in the slacks chooses another Abba track, but then he surprises me when he selects a Cutting Crew single. We exchange our life stories, condensed to about two minutes each. Following this, I let out an unexpected yawn in a quieter moment; I blame the Comatose Curate or whatever it is called. I try to recall the place that looks a bit like yawn in Welsh; I know it's one syllable and begins with 'C', but Chirp, Crisp, Crock and Chasp are all wrong. I decide it's time to leave and promise Stacey I will return; she gives me a big smile and a thumbs up. As I leave, I am briefly blinded by the red and blue from the stained glass windows at the front of the long, thin pub. The Royal Oak scores nine out of ten rather than full marks due to the red and blue of Crystal Palace's colours. Not that I bear grudges.

I return to my hotel for a break and a rest. When the 2022 World Cup draw comes on television, I cannot decide whether to watch it. I know it will be as dull as the Eurovision Song Contest, but I feel compelled to watch it. It ends in time before an appointment I have before dinner. I have discovered a magician is in town tonight, and for £3, I can see someone billed as one of Wrexham's top twenty magicians. Freshened by a shower and the knowledge that England will stroll to the second phase of the World Cup, I set off for YAB, where the magician is performing. YAB stands for Yellow & Blue, not the colours of Wrexham FC. The magician is good. In fact, outstanding. So outstanding that he has disappeared into thin air. Despite walking around in circles, I cannot find the venue.

I decide to take up Stacey's recommendation and fill the space by visiting the Magic Dragon; it's the nearest I will get to magic tonight. I head to the Magic Dragon, where there is a selection of their own brews. Unfamiliar with the brands, the barman invites me to describe the type of beer I like and serves me something that not only meets but exceeds my expectations. It's quiet with a handful of early Friday evening drinkers, two of whom are debating an issue forcibly but in a friendly manner. A group of six arrives soon afterwards, adding colour and background noise to the place. They are an interesting bunch, all different but clearly on the same wavelength. I try to work out their connection and decide they are school teachers on a night out. I wonder if they are trying to guess my reason for being in the pub. Somehow, I doubt it. Having completed my pint, the barman jumps up in readiness to pour me another. He looks slightly crestfallen that his efforts to bring me the perfect pint only culminate in the sale of one measly unit. I thank him and leave for the Fat Boar.

I suppose you may wonder whether I am fat, thus

making my presence in the Fat Boar just a tad funnier. In that case, I should point out that I may be overweight, but I would describe myself as more of a bore than actually fat these days. The Fat Boar is a splendid pub serving excellent food and well-kept beer. The lady ensuring that everything runs smoothly is working her socks off, not that she is wearing socks – or, perhaps, she was before she worked them off. I order fish and chips, and it's as good as fish and chips can be. I wash it down with a beer and a fruity glass of Rioja. After finishing my meal, I notice a sign I misread as 'please be wise and fantasise'. I am unsure about the wisdom of fantasising in a pub, but after adjusting my glasses, I realise sanitising is the wise thing to do. Anyhow, I suppose it depends on what sort of fantasising you do. After first-class treatment in the Fat Boar, I return to the Royal Oak to see whether Abba or, perhaps, Cutting Crew will be playing on the jukebox. The Royal Oak really is my sort of pub.

There's a cheerful atmosphere in the Royal Oak, and much of the talk is about Wrexham's football. Stacey welcomes me back and guesses that I need another Slumbering Monk. I choose something less soporific and am soon discussing Wrexham's chances against Stockport. I meet a guy married to the cousin of Wrexham legend, Arfon Griffiths MBE. Arfon made almost 600 appearances for Wrexham between 1959 and 1979 and won seventeen caps for Wales. I enjoy the friendly company of the Royal Oak, sharing jokes with some of the regulars. Stacey tells me that the pub will be open for pre-match drinks at 10am tomorrow as the game kicks off at 12.30. I give one of those smiles that hopefully suggests thanks but no thanks; I won't be ready for a beer at 10am. Stacey does some more self-promotion and, as I leave, surprises me by giving me a friendly hug. I try to recall whether a landlady at a pub has ever given me a hug. I don't think so.

After my adventures in the Royal Oak, it is time to return to my hotel. Within yards of leaving the Royal Oak, a little voice in my head suggests having one for the road. Where did that idea come from? I was determined to call it a day just thirty seconds ago. I have never really understood the expression 'one for the road'; it doesn't sound like something that would appear in a Public Information Film. I enter the first pub on my route and tell my brain that there will not be another 'one for the road' after this. The pub is busy but not mobbed. I buy a pint and look for somewhere to sit. I see that every table is occupied and begin to wish I had gone somewhere else.

Andy and Kate, sitting at a table for four, notice me vainly looking for a seat to rest my weary legs and gesture to me to sit with them. I do that British thing of being overly polite.

"Are you sure?" and "I don't like to disturb you", as Andy pats the back of one of the spare chairs. They introduce themselves, immediately radiating a warm welcome. They are both in their thirties and look a bit hippyish, although Andy's well-spoken manner makes me wonder if he wears a smart suit in the daytime. I am on these travels to meet people, but I am barely ready for introductions while having 'one for the road'.

Kate introduces herself as 'a sort of journalist'; I don't feel qualified to ask questions that would differentiate her from being a proper journalist. Andy then introduces himself. Even during these semi-formal introductions, I sense they are a bit of a comedy double act.

They ask me if I live locally, and I explain why I am in Wrexham. "Fabulous", says Kate enthusiastically, "Really fabulous", she adds for emphasis. Andy enthuses, too, "It's great doing things that you love." I ask them if they are locals. Andy begins to answer, but Kate jumps in. "No, not at all", she bubbles. "You'll probably think we are so boring", she begins, deliberately extending the 'o' of 'so'. "We are in North Wales to see birds and wildlife. We've never done it before and just said, 'let's do it', so here we are. We are in Wrexham for one night as I've got an elderly relative here". Her words fly at me at a speed that reminds me of how my daughter has an output of words that is double what most achieve. "We just escaped for the evening", interjects Andy with a wry smile. Kate jumps back in, though. "We are doing owls in Llandudno, a bird sanctuary in Holyhead and wetlands in Conwy". "And, the inside of some pubs", adds Andy holding back a chuckle. "You're a naturist, aren't you, Katy?" says Andy with a broad, devilish grin. "I am. I do voluntary work at a pet rescue centre".

I want to ask Kate whether she agrees with the possibility that she may be a naturalist rather than a naturist, but I can't think of how to frame the question. Andy steps in, now grinning. "Is it naturist or naturalist, Kats?" he laughs, employing a third variation of her name in as many minutes. She is not ready for the question. "Naturist? No, naturalist. What are you on about?" She laughs. "Naturists wear no clothes", Andy rescues her, laughing wildly. She hits him gently, playfully; she appears to be used to being the butt of Andy's humour. Andy is keen to tell me that Kate talks to all the animals where she works at the pet rescue centre. "I caught her talking to a tortoise the other day". "He was sweet", Kate explains, justifying her reptilian conversation. Andy shows off a bit by telling me that the collective name for tortoises is a creep. I confess that I did not know that, but it makes sense.

The conversation switches to jobs without much warning. Andy used to be a journalist but has reinvented himself as a marketing executive. Kate – or Katy; I don't feel I can call her Kats – is a freelance writer and journalist who used to work on local television. "We met in a pub after a big VAT fraud court case. Kat had missed two days of the trial, so I helped her out; the rest is history. She had got some of the facts wrong, but I saved her!" Kate laughs and admits she had missed some of the trial as she had been out 'bingeing' for two days on a 'hen do'. "It's true; he saved me," offered Kate, squeezing Andy's arm. "She was offered the role of Bridget Jones but turned it down, so Renee Zellweger, who was the second choice, got it", he laughs. Andy receives another friendly punch to the arm. There is a certain resemblance to Bridget Jones.

Just as I start to worry that Andy uses Kate as the butt of all his humour and puts her down at every opportunity, Kate hits back. "I can tell you a few things about Andy", she begins with a wicked look. I soon learn that Andy whistles while sitting on the toilet. "Too much detail, Kate". Kate moves on without a break to Andy spending hours fiddling with radio transmitters as a hobby. "Real, boring stuff", she comments, "although he's as happy as a pig in muck". Andy pulls an expression that confirms he is as happy as a pig in muck. However, I've never been convinced that pigs are happy in muck. Before I know it, Kate switches to telling me about her 'fun' writing; she is trying to write a romantic novel. "Mind you. I need to find another man to get better ideas for the raunchy sex scenes", she laughs dirtily at Andy's expense. Andy pulls a little boy's face now, but he is clearly used to Kate hitting back.

They suggest another pint. I decline. In thirty minutes, I have met two fun and charming people. I laughed a lot. I feel they gave away a lot more than me, but they say how much they have enjoyed meeting me as I tell the little voice in my head to get lost when it suggests 'one more for the road'. I wish them well on their owl and wetland adventure, although I worry that I make it sound less important than following the FA Trophy. In truth, it is, of course. I leave the pub, infused with five pints of beer, and realise that I must get back to my hotel and note my recollections about Andy and Kate. When I return to the hotel, I make a cup of tea and scribble notes furiously. We will never know whether I recalled all the conversations accurately. It is undoubtedly time for Bedfordshire, even though there is no wooden hill to climb. I briefly wonder whether parents in Luton tell their children to go up the wooden hill to Bedfordshire, but that's something to think about tomorrow.

On Saturday, I am awake early and enjoy a hearty breakfast, which is probably not good for my heart. As the kick-off is at 12.30, I wander around the pedestrianised area for an hour. At 10.15, the town is far busier than it has been for the previous two days. Police stand on corners in pairs, watching football fans wearing the red scarves of Wrexham or the blue scarves of Stockport County. It feels like the build-up to a Championship match and a far cry from my first game at Hashtag United. The centre of Wrexham is busy with Saturday shoppers, but the column of ants marching towards the Racecourse Ground comfortably outnumbers them. I feel a bit aimless in the centre and begin to make my way back to the hotel to collect my ticket for the match.

As I walk towards the ground, a man in his late seventies asks me if I am going to the game. Like many others walking in the direction of The Racecourse Ground, it's a safe bet. We amble together, avoiding youths who are zigzagging through gaps in the crowd. The man has a rounded gait; he probably has a rectangular front door as well. He tells me what a friendly club Wrexham is when I tell him it is my first visit to the ground. We go our separate ways and say our farewells as he is sitting in a different part of the ground. There are still 45 minutes to kick-off, and it's already busy. I go straight to my seat, squeezing past people in the stand's walkway. It's hard work to get the fifty yards to the gangway for my block of seats. Everyone seems to be eating chips drowned in tomato ketchup, drinking beer or queuing up for this dubious pleasure. I take my place and read the match programme. As kick-off approaches, the ground slowly fills up. One of my neighbours arrives at his seat together with what I assume are various members and generations of his family. They sit to my left and in the row behind. He is immediately annoying; I just hope he isn't a jack-in-the-box throughout the game. He sees the Wrexham mascot, a dragon, approach on the pitchside. The man insists that a young family member gets a photograph with the dragon. The young lad doesn't want it, but my neighbour does. Eventually, he grabs the child, who, for all I know, is dracophobic. The child obliges with a false smile while Mr Annoying laughs loudly. He tells another supporter that he's already had two pints this morning. "Thank God, it was only two", I think, as he accidentally elbows me in the ribs while swivelling round to joke with another family member. He really is a jack-in-the-box, except that a jack-in-the-box only pops out once without human intervention.

As the teams come out, there is a roar, coupled with an air of expectation as these top two sides in the National League prepare to face each other. Stockport County have won twenty of their last twenty-one games, slipping up at home to Chesterfield in a 2-2 draw. Wrexham can't match that, but eight consecutive wins are no mean feat. With kick-off a minute away, my neighbour decides he needs to visit the gents - quelle surprise, as they say at Paris St Germain. Off you go, Jacques-dans-la- boîte.

The game starts in a lively fashion, with both teams breaking dangerously in the opening minutes. A Stockport attack requires a hasty clearance to avert the threat. After six minutes, the first clearcut chance falls to Stockport's Antoni Sarcevic, who fails to direct his header, resulting in a goal kick. A degree of caution creeps into the game as the midfield of each side battles for dominance. Will Collar stands out for Stockport, always involved and looking to get on the offensive. Although Stockport have more possession and more control in the first part of the game, Wrexham always look menacing. Paul Mullin and Ollie Palmer run the channels well and keep the Stockport defence on their toes. The battle of the Palmers between Wrexham's Ollie and Stockport's Ashley in the heart of Stockport's defence is fascinating.

After 25 minutes, a clever turn by Wrexham's Luke Young makes some space for the Ollie variety of Palmer to shoot at goal. The shot brings a loud appeal from the Wrexham players and fans for handball, but Mr Bannister, the referee, who replaced the injured Mr Bell in the tenth minute, has none of it and waves the appeals away. Shortly afterwards, Stockport's steady left-back, Mark Kitching, releases Scott Quigley, who screws his shot wide of the post. It's arguably the best chance so far. Wrexham's threat diminishes, despite a neat interchange between Mullin and Young which puts Mullin in some space. Lacking support, he attempts a long-range shot, which Hinchcliffe in the Stockport goal saves well.

With five minutes left in the first half, my neighbour decides he needs chips and sets off to beat the queues. I suspect that those early beers have made him peckish as he tries to insist that everyone in his party has chips; most turn the offer down. The conversation goes on longer than it needs to. I feel a creeping irritation as he stands up again, trying to press his family to eat chips. "For God's sake, they don't want bloody chips", a voice in my head says. As half-time approaches, more good work from the busy Sarcevic gives Quigley a half-chance, but the ball clears the Wrexham bar in a hectic scramble. Stockport end the half in the ascendancy, and Quigley has a shot on the turn saved well by Christian Dibble in the Wrexham goal. It's goalless at half-time, but Wrexham will need to improve in the second half.

During half-time, my neighbour returns with a surfeit of chips. He finds it funny that he has wasted money on chips that no one wants. After the restart, a foul on Wrexham's Palmer results in a free-kick in a dangerous position, but the kick is well saved. Things look more hazardous when Palmer finds some space and runs at the heart of the Stockport defence. He needs to evade one more tackle to have a simple scoring chance, but an outstretched foot is enough to halt his progress. Crosses from Andy Cannon and Oliver Crankshaw from Stockport's right flank look threatening, but their prolific scorer, Paddy Madden, can't get on the end of them as two promising attacks fade to nothing. However, Wrexham are getting into a good rhythm and menacing the visitors' goal. A careless backpass gives Mullin the best chance of the game on 65 minutes, but he is forced wide and screws his shot wide of the post. At the other end, Crankshaw looks likely to score too, but Dibble saves with his foot.

An openness creeps into the play during the middle period of the half, but it doesn't last as full-time approaches. 0-0 looms. Sarcevic, who has had a quieter period, bursts back into the game with a neat turn in the box with ten minutes to play, but a timely tackle from Wrexham's skipper, Ben Tozer, results in a corner. Another routine save from Hinchcliffe means we enter stoppage time with the score still level. Then, the fireworks start. Kitching quickly releases Mullin down the inside left channel when a Stockport attack breaks down. For a second, it looks like he has miskicked, but I realise it is a delicate chip that floats over the stranded Hinchcliffe and drops into the goal. It's yet another goal of the season in the FA Trophy, a pure moment of magic. Wrexham look to be heading to Wembley; the crowd is jumping and singing. Any doubts disappear when a long clearance from Dibble bounces and bounces, evading the Stockport defence. Mullin, once again, is sharp as he flicks the ball over the advancing Hinchcliffe and runs it into an empty net. 2-0. Now, we know that Wrexham are going to Wembley. The final whistle goes seconds later; the crowd still hasn't settled after the two goals. Wrexham are the nation's injury-time specialists.

An ecstatic Wrexham fan tells me 'I am literally at Wembley' as I leave the ground. I want to tell him that he is not. I make my way to the Royal Oak, where I know celebrating fans will be. As I walk in, Stacey spots me and does those up and down arm movements while pointing at the sky with her fingers. She knows there will be a happy bunch of boozers this afternoon. I knock back two pints of Not the Slumbering Monk, before my return to Wrexham station to make my journey south. At the station, it's quieter, although many young Wrexham supporters are catching the same train as me and breaking into song repeatedly. Their songs are generally banal, but I like their variation of the song Stockport fans sang at the Wrexham fans. While Stockport fans sang, "you can stick your fucking dragon up your arse", these lads made it clear that Wrexham "had stuck our fucking dragon up your arse". You will have to decide whether it can be classed as culture. The despondent Stockport fan on the train takes it in good spirit, although he looks suitably dejected.

I have the challenge of changing trains at Chester and Crewe ahead, but I am ready to return home. It's been a magical trip to North Wales.

CHAPTER 11

WEMBLEY

Sunday 22nd May 2022 – Final – Wrexham v Bromley

I'm nearing the end of my FA Trophy trail. There's a tinge of sadness about it. My spellchecker always wants to change FA Trophy trail to FA Trophy trial; it's been anything but a trial. Europe's famous song *The Final Countdown* includes the words:

> *I guess there is no one to blame.*
> *We're leaving ground*
> *Will things ever be the same again?*

Well, there is no one to blame for anything; it was my decision to follow the FA Trophy trail. Edith Piaf singing *No Regrets* would be a more appropriate song. Nonetheless, I will certainly leave a ground at the end of Sunday's game – Wembley Stadium, no less. As for whether things will ever be the same again, well, probably not after all the friends I made on my way to Wembley.

If there is any strange feeling as I board a train on my way to Wembley, it is that I am worried this game will be a bit of an anti-climax. However, I am making a weekend of it and on Saturday, and I will watch the League One playoff between Sunderland and Wycombe Wanderers before enjoying Sunday's non-League Finals Day. This will feature the FA Vase final between Littlehampton Town and Newport Pagnell Town before the big one – Wrexham versus Bromley in the FA Trophy final. As far as I can recall, it will be the first time in my life that I will watch three games in one weekend. I remember playing three games in one weekend many moons ago. However, to be truthful, teammates might have described my performances on the field as more 'watching' than 'playing'.

As my train stops on its way to London, a balding man boards the train in full Sunderland kit with his two young daughters, who look as though they are reluctantly wearing Sunderland shirts. The shirts are either brand new or have been ironed to the highest standards; it's a big day for this family. Well, it is for Dad. When I change trains at East

Croydon, a man in a Queens Park Rangers shirt heads toward me. I can't imagine why he is wearing his team's colours; QPR's season has finished. As he gets nearer, I spot a logo on the blue and white hooped shirt for a Hong Kong bar. I remember making a similar mistake in a café at St Albans. As the ostensible QPR fan disappears out of sight, another man who looks like Rodney Marsh comes alongside me on the platform. Or, more accurately, a man who looks the way Rodney looked fifty years ago. Too much QPRness for one day. You don't get that 1970s Rodney Marsh look very often these days.

Central London seems quiet as I arrive at London Kings Cross. I walk from Kings Cross to Euston station to catch my train to Wembley. I get within a few hundred yards of Euston station, and there is a sudden buzz. As I turn a corner outside a pub, there is an army of Sunderland supporters, almost all wearing red and white striped shirts. Without warning, they burst into song. I can't make out the words, but it sounds like "Sunderland, do it all for me". Or, maybe, it's "Sunderland do it all for me". I'm not sure if it is a statement or a command. I scour Euston Station for a Wycombe Wanderers shirt with its distinctive light and dark blue quarters, but it's a sea of red and white except for a homebound Scot wearing a Celtic shirt.

Not caring for ten pints in Euston with Sunderland supporters before travelling on a noisy, packed train to Wembley, I leave Euston early enough to miss the crowds.

I take a stopper service to Wembley, slower but significantly quieter than the fast train. I am lucky enough to sit opposite someone wearing a 1991 Wycombe Wanderers FA Trophy Final shirt. The man is travelling with two other generations of family members. It appears the gentleman wearing the 1991 shirt may have played in the 1991 FA Trophy Final when Wycombe Wanderers defeated Kidderminster Harriers 2-1 at Wembley. Strangely, it's the first Wycombe shirt I have seen, but it's a rather special one.

I arrive at Wembley Central, which may be central to Wembley but is farther from the stadium than Wembley Park and Wembley Stadium stations. I walk along the High Road, which, unlike Chipstead's High Road, is full of shops, food outlets and the like. It's a long while since I have been to this part of Wembley, but it seems much improved. Indeed, this will be my first visit to the new stadium, which, I am surprised to find, opened in 2007, 15 years ago. As I approach the stadium area, I can also see that there has been a massive upgrade; there are boulevards and a modern feel to the place with cafes, fast-food outlets and bars. I ask a steward if he knows where the Premier Inn is. He looks at me blankly at first, which should have been enough reason to ignore his directions. With initial hesitation, he points out where I should go, but it's his increasing confidence that fools me. Ten minutes later, I am back to where I met the steward. He has gone, but the Premier Inn is less than 50 yards away.

At the hotel entrance, there is a security check to ensure I am a bona fide guest. I use a self-check-in machine with some difficulty, watched by a receptionist. Having completed this task, the receptionist, who had been idle while I fought with unclear computer instructions, gives me a room key. I'm all for technology, but I am not sure what the advantage is to anyone in this context. I am surprised that I can check in early. I dump my bag and head to the Premier Inn's bar, which is not overly busy. I start to talk to some Sunderland supporters, who assume I am a Wycombe supporter. Strictly speaking, I am a Wycombe supporter for the day. When I tried to get tickets for the playoff final, the FA's website directs you to either the Sunderland or Wycombe Wanderers website, depending on your loyalties. As a neutral, I could not get a ticket until I explained to Wycombe's administrative staff that I was writing a book about the FA Trophy. I am grateful for their help. The Sunderland supporters are full of bravado; 3-0, one says, another predicts 4-0. I wonder if their predicted scores align with the number of pints they have drunk so far. It could be 7-0 by kick-off time. Easily. They seem friendly enough, so I drop into the conversation that I am a Charlton Athletic supporter. They all groan simultaneously. Charlton are not the nemesis of many clubs, but they have beaten Sunderland in two playoff finals, once on penalties and, more recently, with the last kick of the game. They take it well and tell me not to support Wycombe Wanderers. They all leave, strangely feeling the need to introduce themselves to me as they leave for some fast food. At least two of them have the same name, Dan. Maybe it was three.

Soon afterwards, I meet a lady in her eighties who has come down from Sunderland. She introduces herself as Shirley and tells me she is doing the trip in style. She has travelled first class on the train, is staying at the Premier Inn and has booked a taxi for a posh restaurant in the evening. "She's normally tight-fisted too", jokes a man with her. I refer to Jack as her husband. "Good Lord, no. He's my brother", she tells me. "My husband wouldn't be bothered with this". Jack is a pleasant gentleman who tells me tales about Charlie Hurley, The Roker Roar and how he used to get in for nothing at Roker Park as a kid by nipping over a fence. He tells the stories as though they happened last week.

With an hour to kick-off, I head to Wembley Stadium; it's a stone's throw from the hotel. The queue to get in is horrible. Fortunately, the Wycombe supporters are patient; it's just a boring thirty minutes or so in a crowd. Inside the stadium, the Sunderland supporters are making a lot of noise. The teams arrive on the pitch to a roar, matching the Roker Roar, perhaps.

In the early stages, Sunderland have the edge; for all Wycombe's hard work, they appear to have no cutting edge. After only 12 minutes, Elliot Embleton gives The Black Cats the start they wanted. Following a strong run from midfield, Embleton unleashes a powerful shot from just outside the penalty area. Stockdale in the Wycombe goal may feel disappointed as the attempt is close to his body, deflecting slightly off his upper arm as it flies in. The game continues in this vein until the 50th minute when Sunderland striker, Ross Stewart, is inches wide with a header. However, with ten minutes left, Ross Stewart controls a ball well and tucks away a low shot into the corner of the Wycombe net. Sunderland deservedly lead 2-0 and are on the brink of promotion to the Championship. I joke with the friendly Wycombe fan next to me that this is next season's Championship relegation playoff. "Too right", he agrees. As a treat, I see the chunky Adebayo Akinfenwa's final game when the 40-year-old comes on as a substitute for Wycombe. He shows more skill than most others, but it's too late, both in the game and, probably, in his career. The final whistle sounds and two-thirds of the ground erupts. I dive for the exit and reach my hotel in less than ten minutes. Out of the window, I see jubilant Sunderland supporters leaping about and Wycombe supporters glumly standing in a massive queue for the train to High Wycombe. I make a cup of tea and sit down for a rest.

In the evening, I use online recommendations to choose an Indian restaurant. Before dining, I try a pub close to Wembley Central station. It has a small front paved area where I can sit in the sun and enjoy a beer away from the crowds. Just as I am considering a second pint, one of the bar staff sits next to me and puffs cigarette smoke in my direction. I leave. I proceed to my chosen Indian restaurant, the Malgudi, which has a great atmosphere. I am the only non-Asian in the busy restaurant. I try to order a fish curry, but the waitress tells me that I would find a meat dish more to my liking. I take her advice and order a lamb dish. The restaurant may be called Malgudi, a mixture of bad and 'goody', you might think, but the food is very much up at the 'goody' end of the scale. It is delicious. On my way back to the Premier Inn, I have a pint in the Wetherspoons pub. I talk to a man raising money for disadvantaged kids to play football under floodlights and chip in a few pounds. I like his ideas, enthusiasm and how he wants to help kids. My enjoyment ends abruptly for the second time when four or five Sunderland supporters decide to stand on a table and shout whatever comes into their heads. It's time to return to the Premier Inn.

In the Premier Inn bar, Sunderland celebrations are in full swing. They are happy rather than rowdy. One man stands out as he keeps bursting into song, shouting rather than singing, "everywhere we go". However, they seem to be the only words of the song he knows. A man I talk to gets a phone call from his wife in Sunderland. It's not to ask how the game went; it's to see where he is. It seems she did know he was in London. Another man insists that I write the name Bradley Hall on my notepad. He is an under-14 Sunderland lad who has just signed for Liverpool and will be "world-class". I write it down as the man is insistent; he checks that the name is correct in my notepad. You will have to wait and see if he is world-class or not.

Just as I am about to return to my room, there is a moment to treasure. Wrexham fans arrive at the hotel preparing for the next day's FA Trophy final. They mix well with the jubilant Sunderland fans. What doesn't mix so well is the arrival of Andre Rieu fans who have seen the great man perform at Wembley Arena. Wearing suits and long dresses, they form a lengthy queue to the bar amongst the Sunderland and Wrexham fans. "Everywhere we go", indeed. It reminds me of a wonderful occasion when I saw Thurrock play Bromley many years ago. Thurrock's ground was on the site of a motorway hotel, which had function rooms. As muddy and sweaty players left the pitch, a bride and groom and a wedding party mixed freely with the players. I just love the incongruity of these situations.

I wake on Sunday morning to the news that Charles and Camilla will appear on EastEnders. Announcing this on FA Trophy Final Day is frankly a bit thoughtless. I walk around the Wembley area but do so with little enthusiasm. Wembley is not the home of either of today's finalists. I pass the Stonebridge Boxing Club, whose strapline is "Stronger Together". I'm not going to argue with that. A family group spanning three generations blocks my path. They are all wearing the colours of Newport Pagnell Town. A banner carried by a young schoolgirl bears the hashtag

#turnwembleygreen. Maybe, it should be #turnwembleygreener as the pitch is already green. However, it's their big day out, and Mum tells me that there are 7,000 of them attending the final. Impressive. My brief tour of Wembley ends with a cuppa in Nero, where an enthusiastic barista takes it upon himself to welcome me to Wembley.

I head to the ground about an hour before the FA Vase final to soak up the atmosphere. As a neutral supporter, I have a seat in one of the plushest parts of the stadium. As I pass the turnstile, it is more like an airport with escalators taking me up to modern bars and facilities. My seat is almost as good as it can be, situated close to the halfway line. Many non-neutrals, wearing their team's colours, also seem to know it's an excellent place to sit. My friend, Jon, soon joins me; Jon witnessed the memorable Cheshunt win at St Albans four rounds ago. The Newport Pagnell faithful are noisy compared to the fans supporting their opponents from Littlehampton. Even though there are vast areas unoccupied which the Wrexham and Bromley fans will fill later, there is still a good atmosphere.

The pre-match entertainment is good enough, but it reminds me of an important piece of advice. If someone shoves a microphone at you coming up Wembley Way, do not feel tempted to screech "Littlehampton for the Cup" or whichever team you support. It's not a good look on a screen that is half the width of the pitch.

From the off, Newport Pagnell Town look the sharper team. However, in the early stages, Littlehampton come close when they get behind the Newport Pagnell defence. The goal that breaks the deadlock is spectacular. A Littlehampton defender heads a corner out, but Kieran Barnes is on the end of it to hit a superb first-time left-footed shot into the top corner of the Littlehampton net. In the second half, chances pass by until Ben Shepherd pokes home a second goal after a goalmouth scramble. 2-0 to Newport Pagnell. Littlehampton miss an 'unmissable' chance on the hour, which proves to be the final straw. As soon as the ball goes down the other end, Jake Watkinson tumbles over an outstretched leg to give Shepherd a chance to seal things from the spot. His penalty sends the keeper the wrong way. 3-0! Littlehampton continue to battle away, but the FA Vase is heading up the M1 this season.

Between the Vase and Trophy finals, there is plenty of time to enjoy a pint in the plush bars. Jon and I move quickly to beat the queues, but there are no queues. I did not imagine having a beer at Wembley would be so pleasurable, even if the beer costs a few pennies more than it does in a Wembley pub.

When we return to our seats, the ground has filled with Wrexham and Bromley supporters. Most Newport Pagnell and Littlehampton fans have left for the nearest watering hole. As kick-off approaches, the volume rises and is deafening as the two teams appear. The Welsh National

Anthem, *Mae Hen Wlad Fy Nhadau*, better known as *Land of My Fathers*, has many of the red and white contingent belting out the lyrics for all they are worth.

Wrexham start the game showing plenty of flair as well as flare, with red smoke billowing behind the Wrexham goal. Ollie Palmer, Wrexham's powerful striker, finds Paul Mullin in the opening minutes. Billy Bingham in the Bromley defence desperately blocks Mullin's cutback. Although Wrexham look more likely to score in the opening stages, Bromley break through Corey Whitely, but his shot narrowly clears the bar. At the other end, Wrexham have a good chance when a long ball from Callum Mcfadzean finds Paul Mullin. Mullin holds the ball up well and rolls it to Jordan Davies, who scuffs his shot when well-placed at the edge of the penalty area. The latter part of the first half sees both teams competing hard in midfield, but there is little goalmouth action. The teams go down the tunnel with the scoreline still 0-0. At half-time, you feel that Wrexham need to raise their game just a little more, and they will run at winners.

At half-time, Jon and I agree that Wrexham look to be the favourites. I comment to Jon that if Wrexham go a goal up, I can see them winning 3-0. The expert predictor has spoken. The second half starts where the first half left off. It's still a tight midfield battle. However, gradually things change as Bromley start to threaten more frequently. Whitely becomes a thorn in Wrexham's side, running at the

Welsh defence and making intelligent runs to find space. Ali Al-Hamadi has a good chance for Bromley, but Christian Dibble in the Wrexham goal makes a good save to his right. Soon afterwards, an accurate pass from Chris Bush in the inside left channel finds Michael Cheek making an astute run, which Dibble blocks again. Bromley are in the ascendancy.

Then comes the game-changing minute. A strong attack by Wrexham ends with Paul Mullin shooting into the side-netting; some of the crowd think it is a goal. Moments later, a long ball finds Whitely bursting from the Bromley midfield. The exposed Wrexham defence allows Whitely to square the ball across the penalty area for Michael Cheek to plant home confidently in the top corner from close to the penalty spot. Cheek wheels away to celebrate in front of the Bromley fans.

Wrexham have 25 minutes to pull the goal back and press with some fervour. Jake Hyde, who replaces Luke Young with five minutes of normal time, is at the centre of the last-ditch excitement. Firstly, a close-range header brings a spectacular save from Bromley keeper Ellery Balcombe. Seconds later, a dangerous low cross from Davies goes through a sea of legs to Hyde, who cannot control the ball as it bounces off his shins for a goal-kick. Seconds later, it looks like third time lucky for Hyde. He has the ball in the Bromley net from Mullin's low cross as he nods home a ball that bobbles into the air from a scramble. As the net ripples, the Wrexham fans leap into the air. Their exuberance soon dies as everyone sees the assistant referee's flag aloft.

The game ends, and the Cup heads south-east, leaving Wrexham to face the National League playoffs. Yet another prediction of mine is wrong, although technically, I am not wrong as I only said that Wrexham would win 3-0 if they went a goal up. I think we'll still call it another lousy prediction.

I am well-placed to see Bromley collect their trophy. I am one row further back and one block to the right of where the trophy presentation takes place. I ask a steward if I can move one block to take a close-up photo. I explain that I am writing a book. He firstly ignores me and then barks, "No". As a result of my plea, he summons reinforcements to ensure that I don't make a break for it. It's a bit of an overreaction, although I suppose they are jumpy after their failures at the Euro 2020 Final.

So, it's the end of the road. It all started at Hashtag United v Chipstead back in September. It has been an enormous amount of fun. It's time for a quiet pint to reflect on my Wembley trail. I hope you have enjoyed making the journey with me.

My FA Trophy Trail and My Pre-Match Predictions

- Sunday 27th September 2021 – First Round Qualifying – Hashtag United v Chipstead 1-4 – Prediction: 3-1.

- Saturday 9th October 2021 – Second Round Qualifying – Aylesbury United v Chipstead 1-1 (Chipstead won 4-2 on penalties) – Prediction: 3-1

- Saturday 30th October 2021 – Third Round Qualifying –Chipstead v Whitehawk 2-1 – Prediction: 2-1

- Saturday 13th November 2021 – First Round Proper – Bishop's Stortford v Chipstead 2-1 – Prediction: 3-0

- Saturday 27th November 2021 – Second Round Proper –Bishop's Stortford v Leiston 5-1 – Prediction: 2-1

- Saturday 18th December 2021 – Third Round Proper – Cheshunt v Bishop's Stortford 0-0 (Cheshunt won 4-3 on penalties) – Prediction: 0-3

- Saturday 15th January 2022 – Fourth Round Proper – St Albans City v Cheshunt 0-3 – Prediction: 3-1

- Saturday 12th February 2022 – Fifth Round Proper – Stockport County v Cheshunt 1-0 – Prediction 4-1

- Saturday 12th March 2022 – Quarter Final – Needham Market v Stockport County 0-3 – Prediction: 0-4

- Saturday 2nd April 2022 – Semi-final – Wrexham v Stockport County 2-0 – Prediction: 1-2

- Sunday 22nd May 2022 – Final – Wrexham v Bromley 0-1 – Prediction: 2-0

Summary of My Predictions

- 1 correct score
- 4 correct results
- 6 wrong predictions

Best Goals During My FA Trophy Trail to Wembley

Winner - Reece Beckles-Richards, Cheshunt v. St Albans City

Runners-up:

- Paul Mullin
- Wrexham v. Stockport County
- Tom Annetts
- Chipstead v. Hashtag United
- Jordan Keane
- Stockport County v. Needham Market

Random Awards

- Most knowledgeable club historian – Jim Tuite, Cheshunt

- Most roles at a club – Trevor Stotten, Chipstead

- Supporter with most uncertain facts – the Stockport fan in the Prince Albert pub

- Noisiest supporters – Wrexham at Wembley

- Noisiest supporters relative to numbers – Cheshunt at Stockport County

- Club that deserves to return to its home – Aylesbury United

- Town that was buzzing most with Cup fever – Needham Market

- Friendliest pub – The Royal Oak, Wrexham

- And, of course, the 2021-22 winners of the FA Trophy - Bromley

Printed in Great Britain
by Amazon